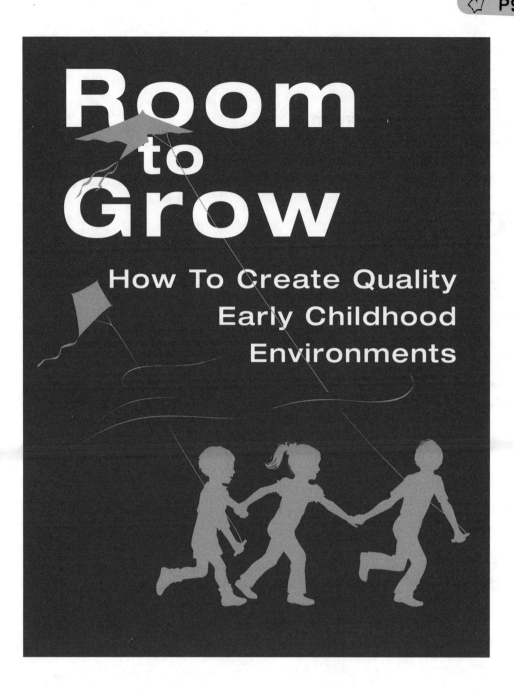

Room to Grow

How To Create Quality Early Childhood Environments

Margaret B. Puckett, Ed.D

Editor

Texas Association for the Education of Young Children

Copyright 2002 by the
Texas Association for the Education
of Young Children

P.O. Box 4997
Austin, Texas 78765-4997

Fax: 512-419-1872
E-mail: taeyc@TAEYC.org
Web Site: http/www.texasaeyc.org

ISBN 0-9640108-2-8

Preface

"Teach me," said the child,

"With simplicity and imagination –

Simply that the paraphernalia and the gadgets

Do not get between us;

Imaginatively that I may sense and catch your enthusiasm,

And the quickening thrill of never having been this way before."

— Leland B. Jacobs

Between the covers of this book is the enthusiasm, creativity, and imagination of many whose child development and early education expertise provides the "way" for both adults and children to experience the satisfactions of growing and learning. Both practical and innovative, the content of each chapter guides the reader to plan and design safe, effective, and appealing spaces for children from infancy to school-age.

This 3rd edition of *Room to Grow* continues the tradition of previous editions in setting forth guidelines for planning, designing, and maintaining highest quality environments and selecting materials and activities that best meet the needs and capabilities of young children. Throughout, emphasis is placed on creating environments that are functional, yet appealing and practical, yet enchanting.

Growing and learning is what children do. The adult who becomes engaged in this process with children and who continually taps the grand and ever-changing knowledge base in child development and education is best prepared to create room to grow.

Margaret B. Puckett, Ed. D., Editor

Acknowledgments

Gratitude is expressed to TAEYC members who volunteered their time and expertise in writing the chapters of this book. Their collective years of experience and thoughtful efforts on behalf of this project has led to a book that represents some of the best of our current practice in early childhood care and education.

Appreciation is extended to Mary Clare Munger, Chair of the TAEYC Publications Committee who has shepherded this 3rd Edition project from its inception. Serving as a liaison between the TAEYC Board of Directors and the Editor, she has provided significant guidance and support. LaShonda Brown and Kathy Brumley must also be acknowledged for their help and support from the TAEYC Central Office. Appreciation goes to the following individuals who reviewed individual chapters: Beth Hatcher, Director of the University Christian Church Weekday School and members of the UCC Weekday School faculty, Glenda Appleby, Sharon Broyles, Margaret Doak, Michele Forbs, Lisa Francis, Deborah Grant, and Ingrid Keller. Also reviewing parts of the manuscript were Elizabeth Donaldson, K-1 teacher at Alice Carlson Applied Learning Center, Fort Worth Independent School District, and Ann Reed, Associate Professor of Education at Texas Wesleyan University. The scholarship, expertise, and daily practical experience of these individuals provided insights and much appreciated guidance. Thank-you is also extended to those who provided photography: Paul Jacobs and the University Presbyterian Church Children's Center in San Antonio, Henry Ortega, Amarillo College, Wes Corzine, Communications Coordinator for Camp Fire, USA, Fort Worth, Texas, Jennifer Denkhoff, Nancy Beaver and the faculty of Eastfield College Parent Child Study Center, and the Texas Association for the Education of Young Children.

Special appreciation is extended to our production team at Branch Smith, Inc., Fort Worth, Texas: Susie Richardson, Sandy Beddow, and Don Page, for their skilled and professional assistance in design, lay-out and printing of the book. It has been a pleasure to work with this team every step of the way.

As Editor, it has been an honor to work on a document so well conceived by my predecessors, Linda Ard and Mabel Pitts, Editors of the previous editions of *Room to Grow*. It has been my extreme pleasure to work with so many truly dedicated professionals across our many related fields. Bringing this project to readers carries with it a certain kind of joy and anticipation not unlike entering class on the first day of school.

Margaret B. Puckett, Ed.D., Editor

Note: The chapters in this book reflect the knowledge, experience, and opinions of their authors and do not necessarily reflect the policies or positions of the Texas Association for the Education of Young Children. Authors are responsible for the accuracy of all statements and references.

Contents

Section I. Getting Started

Section II. Environments for Children Younger Than 3

Section III. Environments for 3-, 4-, and 5-Year-Old Children

Section IV. Environments for School-Age Children

Section V. Professional Development

Section I

Getting Started

Chapter I

All of us respond to the space around us. The space can make us feel comfortable, cheerful, anxious, depressed, excited, or subdued. Space can help us organize our lives or add to the clutter. Space can be beautiful or dreary. Most of us like the space we live in to be suited to our needs, reflect our values, and to be attractive, clean, and ordered.

Using Space

Linda Ard

This book contains sections about infants and toddlers, preschoolers, school-age children, and children of mixed ages in early childhood care and education settings. *Room to Grow: How to Create Quality Early Childhood Environments* was written to help caregivers and teachers to make the best use of space for children. The book's guiding principle is that well-planned physical environments are necessary to support developmentally appropriate practice in all types of programs serving children from birth through age 8. Such programs include, but are not limited to, public schools, Head Start, nonprofit and proprietary child care centers, nursery schools, private schools, and family child care homes. The environments described include indoor and outdoor settings for children, classrooms in school buildings or playrooms in converted garages, classrooms designed for a single age group or those intended to meet the needs of a range of ages. Environments should facilitate cognitive, physical, social, and emotional development in children. The organization of the physical environment can promote development by recognizing and respecting that children learn through play. Children need room to play, room to learn, and room to grow.

Organizing Space to be Function-Specific

In discussing the environment, the authors have been consistent with accepted practice that environments for children should be organized into interest areas or learning centers. This approach is function-specific, much like our homes. Our homes have places for specific functions – preparing food, eating, sleeping, bathing, and relaxing. Similarly, an infant room has areas for feeding, changing diapers, sleeping, playing with floor toys, and developing large muscles. A preschool room has traditional centers such as art, dramatic play, library, manipulatives, science, blocks, and music. The outdoor play area is likewise organized into function-specific areas – quiet play, digging, water play, running, wheel toys, and climbing, for example. Organizing the environment into function-specific areas or learning centers brings many benefits:

- Individual children are able to choose activities that match their developmental levels and interests. When caregivers try to get a large group of children to all do puzzles or art at the same time, individual needs are not respected.

- Children are able to better use materials when the materials are grouped into meaningful areas. The environment gives clues to help children know what behavior is expected. A table, four chairs, and shelves in the manipulatives center, for example, tell children that this place is where four children select materials from the shelf and use the materials at the table.

- Adults are able to guide, support, and challenge children's play by planning specific activities and adding certain props. If the children are learning about animals, the teacher can place books about animals in the library, pictures of the children's pets around the room, animal models in the block centers, and sequence cards about how animals grow in the manipulative center. Opportunities to care for and interact with appropriate classroom pets or "visiting" animals can also be provided.

- Children are able to learn in the way they learn best – through play. Children are active learners who thrive on first-hand experiences. They learn much more about earthworms for example, by holding an earthworm, examining it up close, and feeling it wiggle about than by viewing a picture or hearing about earthworms.

This chapter focuses on creating livable space to meet the needs of children and adults, using space to promote a sense of beauty, and anti-bias considerations in design and provisions. Managing the use of space through scheduling, furniture and equipment arrangements, display and use of play enhancing props, and using low-cost ideas to create and maintain environments for children is also discussed.

Livable Environments

Children frequently spend as much as 80 percent of their waking time in out-of-home environments. Adults may "work" in early care and education environments but children "live" in these spaces. Therefore it is important to create space that is livable.

According to the General Services Administration Guidelines (2000), published in the *Head Start Center Design Guide*, there are certain factors that make space livable:

Security
There must be security measures in place to keep children safe within the center, to safeguard them from outside intruders, and to protect them from hazards. This includes many concerns such as safe water, mold controlled environments, buildings free of lead and asbestos, installation of fire detection alarms and communication systems, locked storage of medications and dangerous materials, and safety hinges on doors and cabinets. Other security measures include video cameras, electronic security systems, authorized entry systems with keypads, card control, or reception area, exit doors with electronic magnetic locks. The playground, restrooms, entrances, and exits should all be easily supervised while children are in the building.

Lighting
Natural lighting should be available in each classroom. It is recommended that the exterior window size be equal to 8 to 15 percent of the floor space. If artificial lighting is used, it should include a variety of fixtures such as dimming controls, separate switching, adjustable directional fixtures and indirect lighting such as lamps. Many programs suffer from over lighting. If there is adequate ceiling height, reflected light from pendant or recesses is strongly preferred to troffer-style downlight fluorescent fixtures. Florescent lamps should have a color temperature of 4,100 degrees Kelvin with the highest possible color-rendering index (CRI). CRI should be 80 or greater. Care

should be taken to insure sufficient lighting during naptime so adults and children can see to safely move about the room.

Color
Strong color schemes should not be used in classrooms for children. Off-white is the recommended with small amounts of color used for accent. Children can become over stimulated by strong bright colors. Since most children's learning materials and their clothing are bright and colorful, there is no need to place bright colors on the floors, walls, or ceilings.

Acoustics
If the center is adjacent to or near airport flight path, major highways, or busy rail lines, it will be important to minimize the exterior noise through acoustical measures. Infants appear to be especially sensitive to continuous or intermittent noise so every effort should be made to keep their environment as free of extraneous noises as possible. Acceptable sound levels for outside play yards are 70 dBA continuous and 80 dBA intermittent and inside sleeping and quiet areas are 60 dBA continuous and 65 dBA intermittent. Sound can be controlled by acoustical ceiling, non-slip throw rugs or permanently installed carpet, accoustical panels installed where needed, and banners and fabrics such as hanging quilts or soft structures, can be used as part of the design. Outside, solid fencing can be used to block out traffic noise and noise from such equipment as air-conditioning units.

Temperature and Humidity
The acceptable temperature and humidity levels during the winter are 69.8 degrees F and 35 percent minimum relative humidity and during the summer are 75.2-78.8 degrees F and 50 percent maximum relative humidity. The temperature and humidity should be measured at 3 feet above the floor.

Ventilation
A humidifier/dehumidifier may be needed to meet the levels suggested above. Each space should be supplied with a minimum of 15 liters/seconds of outside air for each occupant in order to control odor. Outside ducted fans in bathrooms and over changing tables will also help to control odor. The air motion in the occupied space should not exceed 8,000 mm per minute. Air diffusers can be used to minimize drafts on children.

Accessibility

Environments must be accessible for both children and adults. On the playground use hard surfaces or manufactured wood fiber to provide wheel chair and walker access. Aisles and corridors need to be 3 feet wide with a passing space of 5 feet provided at least every 200 feet. The slopes of ramps should have a slope of no more than 1 inch for every 12 inches. The children's toilet should have side and grab bars. Drinking fountain controls should be front or side operable. There must be handicapped parking available as needed for the size of the program and the needs of parents and staff. Additional information on making children's spaces accessible for children with special needs, contact Americans with Disabilities Act (ADA) specialists in your community.

Environments that Meet Children's Needs

When creating environments for children, the first step is to consider the characteristics of the children who will be cared for in a particular space. Having child-size furniture and materials helps children feel the environment is theirs and that they have some power over it. Keep in mind that child-size is not one-size-fits-all. An 8-year old is easily three times the height of a toddler. Everything from the size of a doll, to the height of a chair, to the location of a drinking fountain needs to be scaled to the size of the specific children who will use the space.

The environment should also reflect the skills of the children in it. For example, the dress-up clothes for the 2-year-olds need elastic waistbands for easy dressing and low-heel shoes that are large enough to be worn over the children's own shoes. The dress-up clothes for the 5-year-olds should challenge their skills at zipping, buckling, and tying.

The environment should be designed to allow for varying age-related play needs and behaviors. Toddlers like to play by themselves but next to others so their sand tires should be small enough for one child but placed close to other sand tires. The sand tires for the 4- and 5-year-olds should be large enough for several children working together to bake sand pies or dig a hole for an underground parking garage.

Even smaller details, such as pictures, should be chosen to match the children's developmental level. A picture of a camel's head, for example, would be appropriate for 5-year-olds but not for 2-year-olds. A foreign animal is more likely to be within the experience of many 5-year-olds, but a pet, like that cat that sometimes naps in the neighbor's back yard, would be more familiar to the 2-year-olds. Moreover, the older children could visualize the body that goes with the pictured animal's head, while younger children could not.

The environment should support what children are learning and the way that children learn. Mobile infants spend a lot of time exploring, grasping and putting things in their mouths. Instead of constantly trying to counteract this way of learning, it is better to make the infant's environment as safe and healthy as possible. A caregiver can ensure that only safe teething toys are within the infant's reach and establish a system for insuring that toys are clean. For example, one container can be provided for clean toys and another container for toys that need to be sanitized. When toddlers are always climbing on shelves and tables, their caregivers (while assuring that all equipment is sturdy and steady) should take a hard look at what equipment children have indoors and outdoors to help them practice their large motor skills. When kindergartners have to be reminded repeatedly to drive their trucks in the block center (rather than the music center), it is probably time to enlarge the block center or to create a new area for truck and car driving.

Environments that Meet Adults Needs

Sometimes environment planners forget that adult needs must be met in rooms or spaces where children live and grow. An adult who changes diapers needs an organized, easy-to-sanitize counter that is at a comfortable height. An adult who cares for toddlers might appreciate a counter with steps attached so that a child can climb into position for changing. When such surfaces are at a comfortable height, both adults and children are better served. Toddlers enjoy climbing and being independent, while the adult is spared the risk of possible back strain caused by lifting heavy children.

Adults need a safe place to store their personal belongings. Most early childhood professionals do not consider an adult desk appropriate in an area for children, but a comfortable chair and a place for adult storage is necessary. Adults also need an attractive, comfortable place to take breaks.

In addition to staff needs, the environment can be designed to respect parents' needs. Parents who already feel guilty about leaving their children in someone else's care may feel even more guilty when they open the door and smell wet, soiled diapers. In addition, parents may assume that their children are not valued when they play with broken toys or torn books.

Parents often need help understanding the early childhood learning environment. Some parents might be more impressed with neat rows of desks, workbooks, and computers than they are with a creative playground or a well equipped and creative dramatic play center. Most parents have limited knowledge about how children learn or appropriate early education methods. Lacking this understanding, they tend to over-emphasize the need for children to learn isolated skills such as counting by rote to 100 or reciting the alphabet. Parents may not realize that there are certain cognitive and perceptual skills required to progress from scribbling to the preschematic stage of art or to the advanced mathematical thinking necessary to build a skyscraper out of blocks.

Teachers have a professional responsibility to share with parents in helpful and meaningful ways the rationale for using and designing environments that promote children's learning through play. A stack of lumber on a shelf doesn't mean much to most parents until the teacher takes time to explain what children will learn through building with unit blocks. Some parents may think that allowing 4-year-olds to use a hammer and saw is dangerous, yet the trained professional knows the tremendous value of such an experience and can reassure parents about the program's safety policies.

Parents need to know they are always welcome in the center or family child care home. In addition to a bulletin board or corner for providing information, the space design should include a private, comfortable place for parent-teacher conferences. Nursing mothers need a quiet space to feed babies. Although caregivers spend much of the day sitting on the floor or in small chairs, that type of seating does not convey a welcome message to parents. Parents also usually help younger children remove and store outer clothing, so the cubby space should be near the door and out of the traffic path used by the children.

In many family child care homes, space is used for children during the day and for the caregiver's family in the evenings and on weekends. Caregivers must be creative in adapting the environment. Shelves of play materials can be created in a closet that can be opened for children's use and later closed when the children leave. In the bathroom, a low shelf holds the children's toothbrushes and drinking cups while a high, locked shelf contains the daughter's asthma medicine and Dad's razor.

Many classrooms for children, especially those in churches, must be transformed every Monday morning and Friday evening. In those situations, shelves on rollers that hinge closed and portable bulletin boards make change easier.

Beauty and Order

In recent years, the influence of Reggio Emilio programs in Italy has caused early childhood professionals to focus on the aesthetic value of children's environments. Attractive landscaping, natural lighting and the careful use of color and texture contribute to beautiful environments.

Beautiful environments for children need not be at odds with the natural clutter of children's play. Instead of toy boxes, which encourage children to dump their toys, the use of low shelves helps children to learn to put their toys away in an attractive and organized way. While encouraging order, the storage method should also be reasonable for the children's limited motor skills. For example, children may not use dress-up clothes in the dramatic play center because the clothes have to be folded and placed on the shelf. However, when hooks are installed next to the mirror, the children are eager to play dress-up because they can hang the clothes easily.

Few buildings that house early childhood programs are actually designed for young children. Usually teachers and caregivers have to make the best of existing environments. In doing so, they must remember to create pretty places indoors and outdoors. A pretty place can be a basket of dried flowers on a top shelf, a framed art print hung at the children's eye level, a tire filled with spider plants, or a brightly colored wind sock.

Anti-Bias Considerations

Developmentally appropriate environments are designed to show respect for differences in race, ethnicity, gender, and abilities. Anti-bias settings for children include visuals, objects and artifacts, play and creative materials, books and story themes that reflect a wide range of diversity among children and families. For example, a picture hanging in the infants' room showing an African-American man changing a smiling baby illustrates both culture and gender diversity. Providing both men and women's clothes in the dramatic play center allows boys and girls to participate fully in sociodramatic play. The books, stories, songs, and dance can be purposefully selected to reflect all cultures in a positive way. The art center that provides paints of high contrast colors and textures (e.g., sand mixed with finger paints to create a textured medium) supports the creative efforts of a classmate who is legally blind.

Managing Space

Using space effectively requires many group management techniques, such as planning a schedule. The schedule should meet the needs of the children in care and help the caregiver's day go smoothly. Children are comfortable when daily routines such as eating lunch or resting occur at the same time each day. An appropriate schedule includes times for the arrival and departure of children, meals and snacks, sleeping or resting, self-help skills such as toileting, dressing to go outdoors, washing hands, put-

ting away toys, and transitions from one activity to another. Transitions include singing a marching song as children move from outside play to wash up for lunch.

The key to an effective schedule is balance. The schedule should balance the needs of individual children with the needs of the group. The schedule should have a balance of individual, small-group, and large-group activities. It should balance active play such as dress-up, block building, and riding tricycles with quiet play such as reading books, working puzzles, and finger painting. The day should also have a balance of times when children direct their own activities in learning centers and other times when teachers and caregivers direct activities.

Sample Schedule
(4-year-olds)

Time	Activity
7:30-8:30	**Arrival and greeting.** Children choose from playdough, blocks, maniupulatives, books, and dramatic play items.
8:30-8:45	Snack
8:45-9:00	Circle Time
9:00-10:20	**Child-directed activities – Choices:**

Easel	Dramatic Play
Blocks	Art Table
Music	Puppets
Science	Language
Manipulatives	Woodworking
Mathematics	Writing
Sand/Water	

Teacher-directed activities (small groups):

Science	Language
Manipulatives	Mathematics
Writing	

Time	Activity
10:20-10:30	Clean-up
10:30-11:15	**Outdoor play – Choices:**

Cloud watching	Water Play
Balance beams	Balls
Bubble blowing	Sand play
Planting	Woodworking
Tent	Outdoor blocks
Clay	Digging
Mud	Chalk on sidewalk
Stilts	Easel
Wheel Toys	Kite flying
Cardboard boxes	Dress-up clothes

Rainy Day Choices:

Umbrella walks	Balance beams
Climbing gym	Tunnel
Jump ropes	Tumbling
Creative movement	Balls or bean bags

Time	Activity
11:30-11:50	**Teacher-directed activities** (large groups):

Music	Movement
Story	Wash-up and set table

Time	Activity
11:50-12:30	Lunch
*12:15-12:50	Getting ready for nap Brush teeth Listen to music
*12:20-2:40	Nap
*1:40-2:40	**Quiet activities indoor or outdoors**

Art	Listening center
Books	Puzzles
Clay	Individual activities

Time	Activity
2:40-2:45	**Getting ready for snack**
2:45-3:00	Snack indoors or outdoors
3:00-4:30	**Outdoor play** (see morning choices)
4:30-5:30	**Child-directed activities** (see morning choices)

*Note overlapping times to meet individual needs.

Children should be able to use the learning centers several times a day. At a minimum, 45 minutes should be allotted in the morning and the same amount of time in the afternoon. The children should be able to move from center to center as their interests dictate.

Caregivers and teachers with children older than 3 years use a variety of management techniques to help children use the centers in a constructive and organized way. The goal is to increase the children's freedom and opportunity to choose. One technique is to use large group time or circle time to introduce new materials and activities – introducing sunflower leaves and seeds for the science center and yellow and green paper for the art center when children have indicated an interest in sunflowers, for example.

To help children plan which activities they want to accomplish during learning center time, the teacher can use a planning chart. A planning chart is a poster or plyboard with pictures of each learning center. Under each learning center picture are the numbers of hooks that correspond to the number of children who can use the center at any one time. During group time the caregiver asks children one by one to choose a center, and children indicate their choices by hanging their nametags on the various hooks. For example, after Sally tells the teacher that she wants to go to the woodworking center, she places her nametag on one of the two hooks on the planning chart that are under the picture of the woodworking center.

A variation on the planning chart concept is to place a poster in each learning center with an appropriate number of clothespins. For example, the woodworking center is designed for only two children, so it has only two clothespins on its chart. Under the system, Sally removes a clothespin from the poster and places it on her clothes. Kevin does the same. If a third child wants to work with wood, he or she must wait until Sally or Kevin is finished.

Establishing a system for using the centers and controlling the number in each center supports children's choices while preventing potential behavior problems. Some teachers discontinue the system as soon as the children are able to use the centers without confusion or conflict. Allowing children to choose centers and the amount of time they spend in each is more supportive of learning and less disruptive to focused activity than is a system in which the children are rotated every 15 minutes or assigned to specific centers.

Rule of thumb: For each child in the group, there should be one and a half spaces to play. (For infants and

toddlers it is best to plan two spaces for each child.) According to the rule, a group of 12 3-year-olds should have at least 18 spaces to play both indoors and outdoors. The breakdown might look like this:

Art Table	2
Easel	2
Blocks	2
Manipulatives	3
Music	1
Language	2
Science	1
Dramatic play	3
Water play	2
	18

Caregivers and teachers need to rearrange the centers often to reflect the children's interests or to add new materials and experiences for them. Sometimes the changes are needed because of weather conditions – adding more large motor activities indoors during rainy periods, for example. Since children cannot handle change any better than adults, caregivers should make changes slowly, explaining why they are necessary and if possible, involving children in changing the environment.

Children give many clues about whether the room arrangement works, and observing them carefully can provide much information. A caregiver observes three days in a row; for example, the 2-year-olds remove all the toys from the bottom shelf and crawl into it to play baby. So she brings a large box, pillows, and baby blankets. During the next couple of weeks, the 2-year-olds continue to play baby, learning important concepts such as how big their bodies are in relation to the box.

Adding New Props

Adding new props to any new area can stimulate many interests. New props can include such play enhancers as cookie cutters with a plastic tub of play dough; balls and a laundry basket taken to the outdoor play area; and pots and wooden spoons for marching. A lace curtain and a bouquet of artificial flowers might spark an interest in playing wedding and perhaps, allow a child to sort out feelings about a parent's recent remarriage.

The children will use new props more constructively if they are introduced carefully. During the circle time, the caregiver should pass around the props and discuss what they are, how they can be used, what safety rules should be followed, how to care for them, and where they are stored. When a new and popular prop is brought into the room, it is a good idea to have at least two of the items or an equally interesting activity going on at the same time.

Getting the Most Environment for the Least Money

Choosing equipment and materials requires careful thought and decision because children in group care use toys as tools for learning. A tricycle from a discount store might cost one-third that of a commercial school-type tricycle, but it will not last as long. Inexpensive books from the grocery store are usually not good literature nor well constructed. It is wiser to buy fewer but better quality books and use books from the public library. A beginner set of hardwood unit blocks is a large investment, but it will probably outlast any other toy available. Blocks can be used by several children of different ages and have infinite possibilities for creative construction and meaningful play. It is better to buy toys designed for several children at a time than those designed to be used by only one child. Furthermore, once the money has been spent, it is important to maintain and preserve the equipment. Many of the following suggestions were adapted from *Total Learning Curriculum for the Young Children* (Hendrick, 1998).

Preservation and Maintenance

Furniture

- Buy varnished or lacquered shelves because they require less frequent refurbishing.

- Look for easily cleaned plastic surfaces on tabletops and chair backs and seats. Chairs, in particular, soil easily, so buy chairs that will hold up under frequent washing and do not require repainting.

- Check all furniture regularly to make certain that nuts and bolts are tight.

- Scratched and marred surfaces can be recovered with plastic or thin grade laminate counter surfacing that can be cut with scissors and glued with a special adhesive.

- Buy good quality, substantial furniture or have it made; it saves money in the long run.

- To make money go further, haunt thrift shops and rummage sales for low dressers and shelves that can be cleaned or refinished.

- Buy furniture with casters whenever possible to aid movement and rearrangements. Avoid built-ins that reduce flexibility.

Floors

- Use linoleum or resilient vinyl tile as the basic surface; carpeting is impossible to keep clean in eating or art areas.

- Use carpeting to add warmth, comfort, noise control, and softness to a room; tightly woven ones are easiest to vacuum. Small area rugs can be shaken out and moved easily; make sure they do not wrinkle, and use nonskid mats underneath.

- An old-fashioned carpet sweeper is handy for quick rug cleanup.

- String mops are more effective than sponge mops after water play.

- A drain in the bathroom floor facilitates frequent cleaning and disinfecting.

Files

(Pictures, poetry, flannel board sets, songs, transition activities)

- Mount pictures and other items on stiff cardboard or mat board. Spray adhesive is the most satisfactory adhesive.

- File under topic headings for easy identification.

- These files are invaluable educational resources and cost relatively little.

- Invest in an artwaxer which make pictures very easy to post.

Books

- Purchase books with durable, library grade binding, or cover them with clear contact paper.

- Repair books promptly with mending tape.

- Teach children to handle books with care.

- Add variety by putting away some books for use another day.

- Keep books sorted according to some simple classification system to make finding that special book easier.

- Use the public library as a primary source of books.

Self-expressive Materials

- Set up messy activities away from carpeted areas.

- Store clean-up materials used together in the same place; for example, keep sponges, detergent, and scrub brushes in the finger painting bucket.

- Wash glue and paint brushes thoroughly after each use; store on end with wood handles down.

- Mix powered tempera paint because it is cheaper than premixed. *Do not mix around children because of the danger of inhaling the powder.* Add liquid starch and water in mixing the paint to help stretch it.

- Stack large sheets of paper on a series of narrow shelves rather than on one deep one for easy access. Paper is heavy to lift.

- Store construction paper in closed cabinets to reduce fading.

- Sort donated materials as they arrive.

- Ask print shops for left over paper.

Wheel Toys

- Store under cover.

- Buy toys that do not require painting.

- Check nuts and bolts frequently; oil occasionally.

- Buy the expensive preschool-grade quality of this equipment; check warranties.

- Provide and encourage children to use safety helmets.

Unit Blocks

- Polish with paste wax before use.

- Stack on shelves according to type; never dump in bins.

- Wash really dirty blocks. Do not soak. Dry immediately to avoid roughening and raising the grain.

- Use blocks on carpeting. It deadens noise, is warmer for children to sit on, and protects corners of the blocks.

- Use homemade, softwood blocks as money stretchers. They don't wear well but will do in a pinch. If money is really tight, use sealed and stapled milk cartons; be sure to provide a lot of them.

Tabletop Activity Materials

- Mend broken corners of storage boxes immediately.

- Have a special, centrally located box, and drop stray bits and pieces (such as nuts, bolts, and puzzle knobs) into it for weekly sorting.

- Label puzzle pieces with individual symbols on the back for rapid sorting and reassembly.

- Teach children to keep small, multi-pieced items on the table or use carpet squares – one per child on the floor.

- Count pieces of items such as doctor's kits and simple games before setting out, mark quantities on the box, and recount before putting away.

- Protect teacher-made activities with the artwaxer, clear contact paper, or laminating film.

- Inspect all items regularly for cleanliness, and wash when necessary.

- Store in see-through plastic boxes.

- Store items such as colored beads, pegs, and cubical counting blocks in shallow container to make them readily visible and appealing.

- Draw a picture on the side or top of cardboard boxes so children can "read" what's inside.

Tools
(cooking, woodworking, gardening)

- Store outdoor tools out of the weather and keep them oiled and painted when necessary.

- Teach children to use the tools for their intended purposes. Avoid discouraging experimentation, when curtailing inappropriate or destructive uses.

- Purchase sturdy equipment that really works.

- Store tools of all kinds with care; do not store piled in a box.

Quality environments are livable spaces that meet the needs of children and adults. In these places children develop a sense of beauty and order. They learn to respect differences and similarities in race, ethnicity, gender and abilities. Caregivers and teachers manage children's space through balanced schedules, effective group management techniques, and the thoughtful selection, arrangement, and care of equipment. Children come to trust that such environments are places where they can explore, play out ideas, and spend time with friends or by themselves. Quality early childhood environments give children room to grow.

References

Administration for Children and Families, Administration on Children, Youth and Families, Head Start Bureau (2000). *Head Start center design guide.* Arlington, VA: National Head Start Training and Technical Assistance Resource Center PaL-Tech., Inc.

Bredekamp, S. & C. Copple (Eds.) (1997). *Developmentally appropriate practice in early childhood programs (Rev.ed.)*. Washington, DC: National Association for the Education of Young Children.

Greenman, J. (1998). *Places for childhoods: Making quality happen in the real world*. Redmond, WA: Child Care Information Exchange.

Giulio, C. & M. Zini (Eds.). (1998). *Children, spaces, relations: Metaproject for an environment for young children*. Reggio Emilia, Italia: Reggio Children s.r.l.

Hendrick, J. (1998). *Total learning curriculum for the young child (5th ed.)*. Columbus, OH: Merrill/ Prentice Hall Publishing Co.

Checklist for Evaluating the Use of Space

Rate the items below on a scale of 1 to 4 with "needing improvement" as 1 and "outstanding" as 4.

_____1. The security, lighting, color, acoustics, temperature and humidity, ventilation, accessibility, and color of the environment make the space livable.

_____2. Equipment and materials are the right size for the children who work and play in the space.

_____3. The environment reflects an understanding of the way children of various developmental levels learn and play. (For example, toddlers need open space for ride-on toys, while school-age children need a table and chairs for group games.

4. Preschool children are able to:

_____choose activities on there own,

_____access and use materials appropriately and successfully,

_____stay involved in an activity, and

_____take care of materials.

_____5. Adult storage and a comfortable staff break room are available.

_____6. Parents are obviously welcome and encouraged to visit.

_____7. The environment is orderly, clean, and attractive.

_____8. The environment reflects respect and appreciation for people of differing race, ethnicity, gender, and abilities.

9. The schedule is balanced between:

_____quiet and active play,

_____group and individual needs,

_____child-directed and teacher-directed activities,

_____indoor and outdoor play, and

_____individual, small group, and large-group activities.

_____10. The children have large blocks of time (45 minutes to 1-½ hours) in which to play in learning centers.

_____11. Children understand the rules for using the centers.

_____12. The arrangement of the room or area remains fairly stable.

_____13. The toys, materials, and equipment are carefully selected and maintained.

_____14. Every item can be justified in terms of children's developmental and learning needs.

About the Author

Linda Ard is a professor in the Child Development Early Childhood Program and chair of the Human Services Department at Del Mar College in Corpus Christi, Texas. She is former editor of *Texas Child Care* and past president of the Texas Association for the Education of Young Children. She is currently responsible for building a Center for Early Learning on the Del Mar College campus.

Chapter 2

Teachers plan and prepare a learning environment that fosters children's initiative, active exploration of materials, and sustained engagement with other children, adults, and activities.
Sue Bredekamp and Carol Copple, 1997

The classroom directly supports children's learning. Early childhood educators understand the importance of the physical environment, so they create their classrooms very purposefully. "The way a room is arranged, the centers that are available to children, and the materials provided in each center are critical to the teaching and learning that goes on in that classroom" (Bickart, Jablon, & Dodge, 1999, p. 99).

Arranging Space

Deborah Diffily

Young children spend time each day participating in activities in different groups: the whole class, small-groups, and individual activities. As teachers arrange furniture in the classroom, they create areas for each type of grouping. Typically, teachers begin by defining a large area where everyone in the class can gather together. In the meeting area, the children and their teacher begin the day by listening to stories, singing songs, and making plans. Throughout the day, they may return to the meeting area as a transition between activities; to discuss their work, a plan, or a problem, or play math games; dramatize a story, or engage in partner reading. At the end of the day, the teacher and children usually meet again in this area to summarize the day's activities. The meeting area is one of the most flexible spaces in the classroom.

In planning the group meeting area, teachers make sure the area is large enough for all children to sit comfortably without being crowded. Teachers define the area – with a rug, carpet squares or even couches – so children know the boundaries of the area where they are expected to gather. Children may sit in different configurations during class meetings. For a read aloud, children sit where they can see the book, whereas, for a class meeting or a math lesson, children sit in a circle where everyone can make eye contact with everyone else. Teachers also make sure that this area is free of clutter and that inviting materials are not within easy reach for children sitting in the meeting area. The teacher also places a chart stand or easel, a basket for supplies, and a CD or tape player within reach of the meeting area to facilitate whole group discussions or lessons (Clayton & Forton, 2001).

Teachers also create spaces for small groups. Some of these areas are the learning centers that are described in detail throughout this book, such as reading, writing,

dramatic play, science, blocks, math, and so on. As teachers arrange centers in the room, they are careful to cluster quiet centers and the more active centers and keep quiet centers separated from the more active ones. Children working in the reading, writing, and listening centers tend to be quieter, so these centers are typically placed near each other. Block and dramatic play centers tend to encourage louder interactions between children, so teachers usually place these centers near each other.

There are times when children work in small groups or with a partner outside designated centers. For example, all children may be involved in Writing Workshop or Partner Reading activities at the same time. Small groups of children gather in different places around the room. Some children choose to work on these activities while sitting on the floor. Others prefer sitting at a table. It is not necessary to bring in extra tables and chairs for this kind of small group work. If storage for learning centers is sufficient, tables in centers can be cleared and used by small groups for their work. Other permanent small group areas might be created in the classroom. These include raised carpeted platforms, lofts, and low tables so that children can kneel beside them to work, or low cabinets children can use as counters.

Just as teachers create spaces for large and small group activities, they also create small private areas in the classroom so that an individual child can work alone. A child may prefer to get a clipboard and write while sitting in a small space between filing cabinets. Another child may choose to sit in a corner surrounded by pillows so he can read privately. Still another child may choose to work in the listening center, listening to quiet music as she works.

Spaces created for whole group, small group, and individual activities may need to be adapted when children with special needs join the class. It is not possible to create a classroom that anticipates all special needs.

Wheelchairs require additional space between furniture and extra space in the meeting area. Sharp edges on tables and bookshelves will need to be padded so that a child who is visually impaired avoids possible injuries. Centers may need to be reduced in size to provide space for special adaptive equipment for children who have particular physical challenges. Rather than try to anticipate possible needs, it is best to wait until children with special needs are enrolled in the program. At this time, a conversation with the child's family will ensure that changes made to the physical environment will meet the needs of this child.

In creating the spaces for different groupings of children, the teacher is supporting different types of activities and different ways of learning. There are also many other considerations teachers think about as they set up a classroom:

- The way a classroom looks either welcomes young children and their families or it does not.

- The way furniture is arranged either supports children's self-control or encourages impulsivity.

- The way learning materials are organized either supports children's developing independence or reinforces their dependence on adults.

- The teacher's choice of learning materials either promotes children's learning or impedes it.

Before children ever enter the classroom, early childhood educators consider all of these issues and create classrooms that welcomes children and supports their development and learning (Puckett & Diffily, 1999).

Welcoming Children

The way a classroom is organized sends strong messages to both young children and their families. Posting children's names and/or photographs near the entrance to the room shows that children are valued. At the beginning of the school year, the teacher can post words of welcome to the students, possibly using phrases from each home language of children in that class. Within a few days, children can create their own words of welcome for families and other visitors to their classroom.

Beyond the initial welcome, many different factors communicate how children are viewed by the adults who created the classroom. Children who walk into a well-designed classroom feel like they belong there. The furniture is child-sized and arranged with "traffic flow" in mind. The learning materials in each center are organized and look inviting. The classroom looks interesting

and stimulating without being overwhelming. Special places for personal belongings are obvious.

A well-designed classroom is a pleasant place to be. It is a child-centered environment, but not a cute, cartoon-like atmosphere. Many teachers personalize the classroom using some touches of home. Art prints hang beside children's paintings. Plants are placed strategically around the room. Attractive baskets hold collections of books. A small table with a soft-light lamp positioned between two bean bag chairs gives the reading center the feeling of reading at home. To add to the aesthetics of the classroom, some teachers add upholstered furniture, tablecloths, curtains, silk or dried flower arrangements, fabric-covered walls, and quilted wall hangings.

Planning for an aesthetically pleasing environment is the perfect time to plan for multicultural components in the classroom. Many teachers include artifacts that represent a number of different cultures in their class environments. One teacher discovered a company that imported musical instruments created by indigenous people. She purchased twelve percussion instruments from twelve different countries, and arranged these on a small table in the music center. Another teacher asked a friend to buy baskets, tapestries, and molas during her trip to Guatemala. Within a week of her friend returning from vacation, this teacher had redone her classroom with new wall hangings and baskets holding books placed in every learning center. Still another teacher had traditional cooking utensils and serving pieces from Japan, Korea, and Lesotho, countries in her home center. Three of her students had immigrated from these countries and lent these artifacts to the class. Friends and families of students are often willing to lend artifacts or help acquire artifacts to add a multicultural dimension to the classroom.

Supporting Children's Self-Control

Teachers anticipate children's impulsive behaviors and arrange furniture to prevent them. For example, young children run given the opportunity. Knowing this, teachers arrange the classroom so there are no large open spaces where children can run.

An area rug that defines the group meeting area reminds children where to sit during story time. Low book shelves that define the science area remind children to hold class pets in that area, rather than carry them about the classroom.

Well-defined learning centers help children remember behaviors that are expected of them in each of those centers. For example, placing the block center in a corner and defining the other two sides of the center reinforces where block building is acceptable. Without the physical reminders, block structures can take over the classroom.

As early childhood educators work to create a risk-free, supportive environment, they use schedules to inform the children of class events. Posting the daily schedule gives young children a sense of security as they realize that each day's routine follows a set pattern.

Supporting Children's Independence

Children develop a sense of independence when they can access things that they need. Early childhood educators organized materials and supplies on low shelves so that children can easily reach things they need.

Organization of materials in an early childhood classroom is essential. Children need access to books, magazines, paper, writing tools, art supplies, and manipulatives that enable them to read, write, measure, weigh, count, and compare. Teachers place materials closest to the area where they will be used and typically put most materials in some kind of container. Teachers pay particular attention to the kinds of storage containers available and which ones, or combination of them, best suit the needs of the children. A variety of containers, tubs, baskets, shelves, and boxes used throughout the classroom keep materials organized and readily available to the children. This organization of the manipulatives, books, and community supplies enables the children to work independently.

Labeling containers adds to the accessibility of materials. Even though children can see through clear plastic boxes, it is helpful to label both the box and the place on a shelf where it belongs. For younger children, picture labels are more functional. As children begin paying attention to print, a handwritten word or two can be added to the picture label. Eventually, only the word label is used.

Supporting Children's Learning

Young children learn best when they are active. They learn as they interact with a variety of learning materials and with their peers and teacher (Bredekamp & Copple, 1997). Early childhood educators consider the cognitive, social, and physical developmental characteristics of young children, as well as how children learn best, to create an environment that supports the learning of children who

will use that space. Figure 2.1 shows how typical developmental characteristics of different ages affect the arrangement of classrooms.

Figure 2.1

Developmental Characteristics that Influence Classroom Arrangement

2-Year-Olds:
- begin to scribble with markers or crayons
- begin to choose activities that support development of fine and gross motor skills
- assert their independence

Therefore, Classrooms for 2-Year-Olds:
- have non-toxic washable markers, crayons, and large pieces of paper in places where children can get their own materials
- offer fine-motor skill related materials in different learning centers, e.g. stringing beads in the math center, playdough or clay in the art center, stacking toys in the home center and so on
- support children's growing abilities in self-help skills, e.g., cubbies where each child keeps his or her personal items, snack tables where children get their own snack
- offer gross motor skill related materials, e.g., push and pull toys, crawl through and climbing structures, rocking boat with one or two steps.

4-Year-Olds:
- learn best through physical activity, especially large-motor activity
- are learning to make decisions about their own activities
- have relatively short attention spans
- are beginning to work with others but still choose parallel play on a regular basis

Therefore, Classrooms for 4-Year-Olds:
- make sure that furniture can be moved for large physical movement
- limit the number of materials in any learning center, but change materials as children no longer choose those materials
- provide many different learning experiences from which children select
- offer materials that foster collaborative work, e.g. group murals, block constructions, dramatic play

6-Year-Olds:
- boisterous and quite social
- like games and artistic expression
- are moving from emergent literacy knowledge/skills into conventional literacy knowledge/skills

Therefore, Classrooms for 6-Year-Olds:
- have different areas that support small group work
- provide frequent opportunities for active and concrete exploration, especially with games focusing on different content/skills and creative expression with different artistic media
- have many opportunities for children to self-select reading and writing activities through placing a range of books and a variety of paper and writing tools in each learning center

Adapted from: Clayton, M.K. & Forton, M.B. (2001). *Classroom spaces that work.* Greenfield, MA: Northeast Foundation for Children, pp. 21-43.

Most early childhood educators prepare for children's exploration and learning through centers. Created appropriately, learning centers are environments that effectively support children's learning (Diffily, Donaldson, & Sassman, 2001).

Valuing Children's Work

Commercially produced materials are used sparingly in early childhood classrooms. Instead, children's work is displayed everywhere. When they see their own work throughout the classroom, children know that their work is valued. Being surrounded by their work reinforces the idea that the room belongs to them.

Drawings, paintings, writing, and computer printouts are posted on room dividers, the back of a bookcase, doors, or easels, in addition to the usual bulletin board and wall space. Constructions and works-in-progress have special display places on low bookshelves. Chart tablet pages or posterboard containing "work" of the class – poems the class is learning, dictation of agreements made during class meetings, or graphic organizers such as KWL charts – are posted in appropriate places. (The KWL chart organizes student planning and dialogue about learning into columns describing: What we **K**now; What we **W**ant to know, and What we have **L**earned.) The information is placed close to the children's eye level so they can refer to these charts independently.

Families and visitors to the classroom learn quite a bit about the life of the classroom from the things that are displayed in the room. However, documentation, done in the Reggio Emilia-style, offers adults a clear, direct explanation of the work and learning involved in a particular project (Edwards, Gandini, & Forman, 1998). Samples of the children's work and photographs of that work in progress communicate the learning that is going on in the classroom. When the teacher takes the time to write explanations of the children's work and the photographs, the children's learning is even more evident. In Reggio Emilia, and in American schools that are using this way of documenting children's work, teachers use several methods of recording what children do. "The camera, tape recorder, slide projector, typewriter, video camera, computer, and photocopying machine are instruments absolutely indispensable for recording, understanding, debating among ourselves, and finally preparing appropriate documents of our experience" (Edwards, Gandini, & Forman, 1998, p. 122). Virtually all the documentation gathered in these ways can be posted in and outside the classroom so that others can more easily understand the life of the classroom.

Considering Practical Concerns

Just as early childhood educators consider a number of factors as they arrange a classroom that supports children's learning, they also take into consideration health and safety issues as they create the environment. Some of these concerns are listed in Figure 2.2 and Figure 2.3. All adults in an early childhood program are responsible for ensuring a healthy and safe environment for children; however, it is best if each task is assigned to an individual person. This ensures that these important concerns are carried out.

Figure 2.2

Environmental Support for Children's Health

- Ensure children have independent access to drinking, toileting, and washing facilities.
- Provide ample supply of tissues and wastebaskets.
- Clean toys and learning materials appropriately.
- Clean surfaces regularly with disinfectant.
- Avoid using sponges that spread germs from surface to surface.
- Vacuum carpets and clean floors daily.
- Clean animals' cages twice a week.
- Post reminder signs about how to hold animals and wash hands afterward.

Figure 2.3

Environmental Support for Children's Safety

- Cover all electrical outlets.
- Secure electrical cords to the floor or wall.
- Inspect furniture and equipment regularly and make repairs immediately.
- Keep cleaning materials and other harmful products out of children's reach.
- Provide a locked closet, cabinet, or desk drawer for medication storage.
- Ensure pathways are uncluttered and nonslip.
- Ensure immediate cleanup of any spills.
- Check all plants to ensure no toxic plants are in the classroom.
- Inspect playground equipment daily and make repairs immediately.
- Arrange fall zones for any climbing equipment with mats for indoor equipment and 6" to 8" of sand or pea gravel for outdoor equipment.
- Install and maintain smoke alarms and fire extinguishers.

References:

Bickart, T.S., J.R. Jablon, & D.T. Dodge (1999). *Building the primary classroom: A complete guide to teaching and learning.* Washington, DC: Teaching Strategies and Portsmouth, NH: Heinemann.

Bredekamp, S., & C. Copple (1997). *Developmentally appropriate practice in early childhood programs.* Washington, DC: National Association for the Education of Young Children.

Clayton, M.K, & M.B. Forton, (2001). *Classroom spaces that work.* Greenfield, MA: Northeast Foundation for Children.

Diffily, D. E. Donaldson, & C. Sassman (2001). *The Scholastic book of early childhood learning centers.* New York: Scholastic.

Edwards, C., L. Gandini, & G. Forman, (1998). *The hundred languages of children: The Reggio Emilia approach - advanced reflections,* 2nd Ed. Greenwich, CT: Ablex.

Puckett, M.B. & D. Diffily (1999). *Teaching young children: An introduction to the early childhood profession.* Fort Worth, TX: Harcourt Brace College Publishers.

Checklist for Evaluating the Room Arrangement

Rate the items below on a scale of 1 to 4 with 1 representing "needs improvement" and 4 representing "outstanding."

_____1. The room looks inviting and welcoming.

_____2. Areas for whole group, small-group, and individual activities are clearly defined.

_____3. Active learning centers are grouped together away from quieter learning centers.

_____4. Small, private areas are included in the room arrangement.

_____5. The needs of any child with special needs have been accommodated in the arrangement of the meeting area, learning centers, and areas for small group meetings.

_____6. Materials and supplies are organized, labeled, and easily accessible to children.

_____7. Materials support the developmental needs of the children in the classroom.

_____8. Children's work is prominent throughout the classroom.

_____9. Concerns for children's health and safety are evident in the class arrangement and in the teacher's observations of children.

About the Author

Deborah Diffily is an assistant professor of Early Childhood Education at Southern Methodist University in Dallas. Her primary areas of interest are supporting emergent and scientific development, teaching young children through projects, and working with families.

Chapter 3

Advances in brain imaging techniques are providing researchers with new information about human brain growth, activity, and plasticity. This information can profoundly affect child care and early childhood practices. Emerging research indicates that experience, especially active, creative play, is extremely important in promoting healthy development in children. Implications for education and child development are still tentative, but a significant body of evidence exists to allow for meaningful guidelines for practitioners.

This chapter presents a description of the structure and activity of the human brain, followed by a discussion of "sensitive periods" for brain growth and neurological development, and the effects of neglect, trauma, and play deprivation. The final section centers on the importance of play for brain growth, and implications and recommendations for education and child development regarding appropriate play for healthy development.

Play and Neuroscience

Pei-San Brown and Joe Frost

Brain Imaging Techniques

Several imaging techniques are currently used to measure brain activity and neurological development. Among these are magnetic resonance imaging (MRI), computerized axial tomography (CAT), and positron emission tomography (PET). The MRI is especially good at imaging soft tissue and blood vessels. The CAT scan produces 3-dimensional images used to study the physical and chemical properties of the body. The PET scan reveals not only brain structure and activity, but also brain energy use. The different colors of the PET scan image show how fast the different parts of the brain metabolize energy.

What Brain Imaging Reveals

Blood flow and glucose use in the brain are indicators of brain activity in humans and other animals, and can be measured by using PET scans (Chugani, 1994). Chugani, a pediatric neurologist, has found that the glucose use in typical human brains follows a specific pattern at each age throughout life. Between the ages of approximately 4-10 years, brain glucose use peaks at more than twice that of adults. However, around 8-10 years of age, these levels start to decline in some regions of the brain, and by 16-18 years of age, children's brain glucose use levels have usually reached adult rates (Chugani, 1994, 1997). These findings do not apply to children who have had brain injury, trauma, disease, or developmental delays. Chugani also reviewed research that reported that on average, brain blood flow and oxygen use are approximately 30% to 80% higher in children than they are in adults (Chugani, 1997).

Neuronal Structure and Function

The brain is made up of nerve cells called neurons. As children grow, the number of neurons in their brains does not change dramatically, but each cell grows in size. As neurons grow, they transmit impulses faster. If the neurons are stimulated frequently, the connections between neurons are reinforced, eventually creating permanent neurological paths to and from the brain and the rest of the body (Fitt, 1988).

Both the positive and negative experiences that children have help to establish and strengthen certain neural pathways. However, if experiences are too few in number, it is believed that synapses (the points where nerve impulses passes from one neuron to another), are not strengthened, which means that efficient neuronal pathways are harder to form and neural pathways may not be established at all (Shore, 1997). When the neuronal pathways are not strengthened through timely and appropriate experiences, they are pruned. In other words, synapses that are not used frequently enough will be eliminated. Thus, brain growth can be thought of as a "use it or lose it" process (Shore, 1997, p. 20).

Prime Times for Optimal Development

The brain's circuits are wired most easily during a "critical period," also called a "sensitive period" (Greenough, Black, & Wallace, 1987), "plastic period" (Shore, 1997), and "learning window" or "window of opportunity" (Begley, 1996). This period can be thought of as a prime time for optimal development of certain types of thinking and skills such as learning to play a musical instrument or learning a second language (Shore, 1997). "Once the prime time has passed, opportunities for forging certain kinds of neural pathways appear to diminish substantially" (Shore, 1997, p. 38). The development of the brain's hard-wired circuits depends upon its exposure to different types of stimulation and the timing of experiences to establish and strengthen synaptic connections (Shore, 1997).

Critical periods are flexible, negotiable, and open to interpretation. The following is a list of estimated windows of opportunity compiled from reviews of brain research (Begley,1996; Frost, 2001a; Frost, 2001b; Frost, et al., 2001; & Nash, 1997):

- Motor development, gross and fine motor—before birth to 10 years of age

- Emotional control—before birth to 2 years

- Vision—birth to 8 years

- Social attachment—birth to 2 years

- Vocabulary—birth to 10+ years

- Language—birth to 10 years

- Second language—birth to 10 years

- Math and logic—1 to 4 years of age

- Music—3 to 10 years

- Stress response—birth to 5 years

- Emotions, planning, making good judgments—puberty

Some neuroscientists propose that critical periods are present early in life, more specifically in the first 8-10 years of life, and parents and educators should respond readily and appropriately to them. However, this does not mean that the end of a critical period signals the end of a child's opportunity for development during a particular "window of opportunity." Researchers are now concluding that there are crucial periods when children are most able to grasp certain skills or concepts, but that they continue to learn new skills even past those periods (Early Childhood Today, 1997). Evidence is accumulating that there is not only a period of rapid neural development during infancy, followed by pruning, but such phenomena also exist during the preteen and teen years for such functions as planning, judgment, and emotional regulation (Begley, 2000).

There are differing opinions on whether the evidence for critical periods is accurate. The most outspoken critic of this theory is Bruer (1999). Bruer asserts that neuroscience does not support the idea of critical periods. He states that those who promote the idea of critical periods are making assumptions about the rates and efficiency of children's learning compared to adults' learning. For example, he criticizes Chugani's position on critical periods, stating that Chugani's research was done on epileptic children, and therefore cannot be generalized to the entire population of children.

Bruer and other scholars such as Jerome Kagan, a child psychologist, believe that the emphasis on the early years, especially the first 3 years of life, has spawned unnecessary toys and activities for children. They believe that children might be over-stimulated by parents trying to teach them 20 hours out of the day, and that they are unnecessarily forced to listen to Mozart (Bowser, 1999).

Adults also need to understand that pushing children into school-like academic lessons at earlier and earlier ages can in fact harm children. They need time to play, to grow and develop through hands-on experiences, with just enough stimulation to keep them interested, engaged, and challenged. They also need down time, time during which they are not externally stimulated and during which they can process things internally. Purchasing educational toys for infants does not necessarily benefit them in the future. Most toys that claim to be educational are in fact recommended for children who are actually too young to use them (Consumer Product Safety Commission [CPSC], in press). All the important people and things that children need can already be found in most American homes.

Negative Factors Affecting Brain Growth

Research on neglect, trauma, and play deprivation in humans supports the premise that the first years of life are very important to brain growth and neurological development. "Negative factors in the environment can have adverse effects on cognitive development" (Frost, 2001a, 2001b). Bruce Perry, a child psychiatrist and brain research scholar at Baylor University College of Medicine states that "children who don't play much or are rarely touched develop brains 20% to 30% smaller than normal for their age" (Nash, 1997, p. 51).

Trauma, Abuse, and Neglect

Early trauma and/or abuse can cause extreme anxiety, depression, attachment problems, and can interfere with cognitive development. Traumatic experiences, especially repetitive ones, influence the biology of the brain (Perry, 2001). Physical or emotional neglect, including a chronic lack of stimulation, can impact children's ability to control impulses and violent tendencies. When neglect and trauma damage the brain's ability to regulate itself, the parts of the brain that control the more primitive survival-related impulses (the brainstem and midbrain) become overdeveloped, and the parts of the brain responsible for problem-solving and empathy (the cortex and limbic system) remain underdeveloped (Perry, 1996). What this means is that some children may be quicker to respond (impulsive behaviors) often in negative ways, acting before they think rationally about a situation.

Parental Depression

Parental depression that persists beyond just a few months can have lasting negative impact on children's development (Ounce of Prevention Fund, 1996). Because depression can consume parent's entire thought processes, those with depression often become unable to respond appropriately to infants' cries, and are less likely to provide the necessary cognitive stimulation and emotional support that their children need. Dawson, Hessl, & Frey, (1994) reported that depressed mothers had more negative and less positive affect, were less active and more distant from their infants, were more likely to be controlling and intrusive when they were interacting with their infants. They were also less able to adapt sensitively to their infants' emotional signals Their infants were shown to be more withdrawn and less active than other infants, had shorter attention spans, were less motivated to master new skills, and had elevated heart rates and cortisol levels. When mothers were intrusive or negative with infants, the infants showed less brain activity. (*Note:* Cortisol is a hormone secreted by the adrenal gland. Under stress, anxiety, and depression the levels of this hormone in the blood increase.)

Substance Abuse

Another factor that impinges on children's lives is substance abuse within children's environments, both before and after birth. Alcohol exposure may cause prenatal infants to develop stagnant or atrophied neurons and dendrites, and to have less neuron development in the neural tube, which eventually forms the brain and spinal cord. Infants of alcoholic mothers have reduced brain activity, especially in the left hemisphere of the brain (Janzen, Nanson, & Block, 1995). Furthermore, infants are at greater risk of fetal alcohol syndrome (FAS) if their mothers drink heavily during pregnancy. Fetal Alcohol Syndrome is believed to be related to low birth weight, growth deficiencies, facial abnormalities, some neurological disorders, mental retardation, behavioral problems, and problems with perceptual, linguistic, and fine motor skills.

Prenatal exposure to the by-products of tobacco smoking is also associated with developmental delays and impairments, and behavioral problems (Wakschlag,

Lahey, Loeber, Green, Gordon, & Leventhal, 1997). Postnatal exposure to cocaine is related to problems with attention, information processing, learning, and memory; changes in heart rate, blood pressure and cortisol cycles, and delayed or impaired motor development (Mayes, Bornstein, Chawarska, & Granger, 1995).

Poverty

Poverty aggravates and intensifies risk factors for children's development (Egeland, Carlson, & Sroufe, 1993). Families in poverty often do not have adequate access to safe shelter, sufficient food, and medical care. They tend to experience extremely high stress and are sometimes exposed to violence. Children living in poverty are more likely to have attachment difficulties leading to emotional and social problems, be placed in special education classrooms, and be retained in grade. Some scholars conclude that "decline in functioning observed at each developmental period seems to have been related to adverse living conditions, not inherent factors and traits within each child" (Egeland et al., 1993, p. 520). However, not all children living in poverty languish. Some of them excel academically and/or socially, and their secure attachment to a caregiver is thought to be one of the determining factors (Egeland et al., 1993).

Why Play is Important for Brain Growth and Neurological Development

Providing children opportunities to play with others and a variety of materials supports healthy brain growth and helps to avoid unhealthy neurological development. Epstein, a pediatrician, believes that "touching, holding, rocking, talking, listening and reading, or just playing with a child dramatically influences the youngster's brain development" (Epstein, 2001, p. 1). He believes that children's brain growth and neurological development is influenced by a combination of both genetics and environment. Since the quality of neural development is shaped by a child's experiences (Begley, 2000, p. 25), neglecting play can lead to serious consequences to children's brain growth and neurological development (CHILD, 2001).

Recently, Frost, Wortham, and Reifel (2001) described principles that support the relationship between play and brain growth. They assert that 1) "all healthy young animals play, and that the urge to play is inherent; 2) "the range and complexity of play quickly increase as neurons start hardwiring connections at a remarkable rate;" 3) "the early games and frivolity of animals and humans equip them for the skills they will need later in life,"- skills such as resourcefulness, creativity, and adaptability; and 4) "play is essential for healthy development" (p. 84). Further these authors suggest that although the link between children's development and neuroscience is not completely confirmed, it is clear that children's early experiences, which are usually play-based, influence the formation of neural circuits.

Benefits of Play

Play that is beneficial to brain growth is active, creative, and social. Active play is play that involves the body in gross and fine motor movement, and engages the mind in problem-solving. Creative play also involves problem solving, as well as imagination and flexibility. It also promotes feelings of accomplishment and ownership. Social play is any type of play that takes place in a social context and includes social interaction. Play that is beneficial to brain growth fosters children's physical, cognitive, social, and emotional development.

Physical Development

Movement is important for brain growth and neurological development (Leppo, Davis, & Crim, 2000). Physical movement and the experiences associated with that movement (exploration of the environment), contribute information to the brain and help facilitate neurological connections in a part of the brain called the cerebellum (Leppo, Davis, & Crim, 2000). The cerebellum is associated with spatial perception, memory, selective attention, language, information handling, and decision making, and because movement contributes to the cerebellum's development, it also seems that movement would be beneficial to these cognitive skills (Leppo et al., 2000). Creative movement, free play outdoors, physical education and other open-ended activities that promote gross and fine motor movement enhance children's neurological development. Sedentary activities such as viewing television and playing video/computer games should be limited, and children should be encouraged to be physically active.

Cognitive Development

Open-ended play activities are important for brain growth and neurological development because of their emphases on the process of play rather than a single correct outcome. Pepler (1986) found that play experiences allow children to create multiple solutions to problems,

which helps them develop problem-solving skills. Most of the neurons in the brain are devoted to sensing information, analyzing it, and deciding how to respond to it (Sylwester 1995).

Bruce Perry concludes that children learn in a richer fashion with multi-sensory presentations of content (Perry, 2000). For instance, if a lesson is accompanied by a song, it may help students to remember the lesson because they have perceived it through multiple senses. Perry also believes that children learn best when they are given time to mull over information. He maintains that keeping children constantly occupied keeps children from reflecting on information, preventing short term memories from becoming long term memories.

Music is also important for brain growth and neurological development. Music is thought to help synchronize the hemispheres of the brain. This development is important because it is believed that optimal learning occurs when both hemispheres of the brain work together. Music makes the brain more receptive to learning by altering brain waves. One possible explanation for this is that music's rhythm and harmony simulate vital patterns in brain growth and neurological development. Moreover, because music evokes powerful emotional responses, it can heighten (or lessen) emotional involvement in learning. Heightened emotional involvement may create stronger synapses, thereby making information easier to remember (Davies, 2000).

Children need a multitude of diverse, open-ended materials and toys. Blocks, sand, water, art materials, and musical instruments are all inexpensive open-ended materials that stimulate children's imaginations and hone their problem-solving skills. However, children younger than 4 years of age may need toys that are more representational (e.g., pretend telephone, small cars and trucks, dress-up clothes) to help them engage in pretend play. Children need sufficient time to process and remember information, and they need exposure to new concepts and subject matter content through multi-sensory presentations.

Emotional Development

As described previously, trauma, abuse, and neglect can significantly alter children's brain growth patterns and emotional development. Children's emotional investment in their play is absolute. Play therapist Garry Landreth (1991) believes that much of the time, children are not able to verbally express what they feel and how intensely they feel it. He states that "play is the concrete expression of the child, and is the child's way of coping with his/her world" (p. 13). Because the end product of play is usually less important than the process of play, play involves the child's emotional self in creative expression, and can reveal the child's experiences, desires, feelings, and self-perception (pp. 13-15). In addition, "play represents the child's attempt to organize her experiences, her personal world. Through the process of play, the child experiences a feeling of being in control" (p. 15). Allowing children to guide their own play can promote positive emotional development. Observing children's play in addition to listening to their words can help caregivers more accurately evaluate children's emotional development. Caregivers should also make sure that expectations for children are clearly defined in a way that children can understand.

Social Development

Trauma, abuse, and neglect can adversely affect children's brain growth patterns and social development. "Peer relations contribute substantially to both social and cognitive development and to the effectiveness with which we function as adults. Indeed, the single best childhood predictor of adult adaptation is not school grades, and not classroom behavior, but rather, the adequacy with which the child gets along with other children" (Hartup, 1992, p.1). Children need opportunities for group play with many different playmates, and they need adults who engage in positive social interactions with them.

Activities Not Beneficial to Brain Growth

Some activities often associated with play, such as viewing television and engaging in electronic games, do not necessarily promote brain growth and neurological development. Television-watching is often referred to as a "passive" activity because the viewer has no incentive for being physically engaged. Furthermore, "spoon-feeding" information to the child audience does not usually promote active engagement in information processing. Furthermore, as asserted in a recent position statement, watching violent acts on television, or engaging in violent acts during video/computer game playing, may desensitize children to aggression, and encourage aggressive and anti-social behavior (American Academy of Child and Adolescent Psychiatry, American Academy of Family Physicians, American Academy of Pediatrics, American Medical Association, American Psychiatric Association, & the American Psychological Association,

2000). This joint statement, published by national associations of child and adolescent health states that:

> ...well over 1000 studies, including reports from the Surgeon General's office, the National Institute of Mental Health, and numerous studies conducted by leading figures within our medical and public health organizations, point overwhelmingly to a causal connection between media violence and aggressive behavior in some children. Violence can lead to increases in aggressive attitudes, values and behaviors, particularly in children. (American Academy of Child and Adolescent Psychiatry et al., 2000).

Playing with academically-oriented computer programs and learning to read, write, and do arithmetic before entering school do not necessarily benefit children. Children are spending increasingly less time playing outdoors with other children and more time in front of the computer screen. Benefits from playing computer games do not outweigh the benefits of active outdoor play within a social context. Thompson states, "because these ebbs and flows in the pace of timing of brain growth are part of the developmental timetable, simply seeking to accelerate the rate of neural growth in developing organisms is not always wise" (Thompson, 1997, p. 11).

Conclusion

The relationship between brain research and early childhood education is still speculative. We do not know exactly which play materials and activities might create or strengthen neurological connections. However, we do suggest that caregivers follow the recommendations in the checklist below, adapted from Frost, Wortham, and Reifel (2001, pp. 89-91), to provide children with opportunities for making positive neurological connections. These principles are extended to every environment in which children are present.

Checklist for Evaluating Play Opportunities and Quality of Play

_____1. Children are provided pleasing social interactions with caregivers

2. Children are provided toys and play objects that are:

_____Visually interesting

_____Auditorally engaging

_____Engaging to the senses of smell and touch

_____Open-ended

_____3. Children are provided with a balance of noisy and quiet activities

_____4. Children are provided with a balance of individual and group activities

_____5. Children are presented with content in a multi-sensory fashion

_____6. Expectations for children are clear.

_____7. Activity goals are challenging yet attainable for children.

_____8. Reading, singing, and dancing are available to children everyday, and television watching and video/computer game playing are limited.

_____9. Violent television programs and video/computer games are eliminated from the play environment.

_____10. Children are protected from excessive stress.

References

American Academy of Child and Adolescent Psychiatry, American Academy of Family Physicians, American Academy of Pediatrics, American Medical Association, American Psychiatric Association, & the American Psychological Association. (2000, July 26). *Joint statement on the impact of entertainment violence on children—Congressional public health summit.* http://www.aacap.org/press%5Freleases/2000/0726.htm

Begley, S. (1996, February 19). Your child's brain. *Newsweek*, 55-62.

Begley, S. (2000, Fall/Winter). Wired for thought. *Newsweek Special Edition: Your Child*, 25-30.

Bowser, B. A. (1999, September 29). Young minds. *Online NewsHour.* http://www.pbs.org/newshour/bb/youth/july-dec99/three_9-29.html.

Bruer, J. T. (1999, May). In search of brain-based education. *Phi Delta Kappan*, 649-657.

CHILD. (2001, September). Brain structure and critical periods. *Today's Playgrounds*, 18-19.

Chugani, H. T. (1997). Neuroimaging of developmental nonlinearity and developmental pathologies. In R. W. Thatcher, G. Reid Lyon, J. Runsey, & N. Krasnegor (Eds.) *Developmental neuroimaging: Mapping the development of brain and behavior* (pp. 187-195). San Diego, CA: Academic Press.

Chugani, H. T. (1994). Development of regional brain glucose metabolism in relation to behavior and plasticity. In Geraldine Dawson & Kurt W. Fischer (Eds.), *Human behavior and the developing brain* (pp. 153-175). New York: The Guildford Press.

Consumer Product Safety Commission (CPSC). (In press). *CPSC Toy Guidelines: Research Document.* Washington DC: Consumer Product Safety Commission.

Davies, M. A. (2000, Spring). Learning...the beat goes on. *Childhood Education*, 148-153.

Dawson, G., Hessl, D., & Frey, K. (1994). Social influences on early developing biological and behavioral systems related to risk for affective disorder. In *Development and Psychopathology*. Cambridge: Cambridge University Press.

Early Childhood Today. (1997, August-September). Jane Healy, Ph.D., on current brain research. *Scholastic Early Childhood Today*, 42-43.

Egeland, B., Carlson, E., & Sroufe, L. A. (1993). Resilience as process. In *Development and psychopathology*. New York: Cambridge University Press.

Epstein, B. A. (2001). *The importance of early brain development.* http://www.allkids.org/Epstein/Articles/Brain_Development.html

Fitt, S. S. (1988). *Dance kinesiology.* New York: Schirmer Books.

Frost, J. L. (2001a). *Neuroscience, play and child development.* Paper presented at the International Play Association/USA Triennial National Conference, Longmont, Colorado.

Frost, J. L. (2001b). *Neuroscience, play and play environments.* Presentation.

Frost, J. L., Wortham, S. C., & Reifel, S. (2001). *Play and child development.* Upper Saddle River, NJ: Prentice-Hall, Inc.

Greenough, W. T., Black J. E., & Wallace, C. S. (1987). Experience and brain development. *Child Development*, 58, 539-559.

Hartup, W. W. (1992). *Having friends, making friends, and keeping friends: Relationships as educational contexts.* ED 345 854. Urbana, IL: ERIC Clearinghouse on Elementary and Early Childhood Education.

Janzen, L. A., Nanson, J. L., & Block, B. W. (1995). Neuropsychological evaluation of preschoolers with FAS. Neruotoxicol Teratol 17 (May-June): 273-279.

Landreth, G. (1991). *Play therapy: The art of the relationship.* Bristol, PA: Accelerated Development.

Leppo, M. L., Davis, D., & Crim, B. (2000, Spring). The

basics of exercising the mind and the body. *Childhood Education*, 142-147.

Mayes, L. C., Bornstein, M. H., Chawarska, K., & Granger, R. H. (1995). Information processing and developmental assessments in 3-month-old infants exposed prenatally to cocaine. *Pediatrics*, 95 (April): 539-545.

Nash, J. M. (1997, February 3). Fertile minds. *Time*, 49-56.

Ounce of Prevention Fund. (1996). *Starting smart: How early experiences affect brain development*. Chicago: Ounce of Prevention Fund.

Pepler, D. (1986). Play and creativity. In G. Fein & M Rivkin (Eds.), *The young child at play, Reviews of research* (Vol. 4, pp. 143-154). Washington D.C.: National Association for the Education of Young Children.

Perry, B. D. (1996). Incubated in terror: Neurodevelopmental factors in the "cycle or violence." In M. D., Osofsky, (Ed.). *Children, youth, and violence: Searching for solutions*. New York: Guilford Press.

Perry, B. D. (2000, November 1). *Put brain research to work in the classroom*. Scholastic Teacher Radio. http://teacher.scholastic.com/teacherradio/past_childdev.htm.

Perry, B. D. (2001, April 24). *Effects of violence on how children learn*. Scholastic Teacher Radio. http://teacher.scholastic.com/teacherradio/past_childdev.htm.

Shore, R. (1997). *Rethinking the brain: New insights into early development*. New York: Families and Work Institute.

Sylwester, R. (1995). A celebration of neurons: An educator's guide to the human brain. Alexandria, VA: Association for Supervision and Curriculum Development.

Thompson, R. A. (1997). *Early brain development and early intervention*. Paper commissioned by the Institute for Families in Society, University of South Carolina, under the direction of the Starting Points Team and the Maternal, Infant, and Child Heath (MICH) Council, State of South Carolina.

Wakschlag, L. S., Lahey, B. B., Loeber, R., Green, S. M., Gordon, R. A., & Leventhal, B. L. (1997). Maternal smoking during pregnancy and the risk of conduct disorder in boys: Archives of General Psychiatry, U. S. National Center for Health Statistics, 1996. *The Monthly Vital Statistics Reports*. Washington, DC: The Bureau of the Census.

About the Authors

Pei-San Brown is a founding member of the Children's Institute for Learning and Development (CHILD) and a doctoral student in Early Childhood Education at the University of Texas at Austin. She has been an educator for many years and has conducted research with the Consumer Products Safety Commission (CPSC), the National Institute of Child Health and Human Development (NICHD), the National Aeronautics and Space Association (NASA), the University of California at Irvine, and several departments at the University of Texas. She holds a Masters from The University of Texas at Austin in Early Childhood Education, as well as a Bachelors of Science in Biology, and a Bachelors of Art in Dance from the University of California at Irvine. Her current research is focused on gender construction in early childhood.

Joe Frost is Parker Centennial Professor Emeritus, University of Texas at Austin. He has taught in public schools and helped establish Head Start centers. He is former president of the Association for Childhood Education International (ACEI) and of the American branch of the International Play Association. He taught graduate and undergraduate courses in education and child development at several universities, supervised 52 Ph.D. dissertations, directed research on play and play environments, and authored or edited 17 books and more than 100 professional articles and reports. He was selected Texas Teacher Educator of the Year by the Texas Association for the Education of Young Children (TAEYC) in 1989. He has lectured and provided technical assistance throughout Europe, Asia and North America. His present activities include writing, directing research, and consulting with schools, law firms, playground equipment manufacturers, and government agencies.

Chapter 4

The journey to becoming literate begins early in life. Daily interactions with infants as simple as a smile or a greeting can stimulate a response that begins to lay the foundation for a successful future in a literate world.

Language development begins with the first sounds that babies make when imitating those around them. Experiences of listening, speaking, and responding to others become woven throughout a day. Games, songs, and rhymes delight young minds.

Literacy Development and Young Children

Kay Moberg

Adults are the facilitators, teacher, and caregivers in the classroom environment. The classroom must become a rich literacy environment that encourages experimentation with literacy beginning at birth and extending through the primary grades. Early attempts at literacy including, speaking, listening, reading, and writing must be supported by the literate adults who interact with children.

Another component of a quality literacy environment is the instructional methodology that is used to introduce young children to literacy. Recently, recommendations from the National Association for the Education of Young Children, The International Reading Association, The National Reading Panel, and the National Research Council have presented research and scientific evidence to guide early childhood educators in understanding the critical aspects of early literacy development (National Association for the Education of Young Children and the International Reading Association, 1999; The Partnership for Reading, 2001; National Research Council, 1999).

The essentials components of early literacy instruction are included in this document to promote awareness of the critical skill areas that early childhood educators need to teach young children. They are, Listening, Speaking, and Vocabulary Development; Concepts of Books and Print; Comprehension; Phonological Awareness, Phonemic Awareness, and Phonics.

Research consistently demonstrates that the more children know about language and literacy before they arrive at school, the better equipped they are to succeed in reading. Main accomplishments include: oral language skills and phonological awareness, motivation to learn and appreciation for literate forms, print awareness, and letter knowledge (National Research Council Report, 1999, p.8).

Listening, Speaking, and Vocabulary Development

Adults who provide challenging activities that inspire young children to extend their listening and speaking opportunities are laying a foundation for successful literacy skills. Children rely on supportive, positive relationships with the adults in their lives in order to learn. Some important experiences adults provide for young children are:

Ages Birth to Four Years
- Use eye contact when speaking with children
- Engage in language rich activities such as playing together and talking with each other while diapering, pouring juice, putting away toys, eating meals
- Read board books or wordless books with children sitting close by or in a lap
- Give children simple one-or two-step oral directions to respond to when asked
- Notice if children listen to stories with increasing attention and focus
- Ask children to repeat words and then sentences correctly
- Notice the child's use of new and expanded vocabulary to communicate ideas
- Invite young children to play the Name Game by naming familiar objects
- Name objects in the environment then provide written labels for them
- Expose children to books containing increasingly challenging vocabulary
- Select books with colorful and conceptual illustrations to talk about together

- Use words in conversation with children that they will later recognize and understand when reading
- Engage in meaningful dialogue with children often

Ages Five to Seven Years
- Provide opportunities for children to follow directions efficiently when asked: helping with a task, playing a game with rules, adding specific features to a drawing
- Guide children to listen to stories and books for a specific purpose; naming the characters, setting, predicting events, retelling the story
- Uses new and expanded vocabulary to communicate ideas through discussion, asking and answering questions, and relating events to personal experiences
- Create opportunities for children to perform stories, poems, or plays for others
- Read quality children's literature that encourages children to discuss concepts and ideas presented in the book.

Concepts of Books and Print

Early literacy development requires that young children learn how books and print work. The following concepts can be introduced, reviewed, and recalled as an adult reads aloud to children.

Ages Three to Six Years
- Demonstrate how to hold a book and turn pages of a book correctly. Begin reading holding a book upside down. Ask a child to tell you if you are holding the book correctly.
- Discriminate between different genres of books such as, fiction, nonfiction, poetry, or folk tales. Talk about the author's purpose in writing a book before reading it to the group. For example, "The author wants to tell a story about a boy who wants to fly;" or "The author wants to give us information about trees."
- Demonstrate where to locate the beginning of a sentence. Show a page of a book to the group. Ask a child to show you where you should begin to read.
- Demonstrate that print moves left to right and from top to bottom of a page. During reading, ask a child to show you where you should read next. Use a finger or a pointer to track the print while reading the book. Intentionally begin at the bottom of the page and ask, "Is this where I should begin to read?"
- Demonstrate that written words are separated by spaces. Write a sentence on chart paper with no

spaces, then try to read it. Ask, "What can I do to make this easier to read?"
- Recognize the use of capitalization and punctuation. When reading aloud to children, point out uses of the capital letter in text. Use different inflections when reading sentences with various punctuation marks.

Comprehension

The reason we read is to understand and comprehend the printed word. Building comprehension strategies begins by talking about what is read aloud to children. Thinking aloud allows readers to share their own thoughts and impressions with the group. Asking questions about what was read also leads children to comprehend what was read. Important information to inquire about when reading aloud, reading independently, or responding to literature with children include the following:

Ages Four to Eight Years
- After reading a story aloud, ask questions about the story.
- Take time to ask a child to predict what will happen next in a story then verify the prediction after the story is read.
- Ask questions that require the child to use prior knowledge to comprehend what was read.
- Provide opportunities to sequence events after hearing a story read aloud.
- Discuss the story elements such as character, setting, plot, and events.
- When reading independently use strategies such as rereading and searching for clues to make meaning of the text.
- Use graphic sources to organize information of make sense of what is read: create graphs, story webs, charts, Venn diagrams, maps.
- Provide opportunities for a child to retell a story with a beginning, middle, and end.
- After reading, recall important details.
- After reading, ask a child to summarize or paraphrase the book.
- During reading a story aloud, relate events in a story to specific life experiences for the children.
- Examine how illustrations add meaning to text.
- Provide materials for children to respond to stories and poems through expressive arts.

Children can and should develop some degree of phonological awareness in the preschool years, because it is a crucial early step toward understanding the alphabetic principle and, ultimately, toward learning to read. (Starting Out Right, 1999, p. 9).

Phonological Awareness

Phonological awareness, phonemic awareness, and *phonics* are terms widely used when discussing literacy development in young children. The terms are related but have distinct differences.

Phonological awareness is the broad term that includes *phonemic awareness. Phonological awareness* activities can include rhyming games, word play, segmenting words into syllables, and making rhyming words from the rime part of a word. For example, in the word *fat, -at* is the rime and the onset or initial consonant is *f-.*

Phonemic awareness is the ability to hear, identify, and manipulate the individual sounds or *phonemes* in spoken words. *Phonemes* are the smallest parts of sound in a spoken word. *Phonemic awareness* helps children learn to read and spell.

Phonics is the relationship between the sounds and letters in written language.

Early in a child's life, early literacy skills prerequisite to phonological awareness are developed. As young children acquire oral language they begin to hear sounds in words and notice patterns in language. There are many ways preschoolers begin to develop phonological and phonemic awareness.

Children who have phonemic awareness skills are likely to have an easier time learning to read and spell than children who have few or none of these skills. (Put Reading First, Partnership for Reading, 2001, p.2).

Ages Three to Four Years

- Listen to books read aloud that focus on the sounds of language. Read favorite books several times. Patterned books that repeat a line over and over are excellent ways to extend oral language experiences.

- Listen for rhymes in poems. Read simple poems that have rhyming words at the end of the line and are accompanied by colorful illustrations.

- Enjoy word play using language to create a silly sounding word. When reading a book aloud, reciting a poem, or singing a song, replace actual words with made-up words that are nonsensical.

- Sing songs together. All through the day sing songs

together. Play audiotapes, CD's or sing without accompaniment. Encourage movement to the music's beat. During transition activities, designate a song as a signal.

- Repeat nursery rhymes often. Accumulate a repertoire of rhymes that children can repeat by memory. Discuss the meaning of the rhymes.

Beginning in kindergarten through grade 1, children begin to refine their phonological and phonemic awareness by participating in some of the following activities:

Ages Five to Seven Years

- Listen to two sounds. Are these sounds the same or different?

- Listen to spoken word pairs. Do the words sound the same or different?

- Place a card on a table or clap for each word spoken in a sentence. I like kittens. (Place three cards on the table or clap three times.)

- Tap for each part heard in a word. *"Tom-my"* (Tap twice.)

- Identify pictures in a set of pictures that begin with the same beginning sound.

- Place three to five picture cards in a set for children to select from.

- Isolate and say the first or last sound in a spoken word. Use picture cards as visuals for children to listen for sounds in a spoken word.

- Tell which words in a group of words begin with the same sound. *Doll, dime,* and *door* all have /d/ at the beginning.

- Identify the beginning, middle, or ending sound in spoken words. The beginning sound of the word *gum* is /g/. The middle sound is /u/. The ending sound is /m/.

- Blending sounds in a spoken word, /h/a/t/. The word is *hat.*

- Segmenting a word into separate sounds, /c/a/t/. The word is *cat.*

Letter Awareness and Identification

Becoming aware of the names of letters and learning to identify them indicates that a child is beginning to understand the relationship letters have with written and spoken language. Many activities to strengthen the understanding that what is spoken is written and what is written is read are guided by caregivers in the classroom. During daily routines of reading aloud to children and interacting with them in play, there are many informal and formal opportunities to increase letter awareness.

Alphabetic Principle

The relationship between the sounds in spoken language and letters of written language are learned when phonics are taught systematically. The explicit teaching of phonics begins in kindergarten and extends to first grade.

Letter Awareness Goals and Activities for Children Ages 3-6

Recognize letters in the play environment

Play games such as *I Spy* to locate specific letters in the environment: Hide letter cards for children to find while they are working in learning centers.

Add a variety of alphabet blocks, letter cards, board games, alphabet puzzles, and alphabet books to learning centers.

Create a letter wall at the children's eye level, categorizing letters found in the environment, on cereal boxes or in advertisements.

Identifies letters that match

Play the game *Concentration* using a set of 4 to 8 letters at a time: Write the names of each letter on pairs of cards. Begin matching lowercase letters. Randomly place two of each letter face down on a table in rows of four. Each child takes a turn turning two cards face-up at a time. If the letters match the child keeps the cards and takes another turn.

Learn the names of capital and lowercase letters

Name some letters in alphabet picture books or other books read aloud.

Ask basic questions about the letters in books. Find the letter that begins your name.

With a small group of children play the game *Give Me A Letter*: Distribute one set of 4 to 8 letters to each child in the group. Have them line the cards in front of them so they can see each one. The teacher asks for a letter. The children search their cards to find the letter asked for. The child holds up the matching letter card, names the letter, and then returns the card to the set. Continue to play the game until each letter has been called at least twice.

Discriminates between capital and lowercase letters

With a small group of children, play the *Grab Bag* game: place two of each selected letter in a set of 4-8 letters into a paper bag. Each child takes turns picking a letter from the bag and saying its name. If the letter is named correctly, the card goes in a pile.

Understanding phonics leads to an understanding of the alphabetic principle of reading or the sound-letter relationships in words and significantly improves word recognition and spelling. Systematic phonics instruction includes teaching letter-sound correspondences in a logical sequence in order to read words.

Creating Quality Literacy Environments for Young Children

The literacy environment in a classroom is critical to the successful adult/child interactions that lead to literacy

---

Alphabetic Principle Learning Goals and Activities

Says the sound most associated with individual letters

Use pictures to introduce sounds of letters. Introduce one letter sound at a time. Name a set of several pictures that begin with the same sound. Ask the children to repeat each picture name. Emphasize the first sound of the pictures.

Play the *Looking for a Sound* game: Play the game with picture cards or letter cards. Place a set of letter (picture) cards face down on a table. Turn one letter (picture) over at a time. *What is the name of this letter (picture)? What sound does the letter ___make? What sound do you hear when you say___?*

Blends sounds of letters to read simple words by decoding

Use sound boxes to demonstrate the individual sounds of letters to blend into words. Two or three small connected squares works well.

Touch each letter of the word that you want to sound out. Ask children to make the sound for each letter in the word. Point under the letters quickly to signal to slide the sounds together to read the word.

Read high-frequency words

Use a manila file folders to create a *Words I Know* folder for each child. As high-frequency words that cannot be decoded are introduced or appear in reading passages, a child adds the word to an individual word bank that is kept on the inside of a file folder. The words can be listed alphabetically under individual letter headings.

Write the high-frequency words on cards. Play simple card games to practice reading the words quickly.

Spells words accurately

Play the *Say, Spell, and Write* game: Begin with two or three phoneme words. Say a word, ask children to spell the word aloud, then write the word.

Dictate a short list of words or bring sentences to children to write using their knowledge of letters and their sounds.

development. Adults set the stage for literacy growth by providing an environment rich with activities and materials that actively engage young children. An appropriate classroom environment is arranged so that children have materials they can get to easily. The physical arrangement of shelves and furniture takes into account the areas of the classroom where specific materials will be used.

To prepare children for reading instruction in the early grades, it is best that they be exposed to high quality language and literacy environments in their home, day care center, and preschools. (Starting Out Right. National Research Council, 1999, p.15).

Essential Materials that Enhance Literacy Development

The five most essential materials to include in an early literacy environment at each age level are:

Birth to Age Three Years

1. Board books, picture books, wordless books, story books with simple language or predictable text
2. Plastic tubs to store books on low shelves for toddlers to reach easily
3. Rocking chair for lap reading, singing, or reciting a rhyme
4. Camera to take pictures of other children in the classroom and favorite activities
5. Designated area of the classroom for small groups of children to interact with an adult on the floor.

Ages Four to Seven Years

1. A print-rich environment with labeled objects, shelves, and work areas so children can retrieve materials independently. Print in the environment should have a purpose such as: children interact with the print to read a daily message, take attendance, keep a reading log, read helper charts, or check library books in and out independently. A print-rich environment allows children to use the print that they see.
2. Display areas on the walls of the classroom for projects and murals to be mounted. Create the display area at the children's eye level whenever possible.
3. An area of the classroom where children can use wipe-off white boards and non-toxic markers or chalkboards and chalk to practice writing words and sentences. Keep a collection of letter card and word cards for children to use as models while they write.

4. A classroom that allows for large and small group instruction to take place. Position the tables and chairs so that small groups of children can work together on projects. Designate one area of the classroom for a teaching table to work with a small group of students who are at a similar ability level.
5. Literacy experiences extended to every learning center area in an early childhood classroom and every activity area in a primary classroom.

Extending Literacy Activities to Learning Center Areas

Language arts and literacy experiences can be spread over all of the learning centers affording children a variety of ways to experience listening, speaking, reading, and writing. Since literacy development becomes increasingly critical to learning in all content areas, it is beneficial to children to use their emerging literacy skills in developmentally appropriate ways as they work in their learning centers.

Young children especially need to be engaged in experiences that make academic content meaningful and build on prior learning. It is vital for all children to have literacy experiences in schools and early childhood programs. (NAEYC & IRA Joint Position Statement, Learning to Read and Write: Developmentally Appropriate Practices for Young Children, 1998).

The following suggests enrichment materials and activities to support language and literacy development in the learning center areas of an early childhood classroom.

Dramatic Play Area

Add a note pad for messages, telephone umbers, and grocery lists. Be sure there is a play telephone available to extend language development. Collect magazines, cookbooks, newspapers kept in a basket. Provide a mailbox for children to use to communicate with each other in writing. Include recipe cards, old checkbooks, small writing tablets and add a bulletin board to the center. Encourage children to role-play reading and writing behaviors they have observed.

Library Area

Maintain a classroom library area with a shelf, tubs, or baskets for book storage. Add pillows, small chairs and a table for comfortable places for independent reading. Select a variety of books including books related to topics studied in class, multi-cultural titles, and books with examples of diverse cultures and family environments. Select books that portray men and women, girls and boys in a variety of roles. (Make certain that books used with children are free of biases associated with gender, race, ethnicity, age, or ableness.) Rotate books in and out of the area occasionally. Add any class books or individual books created by the children.

Puppet Area

Provide an assortment of puppets for children to use to interact with during the center. Add books they might want to read using a character puppet. Provide wooden sticks, paper sacks, clean discarded socks, and assorted construction paper to design individual puppets.

Sand and Water Area

Letters and words can be traced in the sand with a short stick Wet the sand slightly to form the letters more distinctly.

Manipulative Area

Provide capital and lowercase alphabet cards, magnetic letters, tactile letters, letter puzzles, and word cards for children to use as models while they practice writing.

Block Building Area

Stock the center with graph paper to sketch structures to build or copy structures after building. Keep assorted writing tools, blank paper, and masking tape at the center including colored pencils, pens, pencils, and markers. Children may label their structures as they are constructed.

Writing Area

Include assorted writing tools, sizes and shapes or paper, folder paper to make greeting cards out of and examples of greeting cards that children can copy words from. Encourage children to label their completed art project or write sentences about their completed art.

Math Area

Add paper and pencils so children can write numerals and record their experiences with various math materials. Encourage children to take class surveys to poll their friends for their favorite flavor of ice cream, pet, dessert, sport then tally the results.

Outdoor Area

Encourage children to take books outdoors to read or refer to while playing. Children may make lists including what they are going to play when outdoors, friends they plan to play with, or write notes to friends to meet them at a specific place outdoors. Make class lists to post so that children can take turns selecting play equipment. Children can write stories or draw pictures about what they enjoyed while playing outdoors.

Meeting the Literacy Needs of Children with Special Needs

It is the responsibility of the adult to accommodate the environment for children with special needs. The environment should be adjusted to allow for adaptive or assistive equipment and furnishings. The teacher can create passageways that allow for the child's freedom of movement from one area to another within the classroom, and can provide small seating or group areas that encourage peer support and social and intellectual sharing among the children. Access to materials and inclusion in all appropriate activities afford the child a measure of independence and builds a sense of competence. The environment both physical and psychological must be supportive and inclusive. The child with special needs must feel included in all activities available to other children in the classroom.

Instruction in oral language development and phonological awareness may need to be adjusted for certain special needs. Slowing the pace for children who are struggling to learn concepts, pre-teaching or re-teaching concepts may be needed, or working with no more than two to four children at a time will help some children learn. Both visual and auditory materials used in the literacy curriculum may need to be adapted for children with vision or hearing impairments. Participation in speaking and listening activities may need to be adjusted in order for every child to be successful. Selection of books with large print and clear illustrations may be necessary for some children. Sound amplifying equipment may be necessary for others.

It is important to consider the instructional level of the child before delivering a lesson. This is particularly important for children with developmental delays who may not achieve literacy skills at the same pace as others and may requiring more time, repetition, practice, and perhaps alternative strategies. Every child has the right to have a positive, successful school experience.

Summary

Early language and literacy experiences such as those presented in this chapter form the foundation for a child's future reading success. Parents, caregivers, and teachers create an atmosphere of joy, enthusiasm, and love for reading through the experiences they present to young children in their care every day. Literacy experiences that build oral language skills and phonological awareness, reading books aloud with children, and development of concepts of print motivate young children to want to learn to read. We have the responsibility to help children obtain the knowledge they need to explore being readers and writers. This goal can be accomplished by providing engaging activities that excite children and ultimately lead them toward success as readers and writers.

Take a critical look at your daily classroom routine and create additional opportunities for literacy experiences. Accept the challenge to share your love of literacy with every child every day.

References

National Research Council (1999). *Starting out right: A guide to promoting children's reading success.* Washington, DC: National Academy Press.

The Partnership for Reading (2001). *Put reading first: The research building blocks for teaching children to read.* Center for the Improvement of Early Reading Achievement, United States Department of Education, National Institute for Literacy, National Institute of Child Health and Human Development.

National Association for the Education of Young Children and the International Reading Association (1998). *Learning to read and write: Developmentally appropriate practices for young children.* Washington, DC: Author.

Checklist for Evaluating a Quality Literacy Environment

Rate the items below on a scale of 1 to 4 with "needing improvement" as 1 and "outstanding" as 4.

_____1. Materials are organized so that they are easily accessible to children.

_____2. Labels and other print are posted in the classroom at children's eye level.

_____3. Children use the print in the environment for specific purposes such as taking attendance, reading the daily schedule, or keeping a reading log.

_____4. Space for large and small group instruction is provided.

_____5. Literacy activities are evident in learning center or instructional areas of the classroom.

_____6. Instructional materials the teacher uses to teach phonological awareness, phonemic awareness, or phonics is organized before the lesson begins.

_____7. The classroom library is well maintained with a variety of books and books meet the reading levels and interests of the children.

_____8. The teacher paces the literacy instruction to the instructional needs of the child.

_____9. Projects and murals representing work by the children are displayed in the classroom.

_____10. Children are read aloud to daily.

About the Author

Kay Moberg is the Director of Reading Development for Voyager Expanded Learning. She has recently completed the development of a kindergarten and grade 1 reading program. She served as Vice-President of the Texas Association for the Education of Young Children in 1984 and was the first recipient of the Texas Classroom Teacher of the Year Award from the TAEYC in 1986.

Chapter 5

The Essential Playground: Playing for Keeps!

Paul Jacobs

Playgrounds are exciting and creative places for adventure, sport, and imagination (Frost, 1997; Rivkin, 1995). Playgrounds provide opportunities that indoor play settings simply cannot (Greenman, 1988). Nature, diversity, and flexibility are but a few of the benefits of outdoor play environments. During the past 20 years there have been ingenious innovations and design in commercial playground equipment (Frost, 1992; Frost, Wortham, & Reifel, 2001).

Playgrounds are exciting and creative places for adventure, sport, and imagination (Frost, 1997; Rivkin, 1995). Playgrounds provide opportunities that indoor play settings simply cannot (Greenman, 1988). Nature, diversity, and flexibility are but a few of the benefits of outdoor play environments. During the past 20 years there have been ingenious innovations and design in commercial playground equipment (Frost, 1992; Frost, Wortham, & Reifel, 2001).

These innovations have captivated the imagination of playground designers, school administrators, teachers, and parents. Unfortunately, the high costs of these innovations may have actually deterred the development of creative playgrounds. The new, innovative commercial playground equipment tends to overshadow the creative potential of simple, inexpensive playgrounds. Teachers should be confident that they are capable of creating affordable and creative playgrounds (Jacobs, 1997).

Playgrounds do not have to be expensive. While purchasing high quality, commercial playground equipment can be quite expensive, some of the most innovative playgrounds in the world have been created out of very modest materials using practical and simple principles (Hurtwood, 1968). This chapter proposes a return to promoting the basic elements of play: child development and play development. The design of good playgrounds must take children's development into consideration (Frost, Wortham, & Reifel, 2001).

What should a playground do? That is the primary question. A well designed playground can encourage children's physical development (endurance and coordination) and cognitive development (creativity and problem solving). Playgrounds can also encourage social development (social interactions) and emotional development (self-confidence). When a playground is planned with children's development in mind, then it is simply a matter of providing the time, space, and materials for children to play (Jacobs, 1997).

Essentially, playgrounds should be designed for adventure (Lambert, 1992). Adventure does not require fancy, high-tech playground equipment (Shell, 1994). In fact, some of the most creative and adventurous playgrounds in the world are called, "adventure playgrounds" (Lambert, 1992). These are simple playgrounds with "junk" materials for children to create their own play. The "junk" that a creative playground contains can be easily solicited from the community and families who may need to do some serious "spring cleaning." Examples of "junk" include round edge spades for digging, clean plastic planters for digging and planting, wagons for hauling, plastic dishes for pretend play, and so on.

When planning a playground layout, there are four essential elements to be considered. These four elements are 1) equipment and/or provisions, 2) safety, 3) play value, and 4) management. These essential playground elements can be imagined as a table with four legs. The playground represents the tabletop, and each leg represents one of the elements, equipment/provision, safety, play value, and management. Each leg supports the table and complements the other legs.

Equipment and Provisions

A playground without toys and materials is a bleak playground. Equipment and provisions are what is on the playground for children to use in their play. However, there are a variety of ways to provide equipment and provisions that meet children's developmental play needs without breaking the bank. A large sand area with plastic storage tubs or a box for sand toys is an excellent, inexpensive way to stimulate play. Adding creative and dramatic play props along with the playground's natural features creates setting for creativity and a playground that is easy to maintain. With a little imagination and creativity, caregivers can add exciting and stimulating activities that compliment these simple provisions. Garage sales and "community wish lists" are excellent ways of locating provisions for a playground for adventure.

Safety

The element of safety refers to the quality of the equipment, behaviors of children, and adult supervision. The playground is a very physically active environment. The provisions must be sturdy, durable, and well constructed. The children need instruction, guidance and limits to help them use the playground safely. They will use the playground in ways that meet their needs, but their behaviors may place themselves or others in harms way. Caregivers can create playground rules that are sensitive to children's needs for active play and their developmental abilities. Of utmost importance to safe playground activity is a low adult-child ratio. There should be at least two adults on the playground with the children. Caregivers should anticipate children's behaviors and take measures to prevent accidents by removing hazards and making play behavior expectations clear. The adult should be mentally alert on the playground and ready to respond quickly to unanticipated problems.

Play Value

Play value has to do with how well the equipment and provisions encourage creative play. Children will use the playground in ways that are meaningful to them according to their developmental abilities. Therefore, the equipment and provisions ideally should match their emerging abilities and interests. Using portable equipment and provisions is the most flexible and affordable way to meet playground needs for children with a broad range of interests and developmental abilities.

Playground Management

Management is the teacher's role and responsibility. Management involves setting up and maintaining a safe and adventuresome playground. Playground management can be challenging because playgrounds are subject to harsh outdoor weather conditions. Also, typically, as shared space playgrounds are exposed to higher numbers of children each day than is a classroom. Good playground management requires a "team effort." For effective management, adults in a school or center should together plan and coordinate the use, provisioning, safety, play value, and management of the playground.

Often caregivers hope that purchasing a large climbing structure and swing set will suffice. For a while this works fine and the children enjoy the equipment. But after a couple of weeks, the children often begin to master the challenges of the climbing structure. Then they may begin risky behaviors such as climbing on the roofs of the climbing structure and jumping off, or becoming competitive in their swinging. Adults then find themselves in the uncomfortable position of having to do "crowd control" rather than encouraging and facilitating constructive and creative play.

The creative playground is one in which the four elements function together to support constructive play. Without each individual element, the playground is like a four-legged table with a missing leg. One might still work at the table, eat on it, and set things on it, but it will never be very sturdy. Good playgrounds require all four elements to be effective. Developing a playground management system is an important way to monitor the success of the playground's use, design, and development. Rather than simply looking through a playground catalogue for playground equipment, keep a record of how the children are using the playground. What safety issues arise? What maintenance problems have emerged, and what concerns have arisen regarding supervision?

Of utmost importance, children need a play environment that is responsive to their developmental play needs (Jacobs, 1997). They need equipment that supports growth and development in all domains, i.e., physical, social, emotional, cognitive, language, and literacy. Unfortunately, the history of playground development has been typified by a focus on the physical development of children (Frost, 1992). Meeting children's play needs means providing opportunities for intellectual, social, and emotional, as well as physical development. When planning the design and functions of a playground, adults need to give specific attention to the diverse developmental abilities of children using the playground, recognizing that children of the same age are not all alike. Additionally, a playground will quite likely need to be adapted for children with special needs.

Because children do not all develop at the same rate or in the same way, playgrounds need to be equipped for

flexibility (Frost, 1992). Designing or creating a playground that is both functional and flexible may seem daunting especially if the playground must be adaptable for children with varying developmental challenges (Hurtwood, 1968). Following a few simple principles of playground design can bypass many of the problems that teachers and administrators face in providing an adventurous playground.

Playground principle one: Keep it simple. Making a playground adventurous means keeping it simple (Frost, Shin, & Jacobs, 1998). The most effective adventurous playgrounds arise from the ideas and energy of the children (Lambert, 1992). Providing essential elements and materials accessible and stocked for children's use is a key. Just as families plan well and pack "light" for long road trips, well planned playgrounds can be "light," physically and economically. Simple means providing essentials not frills.

Simple, yet versatile, playgrounds have only a few key requirements. First, playgrounds need storage. Storage can be large buckets, bags, or outdoor sheds. The storage should be easily accessible to the children. Even more appropriate is to create a variety of different storage options. Having a basic storage shed is a good idea, and stocking it with bags of balls, buckets of sand toys, and baskets of dress up clothes keeps equipment and materials well organized.

Second, playgrounds need a route for tricycles and other wheeled toys, and perhaps pathways for children to navigate in and about the play areas. Designated pathways assist children with mobility challenges in getting around and using the playground spaces. This is an often overlooked feature but a very important part of a creative playground. A secure, reasonably level path needs to wind throughout a playground as if it were scribbled onto the playground in crayon. An inexpensive alternative to concrete or asphalt paths is a discarded conveyor belt. The most important feature of a tricycle path is that it goes somewhere.

The third element of a simple playground design is loose parts or junk materials that parents or teachers may bring from home (Nicholson, 1971). Loose parts may include pots and pans, colanders, paintbrushes, telephone receivers, and other safe and engaging odds and ends. Loose parts can also be purchased relatively inexpensively from dollar stores or garage sales. Because loose parts are often recycled items, there is also an element of conservation in a playground of loose parts.

Playground principle two: Keep it natural. It is rare that an adult does not have some fond memory of a favorite tree, picking apples at Grandmothers' house, or perhaps, hiding out in the bushes playing hide and seek. Nature provides an excellent resource for promoting play (Greenman, 1988; Moore, 1988). Trees provide shade on a warm day, depth to a smaller playground, and home to birds, squirrels, and other animals. Shrubbery, too, provides shade, depth, and home to animals. Shrubbery also provides color, aroma, and definition to a playground. Admittedly, there are regions and climates where large oaks either do not or cannot grow. However, each region and climate has a unique capacity to nurture children's fascination and interaction with nature. Creating gardens, xeriscapes, and other indigenous-friendly natural areas add a complex, rich, and supportive backdrop for play.

"Children don't need equipment, they need opportunity" (Shell, 1994). Providing natural material such as sand, water, dirt, and grass creates an ideal climate for creative play. Adding loose parts to these natural elements has the potential to create a cornucopia of play opportunities (Nicholson, 1971). Children seek out natural elements in their play, and providing them in a safe and manageable environment creates an ideal opportunity for play to take root and flourish (Moore, 1998).

Playground principle three: Keep it moving. One of the most pervasive and yet inexpensive principles of creative playgrounds is movement. Running water does not grow stagnate. So, too, does a stimulating playground remain fresh. Playgrounds need to be constantly changing. The changing seasons of the year give playgrounds a helping hand in this regard. However, leaves falling from the trees or chilly weather is only the beginning. Playgrounds need changing ideas. As children grow and develop, their play changes and evolves (Frost, Wortham, & Reifel, 2001). Functional practice play gives rise to dramatic play. Dramatic play gives rise to games-oriented play.

Being responsive to children's play behaviors enables teachers and caregivers to "ride the tide" of children's play and embellish their play with loose parts and other material. Introducing new activities that are not consistent with children's active play themes can be counterproductive. On the other hand, children sometimes need a fresh perspective that a teacher can provide. Teaching a new game creating new props, or just participating briefly can re-invigorate children's play. The key to keeping it moving is responsiveness and timing.

Playground principle four: Keep it safe. Playground safety is no accident (ASTM, 2001; Frost & Sweeney, 1996; U.S. Consumer Product Safety Commission, 1994). If we want children to benefit from play, they need an environment that is free of hazards. Adventurous playgrounds need risk free challenges.

Precautions must be conscientiously taken to ensure that a playground is free of such hazards as sharp edges, protrusions, tripping hazards, unsafe debris, toys and equipment in disrepair, or equipment designs that could entrap any part of a child's body or clothing, or enclosures that could entrap a child. Safe playgrounds free children to test their skills and abilities.

The U.S. Consumer Product Safety Commission (1994) developed the *Handbook for Public Playground Safety* to guide the design and installation of safe playground equipment. Intended as a consumer-oriented guideline, it provides guidance in the design, safety, and installation of playground equipment. While the *Handbook for Public Playground Safety* applies specifically to anchored equipment, such as climbing equipment and swings, its guidelines are just as applicable to loose parts, playhouses, storage buildings, fencing, and nature.

Safety is inexpensive. Child injuries are costly. Following safety guidelines can promote safe and creative play and avoid many preventable accidents and costly injuries. However "safe" the playground may be in design, equipment safety handbooks cannot take the place of adequate and appropriate supervision. Another important set of playground safety standards, the *ASTM Specifications for Playground Equipment for Public Use* is highly technical and intended for commercial manufacturers. It is revised periodically. A word of caution: Any attempt to construct playground equipment makes an individual a "manufacturer" under the law, and in such case, the ASTM standards are applicable. When purchasing equipment, written verification from playground manufacturers that their playground equipment complies fully with the ASTM standards must be requested.

Playground principle five: Keep it supervised. Creative and adventurous play needs adult involvement to facilitate and encourage engagement, but also to ensure the safety of all children. It is against the law in most communities, schools, and child care centers to leave children unattended in classrooms or playgrounds. As a general rule, there should always be at least 2 adults on the playground for a group of 20 children. Ratios of adults to children required for age and number in the class that are set by licensing and/or accreditation standards must be honored on the playground. Adults should be able to see or hear all activity on a playground, and be able to get to a child in distress readily. That, of course, means that teachers need to be *active* in their supervision. Sitting on the playground visiting with other adults is not supervision. Teachers must also supervise by moving about the playground. When playgrounds are supervised by too few teachers or caregivers, unsafe play and injuries result.

But children also need adults who understand when to intervene or participate and when to simply observe. The art of playground supervision has been captured well in the Kenny Rogers' country-western song, "The Gambler," when he sings, "You've got to know when to hold them. Know when to fold them. Know when to walk away. Know when to run. You never count your money when you're sitting at the table. There'll be time enough for counting when the dealing's done." Adult supervision means anticipating children's behavior and responding appropriately. We should never gamble with children's safety and well being!

Playground principle six: Keep it up. The key to keeping up with a creative playground is long-range planning (Frost, 1992; Jacobs, 1997). Just like being a pet owner, taking care of a playground is a commitment. Playgrounds and their equipment no matter their initial costs, undergo considerable wear and tear. Teachers and administrators need to make sure that all playground equipment is kept in good condition.

Also, children's play can fall into neglect. Play is like a living person, plant, or animal. It needs to be nurtured. Conscientious parents plan for their child's tomorrow in the decisions they make today. Likewise, playgrounds need teachers and administrators to plan ahead and decide how they want the playground to grow and develop. A playground is an evolving play environment that should be designed to reflect children's interests and abilities.

Playground Essentials

How can a playground be equipped to meet a wide range of ages and developmental abilities on a limited budget? Playground planning may be looked at as a pyramid of blocks. We begin at the base of the pyramid and work toward the top. Some playgrounds will only have space for the first 3 or 4 levels but the pyramid is designed to provide a child-centered playground based upon child development theory and experience.

Basically, a playground needs storage, loose parts, and natural materials. Children can meet their developmental play needs with these simple elements. Where budgets allow, play enhancing and dramatic play props, climbing equipment, and swings are nice additions. But remember that children's developmental needs can be met with a variety of inexpensive materials. So, while commercially manufactured equipment is attractive, it may not be essential.

Another helpful tool is the *Playground Environment Development Inventory Appraisal* or PEDIA (Jacobs & Moore, 2001). It is designed to encourage creative playground planning and development. The PEDIA reflects the four elements of good playgrounds: equipment/provisions, play value, safety, and management. It is divided into equipment, provisions and layout; teachers' responsibilities; management; and playground curriculum. A good playground does not have to have all of the items recommended. The PEDIA is best used as a planning tool for on-going development and assessment of the playground's play value:

Equipment, Provisions, and Layout of Playground

- Are there adequate provisions for storage?

- Is the playground comfortable for adults and children to interact?

- Is the playground (zoned) for different levels of activity?

- Are the zones complimentary?

- Is there grassy and/or hard surface space for ball games and/or other games?

- Is there a large sand/dirt area(s) for digging and water play?

- Are there natural areas?

- Is there a large area with loose parts, creative materials, games, props, and dramatic play props?

- Are there portable toys/objects?

- Are there game props?

- Are there creative materials?

- Are there construction materials?

- Are there wheel toys?

- Are there natural materials?

- Are there a variety of dramatic prop storage containers?

- Is there a variety of auditory & visual stimulation?

- Are there large dramatic structures?

- Is there soft, resilient use-zone material under and around swinging and climbing equipment 12 inches deep?

- Is there appropriate space for play?

- Is there appropriate time for play?

- Is there appropriate supervision?

- Are there reasonable provisions for children and adults with disabilities?

- Is the playground complex and comfortable?

- Are there appropriate restraining provisions?

- Is the playground equipment in compliance with recognized standards of care and quality beyond state licensing or health department standards?

- Is the playground checked for maintenance?

- Is the playground free of natural and man-made hazards?

- Is the playground reasonably adaptable for emergent play and children with a range of abilities?

- Is the playground challenging?

- Do children and families have access to the playground after school hours?

- Is there a safe and comfortable transition between the playground and the building?

- Are there provisions for injuries?

- Is there signage on the playground that children can understand and follow?

Teacher Responsibilities

- Are teachers alert and aware of activities on the playground?

- Does the teacher facilitate play in a variety of ways?

- Does the teacher observe play in a variety of ways?

- Does the teacher participate in play?

- Are the teachers able to observe activities with minimal obstruction?

- Does the teacher prepare the children for playground play?

- Do the teachers receive on-going professional development?

Management: Daily Routines

- Is the storage accessible to children?

- Are children encouraged to set up and put away the playground provisions?

- Are the (golden) rules for the playground few and simple?

- Is there a maintenance schedule?

Playground Curriculum (Planning for Play)

- Is there a connection between playground play and classroom play?

- Does the playground promote a variety of forms of social play?

- Does the playground promote a variety of forms of cognitive play?

- Does the playground promote a variety of forms of physical play?

- Are the children spread comfortably across the playground?

- Do children spend ample time each day (weather permitting) on the playground?

- Do the teachers, parents, and administrators view the playground and classroom as mutually complementary environments?

- Is the playground valued by teachers, parents, and administrators as a learning environment?

Conclusion

The playground is an exciting and evolving play environment. The playground is unlike any other environment where children play. Unfortunately, the proliferation of new and creative, yet expensive, playground equipment has shaped our perceptions of what good playgrounds should look like. As a result, too many schools, parks, and child care centers retain outdated, antiquated playground equipment that pose health and safety risk to young children because they cannot afford the "ideal" playground.

Playgrounds do not have to be an expensive showcase of state of the art, commercially manufactured playground equipment. If administrators, teachers, and parents follow these simple principles and are thoughtful about how children grow, develop, learn, and play, then playgrounds can be developmentally appropriate and affordable. Research and experience has demonstrated that children need the opportunity, space, time, materials, and freedom to engage in their own creative play. We need to take advantage of the lessons we have learned about children's outdoor play and focus on promoting play through the wise choice of playground equipment and provisions.

References

American Society for Testing and Materials International (2001). *Standard consumer safety performance specifications for playground equipment for public use*. West Conshohocken, PA: ASTM International.

Frost, J. L. (1992). *Play and playscapes*. Albany, NY: Delmar.

Frost, J. L. (1997). Set the stage for learning outside. *Scholastic Early Childhood Today, 11*(7), 46-47.

Frost, J. L., & P. J. Jacobs (1996). Play deprivation and juvenile violence. *Play Rights, 18*(4), 6-10.

Frost, J.L. & T.B. Sweeney (1996). *Cause and prevention of playground injuries and litigation: Case studies*. Wheaton, MD: ACEI.

Frost, J.L., D.J., Shin, & P.J. Jacobs, (1998). Physical environments and children's play. In O. Saracho & B. Spodek (Eds.). *Multiple perspectives on play in early childhood* (pp. 255-294). NY: SUNY.

Frost, J., S. Wortham, & S. Reifel (2001). *Play and child development*. Upper Saddle River, NJ: Merrill-Prentice Hall

Greenman, J. (1988). *Caring spaces, Learning places*. Redmond, WA: Exchange Press.

Hurtwood, L.A. (1968). *Planning for play*. Cambridge, MA: MIT Press.

Jacobs, P. (1997). How to head off conflicts. *Scholastic Early Childhood Today, 11*(7), 52-54.

Jacobs, P. & M.R. Moore (2001). *Playground environment development inventory appraisal*. Manuscript in preparation.

Lambert, J. (1992). *Adventure playgrounds*. Winchendon, MA: Out of Order Books.

Moore, R. (1993). *Plants for play: A plant selection guide for children's outdoor environments*. Berkley, CA: MIG Communications.

Nicholson, S. (1971, October). How not to cheat children: The theory of loose parts. *Landscape Architecture*, 30-34.

Rivkin, M. (1995). *The great outdoors: Restoring the children's right to play outside*. Washington, DC: NAEYC.

U.S. Consumer Product Safety Commission. (1994). *Handbook for public playground safety*. Washington, DC: USCPSC.

About the Author

Paul J. Jacobs, Ph.D. is assistant professor of early childhood education at the University of Texas at San Antonio. He is also a playground consultant and designer. Dr. Jacobs has taught in numerous child care settings including half-day preschool, faith-based child care, and corporate child care programs.

Section II

Environments for Children Younger than 3

Chapter 6

"Look, Elizabeth. See the infant in the mirror," says the caregiver lying on the floor beside the 6-month-old. Pointing to the child's image in the long mirror hung on its side along the base of the wall; the caregiver continues the conversation, *"Pat the infant in the mirror, Elizabeth. Are you kissing the infant? Elizabeth, that baby is you. Elizabeth smiles and continues to pat* 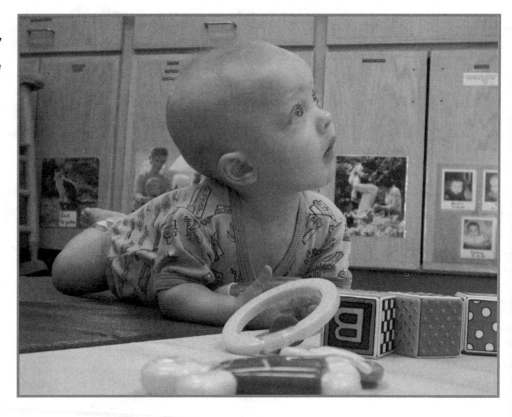 *the mirror. A few feet away, 8-month-old Ricardo watches for a moment. Abruptly, he crawls across the carpet and pulls up on the caregiver's back. "Hey, who's this?" says the caregiver. Soon Ricardo joins Elizabeth in front of the mirror. He leans forward and grins broadly.*

Infants

Phyllis Jack Moore and Arminta Jacobson

The Nurturing Adult

A quality environment for infants is much more than timely feeding and diapering. Quality in infant care depends primarily on a warm, caring adult who smiles, talks, sings, hugs, plays, and offers encouragement at the infant's own pace. Caregivers meet the infants' needs by giving individualized attention that is based on each infant's temperament and uniqueness (Shonkoff & Phillips, 2000). The caregiver recognizes that certain characteristics are biologically based. These characteristics include activity level, reaction to changes in routines, reaction to stimulation, and persistence or distractibility. Acknowledging emerging research on early brain growth and neurological development, the caregiver is aware of the importance of quality experiences during the earliest months and years. Early experiences play a critical role in wiring the brain's neurological circuitry (Shore, 1997). Interactions with a warm caring adult are essential to healthy brain growth and neurological development.

The Competent Caregiver

It is a myth that the only qualification necessary for caring for infants is having had children of one's own. It could be suggested that a competent caregiver needs to be as energetically fit as a professional football player and as knowledgeable as an infant's physician.

Due to cultural diversity among parents and caregivers within child care settings, it is important to remember that parents hold varying culture related views on feeding, toileting, napping, dependence and independence skills, and other child rearing practices. As the caregiver performs these types of routine activities with infants, she may impart through a subtle transfer her own personal values, beliefs and practices. The adult must be aware that this subtle transfer can occur and thus, be sensitive and responsive to the cultural preferences of parents. Just as the infant is beginning to learn at a rudimentary level the practices of his culture, he may become confused by the caregiving practices of individuals of a different culture. It is important for the caregiver to determine how to help the infant remain firmly rooted in his own family culture, which includes learning family language, values, traditions, and expectations, and eventually becoming a fully participating bicultural member of a larger community (Cryer & Harms, 2000). Culture-responsive goals for the competent caregiver include (a) better understanding of various cultural practices; (b) increased communication with families to clarify values and practices, (c) negotiation of cultural conflicts by respecting the parent's viewpoint, and (d) willingness to change some practices in the best interest of individual children.

The caregiver should also become tuned to the "rhythmic dance" that develops between significant adults and the infant. Well known pediatrician, Dr. Berry Brazelton (1983, 1992) calls this special relationship "a dance" because the movements are smooth, natural, and coordinated. The caregiver coos, moving close to the infant's face and the infant pulls up toward the caregiver trying to imitate the coo. The nurturing adult soon learns to recognize individual patterns of infant responses such as staring, cooing, crying, and smiling, and becomes an "expert" on the child's interaction signals. The caregiver skillfully adapts her own responses of talking, smiling, and gestures to meet the infant's interaction attempts. These successful interactions enhance one of the primary goals of infancy, the ability to trust. According to Erik Erikson's psychosocial theory, an infant learns a balance of trust (allowing intimate relationships) and mistrust (for self-protection) in the first year of life (1963). An attentive adult who responds quickly and consistently helps the infant recognize that he is not alone, and the world is a secure, loving place.

Allowing a child to just 'cry it out' is misguided and inappropriate because crying is the infant's way of communicating basic physical and emotional needs. By responding predictably and appropriately to infants' cries, caregivers help infants to gain a sense of trust in those who care for them and a sense of trust in their own abilities to communicate their needs to others. Comforting infants when they cry helps to relieve infant stress and assists them in learning to calm themselves.

Even though diapers are dry and tummies are full, infants may still cry. Just like anyone else, infants need companionship, social interaction, and a sense of belonging. A caregiver's predictable responsiveness provides the continuity necessary for an infant to feel nurturance and adult dependability. Over time, this leads to development of a sturdy sense of trust and emotional security. In a nurturing and responsive context the infant gradually learns some control over the environment and gains a sense of self-direction.

The caregiver is a source of learning opportunities and enrichment, for infants, setting up the physical environment and planning daily activities that are developmentally appropriate and individualized for maximum learning. Providing opportunities for interaction with an enriched and appropriate environment is important for infant cognitive development and an important role for caregivers.

Adult-Child Ratio

The National Association for the Education of Young Children (NAEYC) recommends an adult-child ratio of 1 to 4 in a group of eight infants ages birth to 12 months old; or 1 to 3 in a group of six infants (NAEYC, 1998). For consistency and predictability, care should be provided by the same one or two adults and if possible, with one caregiver serving continuously as the primary caregiver. In this way the attachment process and emotional security are encouraged and enhanced, and the infant's developmental needs are readily recognized and addressed. At least one adult must be present with the infants at all times to assure their protection and safety.

The smaller the group of infants, the better it is for infant development. Keeping group size to a minimum (certainly no more than eight infants in a room with the appropriate number of adults) lowers the noise and activity level of the room, and allows caregivers greater opportunity to know each child. There will be a variety of behavior patterns and developmental levels exhibited among infants in the group. This means, for example, that younger infants must be protected from the older

crawlers or walkers whose physical and social interaction skills are uncoordinated and awkward. Actually, the younger, more dependent infants as well as the older, more mobile and curious infants require an adult's close attention. If the age variance among the infants in the group is wide, small groups could develop naturally based on each infant's daily routines, developmental capabilities or emotional and social needs.

Partnerships with Families

Parents and their infant's caregivers are partners in providing a positive caregiving environment, sharing knowledge of the child, and celebrating accomplishments. The more effective the communication between the parent and caregiver, the better the care for the infant. Daily communication, verbal and/or written, about food intake, urination and bowel movements, sleeping patterns, and medication keeps both caregiver and parent informed about the child's health and other needs. A valuable but often overlooked communication tool is the developmental record. By recording daily observations of the child and comparing them with previous notes and records, the caregiver can evaluate an infant's progress. Developmental observation records provide an effective way to share information periodically with the parents.

Many working parents often feel guilty about leaving their infants in the care of someone else. The caregiver's sensitivity to parent concerns and feeling can help to reduce parental stress. Thoughtful comments about everyday events allow parents to feel a part of the child's total day. Parents treasure such things as video recordings or photographs of an infant's daily activities. The caregiver must be careful to strengthen the parental role, not take it over. First time parents, particularly, appreciate a sensitive and supportive caregiver who can answer questions, listen to their concerns about their child, locate resources and referral information, or simply provide a sympathetic ear.

Some infants may have special health care needs. Caregivers must work with parents to understand the child's special needs and when appropriate, assist in locating specialized care, diagnostic and intervention services, family counseling, or other support systems. As successful communication develops, the parents' respect and trust in the caregiver can grow. This mutually supportive relationship influences the child's overall well-being and positive adjustment to child care. For the development of a long-term relationship between parent, caregiver, and child, some programs develop continuity of care strategies. For example, some programs arrange for caregivers to remain with their same group of children over several years, while changing the learning environment as children get older to accommodate new developmental needs and capabilities. The most significant advantage to continuity of care is to promote deeper levels of understanding and support for individual children. The adult gains greater understanding of the personality and developmental needs and nuances of individual infants and toddlers. Opportunities to know children in this way helps to build and bond relationships with parents and the children, and enhances the caregiver's knowledge and skills in caring for infants and toddler through a wide span of developmental stages.

Daily Routines

Planning and scheduling are just as important in the infant room as in other preschool rooms. The format is similar, with periods during the day for feeding, resting, self-selected play (pull toys, dolls, crawling), informal play between caregivers and infants (music, stories, nursery rhymes, finger plays), and outdoor play. A dependable routine and "rituals" (e.g. special words, chants, songs, and ways of helping a infant go to sleep) help establish a sense of trust because of their predictability, and help the infant gain a sense of order and time. The schedule is more flexible and responsive to individual infants' sleeping and feeding patterns, temperament, and rate of development. The schedule should be adapted to meet the individual pace and physiological needs of infants rather than infants being forced into a rigid schedule.

Within the daily schedule, the caregiver plans individualized activities based on each infant's particular developmental needs and carried out when the child seems most responsive. For example, a child who is trying to crawl may be encouraged by a rolling ball (Caulfield, 2001). The caregiver pays attention to each child's interests and goals and is responsive to each child's lead. Formal group times typically seen with older children are inappropriate at this age. In addition, the caregiver responds to cultural diversity among children by learning some of the traditional music and games familiar to the infants' families and incorporating them into their daily caregiving interactions and routines.

The overall program addresses each infant's physical, intellectual, social, and emotional needs. Although the caregivers plan times for specific skill development, a great deal of informal learning occurs throughout the day. Diapering, feeding, and dressing are excellent opportunities for talking to infants and playing with them. In fact, talking and playing go on informally between adult and infant throughout the day. As a newcomer to the world, an infant needs words for each object and activity encountered.

Although most of the infant's time is spent with adults, other children can also influence learning. An infant takes part in a variety of social exchanges with other children when they begin to crawl, climb, and walk. In a group setting, an infant learns from imitation and the rudimentary practice of give-and-take.

In addition to daily developmental records, caregivers keep an individual cumulative record of developmental goals and accomplishments for each infant. As a child attains new skills, the caregiver records the progress. Progress records are helpful in overall goal setting and program planning for each child. By reviewing progress reports, caregivers can make assessments over an extended period of time. These assessments can alert adults to developmental needs or problems as they occur. One caution: adults should refrain from comparing infants with others in the group. Assessment should focus on individual progress from the beginning of the cumulative record to the present observations. Emphasis should be on the progress of each child's growth rate and unique patterns of development.

Health and Safety

Promoting and protecting infant health is a basic responsibility of every program. All washable floors, equipment, and toys are cleaned daily with a solution of ¼ cup bleach to 1 gallon water or an appropriate commercial antiseptic solution. Clothing, bedding, and diapers are changed as soon as they are soiled. Caregivers follow a standard procedure designed to prevent the spread of germs when changing diapers. It is essential that caregivers thoroughly wash their hands before and after each diapering. Ideally, they should use disposable towels, wipes, diapers, and soap dispensers as a method of disease control. The diapering table must be sanitized after each diaper change. Disinfectants and other potentially dangerous supplies must be located out of the infant's reach and placed in a locked cabinet when not in use. Daily vacuuming and regular carpet shampooing help to maintain a healthy environment. It is also necessary to wash weekly the shelving, lower walls, and corners where mouths and sticky hands explore.

Perishable food and medicines are stored in a conveniently located refrigerator. Each item is labeled with the child's name. Food for infants is prepared in compliance with accepted food service and nutrition standards.

Caregivers confer with parents about feeding plans and adjust the plans as the child's nutritional needs change. Particular attention is given to food allergies.

An infant should be held by an adult when being bottle-fed. An adult's nurturance during this time is important emotionally, but holding brings health benefits as well. Infants who lie down while feeding tend to develop ear infections. Further, they are placed at risk for choking and aspirating milk into their lungs. Another hazard to be avoided is bottle-mouth syndrome, a severe form of tooth decay caused when the sugar in milk coats the teeth of infants who are put to bed with a bottle (Weiser, 1991). Infants who are routinely put to bed with a bottle may relate sleeping to drinking milk or bedtime eating, developing food habits that are difficult to change. Such food habits contribute to excessive weight gain and obesity.

When infants learn to sit in high chairs, they should be encouraged to feed themselves finger foods. As they gain skill, they develop a sense of independence and pride of accomplishment. Cooked soft vegetables and ripe bananas provide an excellent opportunity for practice. *Caution:* hard candies, nuts, popcorn, celery, grapes, coin-cut hot dogs or raw carrots, raisins, and other small or slippery items that could lodge in the throat should not be given to infants. Caregivers should wash their hands thoroughly before preparing the infants' food, and should wash the infants' hands and feeding area before and after each feeding.

One fact of life is that an infant is curious and will explore. If, for example, a pin or small bit of paper is within reach, an infant will find it and immediately put it into her mouth. Adults should constantly check for and remove small, loose items that have fallen on the floor and could be swallowed. Toys should also be checked for broken or loose part and placed out of the infants' reach until they can be replaced or repaired. Electrical outlets should be plugged with safety caps, and electrical and drapery cords should be concealed and out of a child's reach.

Even well designed equipment can be hazardous if improperly assembled or used in inappropriate ways. Infant seats, for example, are only for younger infants and should be used sparingly allowing infants more freedom of movement to encourage and support motor development. The child should be strapped in and the seat placed on the floor rather than on a counter or table. Larger infants can tip the seat over fairly easily, and even smaller ones can lunge forward unexpectedly and topple. The sides of cribs should be in locked position when infants are inside. The mattress height should be adjusted so that an infant who can stand will be less likely to fall out. Loose rugs or unsteady furniture should be removed to protect crawlers and climbers. Furniture with sharp corners or equipment with splintered surfaces should be eliminated.

Caregivers must keep first aid information and emergency phone numbers close by at all times. Evacuation plans should be carefully considered and practiced before an emergency develops. A reinforced wheeled crib, which is easily identified and will fit through all doors, can be used as a vehicle for moving nonwalkers to safety (Wilson, Douville-Watson, & Watson, 1999).

The key to infant health and safety is a knowledgeable, ever-observant caregiver. Caregivers arrange the room so that they can see all areas and adequately supervise infants at all times. For example, a changing table which requires a caregiver to have her back to the room would prevent her from keeping an eye on the other infants.

The Infant Environment

Another aspect of optimal infant care is the overall room arrangement. The organization of the space will either enhance or impede successful care of infants. The following can serve as a checklist for making the space more functional and efficient for infant care:

(a) The crib area is separated from the main play area so that as little distraction as possible occurs while infants are sleeping; yet adults can still view infants in their cribs.

(b) The changing area has a sink equipped with soap, paper towels, and proper pump-spray disinfectant. Storage units for diapers and supplies are within adult reach so that the adult can keep one hand on the infant at all times during changing.

(c) The feeding area is near a sink or kitchen, preferably with a tiled floor for easy cleanup.

(d) A large carpeted area is available for infant exploratory play.

(e) Individual cubbies are provided for each infant's personal belongings.

(f) Problem-solving toys are easily accessible to the infants throughout the day. Children can choose and reach their play materials.

(g) Equipment for large muscle development and gross motor coordination is provided and located away from the main traffic flow areas.

(h) Space is provided for individual children to quietly

play alone. This space might be as simple as a cardboard box or large cushioned corner.

(i) Sturdy furniture is available for nonwalkers to pull themselves up or balance themselves while cruising or attempting to walk.

(j) A reception area is located near the door for caregivers to receive messages from parents and where record keeping can take place. Furnishings for this area include a table, bulletin board, chair, file cabinet, and "in" and "out" baskets for written communications.

(k) Ideally, the room has windows close to the floor to allow infants to view the outdoor passing parade of squirrels, cars, and people as a part of the learning environment.

The most accepted practice for arranging rooms for preschoolers is to create learning centers. This arrangement allows children to choose from a variety of developmentally appropriate activities in well-defined areas in the room. An infant environment contains many of the same components (books, manipulative toys, large motor equipment) of learning centers, but infants use them in a much different way. With careful planning, caregivers can establish an interesting, challenging environment and maintain a homelike, nurturing atmosphere (Bredekamp & Copple, 1997).

The following is an example of a well-functioning infant environment: At the room's entrance are a chair and table for parent check-in. On the wall behind the table is a bulletin board for posting messages, the daily schedule, an evacuation plan, and emergency phone numbers. Individual bags for infants are hanging from hooks attached to the back of a room divider.

The room divider is wooden, stands 4 feet high, and is shaped like an L to separate the active play area from the sleeping, diapering, food preparation, and reception areas. Large, colorful, realistic pictures of children and friendly animals are mounted on the divider's sides for added interest. Photographs of the infants and their families are placed here and laminated with plastic film. The divider serves as a sound barrier for the sleeping area and a physical barrier to keep curious infants inside the 20-by-15-foot play area. However, it still allows caregivers to view sleeping infants on the other side.

At the left side of the room, the cribs are spaced end to end a few feet apart along the outside wall so that infants have a view from the windows. The windows are covered by shades that have simple removable figures attached to them. These shades are raised and lowered according to sleeping patterns. Some beds have a mobile hanging across the top, while others have a mirror or other simple mobile hanging on the side, depending on the child's stage of development. Each crib is labeled with the child's name. From the ceiling over each bed hangs a mobile of butterflies and birds, which has been made by the caregiver. They have been constructed so the features are placed horizontally in full view of the infant. These are changed throughout the year according to the season or a theme. Other mobiles are placed in strategic areas in the room to catch a curious infant's eye; for example, above the changing table.

The changing table stands between the sleeping area and the bathroom. At the table's side is a locked storage cabinet attached to the wall. Above the table on the wall is a nonbreakable plexiglass©-covered frame containing a large, simple picture, which is changed periodically. Caregivers point out picture details as they change diapers to stimulate interest and language development. The food preparation area has a sink, locked cabinet storage, laminate countertop, refrigerator, and a walk-in supply closet.

The right side of the room contains the most active and stimulating area, the carpeted play space. One enters the area through the divider's safety gate. One corner is filled with large pillows and a rack of vinyl and thick cardboard books. Low, open shelves contain a variety of manipulative toys that span several levels of development. The toys are bright, safe, and durable and can be used for mouthing, banging, stacking, and dumping - all valuable infant developmental skills. On the top shelf is a tape/compact disc player with music that includes classics as well as nursery rhymes and music familiar to the various cultures of the families served.

Occupying the far corner is an adult platform rocking chair as well as large (1 to 2 feet), brightly colored, vinyl foam cubes, which are used by active crawlers and climbers. Placed nearby is a large, soft vinyl-covered foam animal, which a child can sit or lie on while talking with an adult, who may be holding another child at the same time. The high chairs are grouped inside the play area against the divider at the location nearest to the food preparation area but away from heat sources. Tile has been extended under the divider for easy cleanup.

In a room such as this, child traffic can flow easily. Crawlers and walkers have many opportunities to choose from the dolls, balls, nesting cups, mirrors, musical toys, and other materials placed on low open shelves. On the floor are several boxes and textured carpet squares for infants to crawl into, on top of, and around. This environment has been planned to meet the needs of infants. It is flexible, safe, durable, and calm as well as stimulating, efficient, cheerful, inviting, responsive to the child, and above all else, nurturing.

An outdoor area planned for infants provides the healthy benefits of fresh air and sunshine, the added sensory experiences of air and trees moving, and changing outdoor sounds, colors, and light. The infant care area opens directly into a protected courtyard or fenced area of the play yard. A tree or covering is available to provide shade on hot days. The surface is grass or commercially made resilient surfacing, providing a safe place to crawl, and a slight incline for a physical challenge. There are no safety hazards such as wood chips, pea gravel or toxic plants. Balls, blocks, and push toys can be brought outside for play. A stroller can be used to explore with an infant the grounds or nearby neighborhood for a change in environment and sense of moving through space.

Matching Activities and Play Equipment to Developmental Stages

Caregivers must be knowledgeable about developmental stages and particularly the rapid changes that occur in infancy. As a caregiver observes an infant's new ability, she can plan individualized activities that meet a child's developmental needs. Providing the right match between child and activity creates the "teachable moment," which allows the child to discover new concepts. The caregiver helps the child learn by showing them, encouraging them, or giving them the physical or emotional support they need (Shonkoff & Phillips, 2000).

The activities below are listed according to chronological age and matched with developmental learning usually occurring at a particular age. However, each infant is on his or her own developmental time-table and may be a few months ahead or behind another child at any time. Variation in rates of child growth and development is normal and expected.

Something to keep in mind is that infants learn through their senses and movement. Activities, play equipment, and environments that encourage infants to use all the senses (sight, hearing, touch, smell, taste) and to move about using their emerging motor abilities contribute to growth, development, and learning. Infant toys and environments (human and physical) must be safe and easy to explore, responsive to individual needs, foster curiosity, help with mastery of skills, are repetitive for practice of skills and knowledge, teach about cause and effect, and encourage early literacy through conversation, books, pictures, and songs. Infants with developmental delays or challenges may need special equipment, such as toys that make sounds when moved for hearing-impaired infants, appropriately designed climbing or mobility equipment for children with motor coordination challenges, and large print and picture books for children with visual impairments.

Newborn to 3 Months. Most of a newborn's day consists of sleeping and eating. During waking moments, infants use all their senses to learn about the environment. They suck on fists, stare first and then track objects, particularly human faces and bright colors that are within close range (8 to 12 inches), lift their heads, recognize their mother's voice and scent, grasp objects, and coo in reciprocal response patterns. Soft lamp light, small washable toys to hold, simple pictures with bold lines and mobiles hung on the sides of cribs are suitable for newborns. By three months, infants give broad, long-lasting social smiles and enjoy the give and take of playing with adults and toys.

To provide a varied and interesting environment, caregivers frequently move infants around the room. They carry them about and move cribs and infant seats to change the infant's view. Infants will focus on stimuli longer if they are held upright or in a semi-reclining position rather than lying down (Fogel, 2001). Mobiles are designed and placed with major features facing the infant. According to Burton White's research, a newborn lying face up spends around 90 percent of the time looking right and 10 percent looking to the far left (White, 1975). This implies that a mobile or hanging toy should be placed at the sides for newborns rather than across the top of the crib. When the infant is able to hold his or her head at the midline, the mobile can be positioned across the crib top. Rod mobiles use a variety of interchangeable toys that add extra interest as the child begins to reach and grasp. Caregivers can talk to an infant, moving large face puppets and dolls from side to side in front of the infant's face to encourage visual tracking. Experience with moderately intense and moderately complex stimuli, just right for newborns and young infants, enhances brain growth and neurological development (Fogel, 2001).

The all-time favorite rocking chair accompanied by a caring adult provides a welcome comfort to the distressed infant. Soft singing, chanting or reading simple verses or nursery rhymes, sharing simple picture books, engaging in pleasant conversation, a soothing massage, or gentle cuddling are all important ways to comfort an infant and each goes a long way in helping the child develop a sense of trust and emotional security.

Three to 6 Months. Infants at this age reach for objects with both hands; place everything in their mouths; play with, and are fascinated by their hands; practice making vocal sounds through babbling; begin to laugh; catch, hold and mouth their toes; look around in all directions; and are more alert for longer periods of time. Appropriate activities include opportunities to reach and grasp rattles and other small interesting toys. Since infant interests and capabilities change so rapidly, it is important to buy items that have a variety of functions. For example, small, soft vinyl-covered blocks might have a musical sound inside, pictures on the outer sides, and straight edges for stacking. Stuffed animals, music boxes, chime balls, cradle gyms, and washable quilts with different textures, colors, and shapes provide sensory experience for solitary play. Adults can dance and move to music with infants, and as they hold them in their laps, point out simple pictures in books and magazines. As infants babble, adults can respond with a variety of sounds as well. They can introduce "Peek-a-Boo," "This Little Piggy," and other simple games.

Six to 9 Months. Infants at this age are able to roll over, perhaps stand with help, and may even creep, scoot, or crawl. They can usually sit alone and enjoy turning, banging, and dropping toys to see what happens. They know the difference between familiar adults and strangers, which means they will cry and become distressed when exposed to unknown faces. That is why this time is often called the period of stranger anxiety. Teeth are beginning to appear and they are learning to feed themselves simple soft finger foods, and enjoy holding a cup. They can drop objects in containers and do simple tasks such as empty all the objects from a drawer. They still babble and are beginning to use one-syllable sounds, such as "ma," "da," or "ba." They understand the meaning of some words and are beginning to associate these words with people or objects.

During this time the caregiver introduces carefully selected, developmentally appropriate, manipulative toys. Stacking and nesting toys are a challenge; pop-up and squeaky sound books are inviting. Infants can hold an unbreakable mirror not only for mouthing and banging but eventually for viewing their own faces. They enjoy rolling a ball and imitating the many actions an adult introduces. For example, they clap hands to music, shake musical instruments, or move their heads "this way or that way." As they begin to understand words, it is important that the adult talk and describe various experiences to the infant while they are occurring, e.g., changing diapers, feeding, bathing, or dressing. Language development increases as the child associates these and other experiences with words.

Nine to 12 Months. Infants between 9 and 12 months are motivated to master the use of their bodies. They begin to walk with help, climb, crawl efficiently, stand, usually without assistance, and can lift arms and legs to help in dressing. They imitate actions of adults and other children and have learned simple problem-solving tasks, such as pulling a toy toward them. They have developed "object permanence," a cognitive ability that allows them to remember where an object is although it is no longer in sight. For example, they enjoy placing objects in a box, putting the lid on top, taking off the lid, and getting the objects out again. They speak in one word sentences, using one word to convey a message, e.g., "go," which can mean "It is time to go," "I want to go, now," "The car is going," or something similar.

The caregiver introduces pull toys, soft blocks for carrying and stacking, as well as other objects for opening, closing, or manipulating. Infants enjoy placing clothespins in a plastic container or opening and closing a hinged box. They like playing "Peek-a-Boo" and finding an object that the adult has covered and is now out of sight. Finger plays, musical games, and nursery rhymes are valuable language experiences. The adult continues to read stories and encourages children to point to objects pictured in books.

Toys and Equipment

When buying toys, and materials for infants, adults must consider whether they are safe, durable, and washable and can be open-ended enough to provide a variety of activities over several developmental stages. For example, a puppet can be used by an adult with an infant as well as in a puppet show by a school-age child. Versatile toys that allow children to express their imagination will be used most often. Balls, blocks, play dough, and 'kitchen cabinet specials' such as butter tubs and plastic measuring spoons are appropriate examples. Larger equipment also needs to be durable, safe, and the appropriate size and complexity for the children who will use it.

Playpens and swings are questionable in a quality infant environment. Infants need many opportunities for rolling, scooting, and crawling to develop gross motor skills. They also need close physical and emotional contact with others as often as possible. Playpens and swings restrict an infant's exploratory and social experiences essential for optimal development and also restrict crawling opportunities necessary for perceptual motor development. Walkers should not be used as infants are more at risk for accidents in them. It is believed that the extra weight placed prematurely on the lower body, legs, and feet may be harmful to developing muscles.

Activities

Happy Face
(Newborn to 3 months)

Objective: To provide visual stimulation

Materials needed: Two 7-inch circles of solid- colored cloth, discarded clean nylon hose, felt scraps, elastic strips long enough to stretch across the width of a crib, glue, needle and thread (or sewing machine), scissors

What to do:
1. Cut facial features from felt scraps, and sew them to one side of a 7-inch circle of cloth.
2. Stitch the face to the second piece, leaving enough of an opening for stuffing. Stuff the inside with hose.
3. Stitch the opening closed.
4. Stitch elastic strips on each side of the face.
5. Stretch the face across the crib and tie each elastic end to the crib. Infants will enjoy looking at the face.

Variations:
As infants begin to use their hands, they will bat, punch, pull, and push the happy face pillow.

Musical Mittens
(Newborn to 3 months)

Objective: To provide visual and auditory stimulation

Materials needed: Brightly colored infant mitten, small jingle bell, heavy-duty thread, needle

What to do:
1. Turn mitten inside out.
2. Place the bell in the end of the mitten and fold mitten to totally cover the bell. Then securely stitch all around, carefully covering all of the bell.
3. Using a second thread, sew around the bell again, making sure all areas are enclosed. (This eliminates the possibility of the bell breaking loose.)
4. Turn the mitten right side out, and place it on the infant's hand. As the infant moves the hand, he or she will see bright colors flashing by and hear a pleasant tinkling sound.
5. Check the mitten regularly to make sure the bell is attached securely.

Self-Concept Mirror
(3 to 6 months)

Objective: To recognize the face and develop self-concept

Materials needed: Mirror paper (available in automotive shops), 2 pieces of tag board (approximately 8 by 10 inches), glue, plastic tape, scissors

What to do:

1. Cut two pieces of tag board so they are the same size.

2. Cut two pieces of mirror paper to fit the tag board, and glue the paper to each side of the tag board. If you wish reinforcement, cut a tag board frame and glue it to the outer rim.

3. Fold tape over the sides of tag board to protect tiny fingers from cuts from the edge of the mirror paper.

4. Use the mirror to play "Peek-a-Boo" with an infant by showing the child his or her face and removing the mirror. When the infant is able, he or she can hold the mirror and play "See (or kiss) the infant."

Picture Cards
(6 to 9 months)

Objective: To encourage visual stimulation and develop eye-hand coordination

Materials needed: Three to 4 pieces of 3-inches square tag board, variety of simple, one-item pictures of familiar objects, glue, 2 large binder rings

What to do:

1. Glue pictures on tag board.

2. Punch a hole in top of each tag board and place on binder rings. (Three to four pictures are a challenge for this age.)

3. Point to each picture and name it while turning the boards.

Ball Activities
(9 to 12 months)

Objective: To encourage motor development and increase eye-hand coordination

Materials needed: Discarded clean nylon stockings, needle, thread

What to do:

1. Cut a 6-inch piece from the top of a sturdy stocking. Cut other stockings into strips.

2. Stuff the strips into the stocking piece, shaping it into a ball. Stitch shut.

3. Roll the ball to the infant and try to get him or her to return it.

Variations:

Roll or drop the ball into large box or clean wastebasket. Dump it out and try again.

Use a variety of balls such as tennis ball, large rubber ball, and beach ball.

References

Brazelton, T. B. (1983). *Infants and mothers: Differences in development.* New York: Dell Publishing.

Brazelton, T. B. (1992). *Touchpoints.* Reading, MA: Perseus Books.

Bredekamp, S., & C. Copple (Eds.) (1997). *Developmentally appropriate practice in early childhood programs* (Rev. Ed.). Washington, DC: National Association for the Education of Young Children.

Caulfield, R.A. (2001). *Infants & toddlers.* Upper Saddle River, NJ: Prentice Hall.

Cryer, D., & T. Harms (2000). *Infants & toddlers in out-of-home care.* Baltimore: Paul H. Brookes.

Erikson, Erik H. (1963). *Childhood and society* (2nd ed.). New York: W. W. Norton and Co.

Fogel, A. (2001). *Infancy: Infant, family, & society* (4th ed.). Belmont, CA: Wadsworth/Thomson Learning.

National Association for the Education of Young Children (1998). *Accreditation criteria and procedures of the National Academy of Early Childhood Programs.* Washington, DC: Author.

Shonkoff, J. P., & D. A. Phillips (Eds.) (2000). *From neurons to neighborhoods: The science of early childhood development.* Washington, DC: National Academy Press.

Shore, R. (1997). *Rethinking the brain: New insights into early development.* New York: Families & Work Institute.

Weiser, M.G. (1991). *Infant/toddler care & education* (2nd ed.). Upper Saddle River, NJ: Prentice Hall.

White, B. (1975). *The first three years of life.* Englewood Cliffs, N.J.: Prentice Hall.

Wilson, L. C., L. Douville-Watson, M.A. Watson, (1999). *Infants and toddlers. Curriculum and teaching* (5th ed.). New York: Delmar Publishers.

Checklist for Evaluating the Infant Environment

Rate the items below on a scale of 1 to 4 with "needing improvement" as 1 and "outstanding" as 4.

_____1. A nurturing caregiver provides supervision at all times.

_____2. All washable floors, equipment, and toys are sanitized daily.

_____3. Perishable foods and medicines are labeled and stored in a convenient refrigerator.

_____4. The environment has been thoroughly checked for safety; it contains no items that infants can choke on, no dangling cords, and no exposed electrical outlets; and equipment is in good repair and used properly.

_____5. The crib area is separated from the main play area so it is quiet where children sleep. The crib area is within a caregiver's view.

_____6. A large carpeted area is available for infant exploratory play.

_____7. Problem-solving toys are readily available and matched to developmental stages of the infants in care.

_____8. Equipment for gross motor development is located outside the main traffic flow as much as possible.

_____9. Sturdy furniture is available for nonwalkers to pull themselves up or balance themselves while walking.

_____10. The infant care area opens into a protected outdoor play area specifically designed for infants.

_____11. The overall environment reflects the diverse cultures of the infants in the program.

_____12. A reception area for parents is located near the door, providing information about the program, daily interactions with the infants, and opportunities for parental feedback.

About the Authors

Phyllis Jack Moore is a work/family strategist, providing consultant services in employer dependent care issues and public/private initiatives. Career experiences include development of several statewide and community initiatives, classroom and college teaching, and owner of a retail materials firm. She is a past president of TAEYC and field representative for the National Association for the Education of Young Children. She holds a master's degree in early childhood education from the University of North Carolina, has studied for her doctorate at the University of North Texas. She has been recognized with the All State's Good Hand's Award; Who's Who in America; Brous Award, Fort Worth AAEYC; and as a UNC leadership fellow in early education.

Arminta Jacobson is Associate Professor of Development, Family Studies, and Early Childhood Education as well as founder and director of the Center for Parent Education at the University of North Texas. As a charter member and past president of Denton Area Association for the Education of Young Children, she has been active in TAEYC. She holds a masters degree in Home Economics Education and a doctoral degree in Child Development from Texas Woman's University.

Chapter 7

Environments for Toddlers

Deborah Rogers

In the space of just one short year,
the human infant evolves from an
immobile, dependent recipient of
care and nurturing to a moving,
exploring, active agent of his own
development and learning. Between
about 12 and 14 months the infant
becomes what is known as a mobile
infant or toddler, and the structure of
their physical environment changes,
as well. Children in this age group are
developing and changing rapidly and
their surroundings must support both
their new mobility and their drive to
explore. At the same time, their
needs for physical care and emotional
nurturing are still strong, and so
must be taken into account. It is this
dual focus of toddlerhood, the need
for security and the drive for independence, that shapes many of
the caregiving decisions that we
make for ones and twos. In designing their
environments, caregivers must allow for active
exploration in an atmosphere of safety and trust.

Toddler Development

Children in the second year of life continue in Piaget's sensorimotor period of cognitive development. The toddler is actively acquiring new information from her surroundings through exploring with her senses and using motor skills to act on objects that she encounters. The toddler often exhibits the insatiable curiosity of a scientist as she touches, bangs, pulls, pushes, dumps, throws, mouths, rubs, shakes, and otherwise thoroughly investigates every item in her reach. There must be support for this activity, with ample safe and appropriate items for the toddler to examine. The increasing mobility of toddlers and their drive to explore their surroundings, make it important that their classroom spaces offer opportunities to master their environment. Along with this need to explore and to learn about everything around them, toddlers have an increased need for autonomy and a feeling of independence. An appropriate toddler space would support this drive, while providing for safety and encouragement.

As children move into their next year symbolic thinking emerges. While they still need interesting objects to explore and are very active learners, they are increasing in their ability to symbolically represent objects and activities. They will imitate complex patterns of behavior or language, such as rocking a baby doll or acting out a finger play. The ability to form mental images of people and events is emerging, and toddlers are able to put language to their thoughts or feelings. The environment for older toddlers will continue to offer many opportunities for exploration and experimentation, with added support for symbolic play such as dress up, blocks and books.

Motor development is an important aspect of toddler life, and movement is essential to learning and well-being. As the toddler masters each new physical skill, both small and large motor, he is compelled to practice. The toddler who has discovered the ability to release an object first by dropping and then by throwing, will perform this behavior endlessly. Likewise, the child who masters the sliding board in the classroom will be obliged to do it over and over again. Being still is not only very challenging for a child of this age, it can be torture! The need to be moving is an integral part of their learning, and something that should only be limited during meal times and caretaking tasks such as diaper changing or washing up. Waiting for a turn, standing in a line, or sitting still for extended time in large group activities are expectations that are not appropriate for a child in this age group.

As the toddler is developing intellectual and motor skills, social and emotional development is progressing, as well. The development of trust caregivers and surroundings is an important aspect of healthy growth. Separation can still be an issue for a child in this age group, and caregivers must be sensitive to the attachment between the toddler and parent. The drive for autonomy that can at one moment seem so strong in the toddler who is declaring an adamant "I do it myself," can seem to dissolve in the child who is sobbing for their missing loved one. The sensitive caregiver will provide support and nurturing care for both sides of the toddler personality, encouraging growth and accepting regression. Consistency and continuity is essential in a program for toddlers, and caregivers need to be able to provide affectionate, nurturing support for the child's growing need for autonomy. Caregivers should structure the environment and activities to support toddler independence, acting as a guide and resource, not a dictator. The emotional states of toddlers can often seem unbalanced, and as such may be difficult for caregivers to handle. The loving support that they receive for all of their many "moods" can set a positive emotional tone for the entire program.

For a program to support the developmental needs of toddlers, caregivers should become familiar with the "ages and stages" information about one and two year olds. Knowing the course of normal child development can help caregivers make appropriate choices for room arrangement, materials, and activities for the children in their care. While a toddler room will resemble an infant room in its support for physical care taking, it will also begin to take on some aspects of the preschool classroom with the presence of simple "centers." By being familiar with the developmental needs and issues of not only the age group served, but also the individual children in the program, caregivers can effectively meet the needs of all of the children.

Basic Considerations for the Environment

When designing the physical environment for toddlers, there are two areas to be considered: the built in features such as the walls, floors, plumbing and storage, and the arrangement of the equipment, furniture and activity areas within this set space. Taking into account the developmental needs of toddlers, their physical space should allow for movement, support sensory exploration, and encourage independence and self-help skills. The environment should be engaging and interesting without being overstimulating. When adding décor items such as pictures or displays, it is important to see the space from the child's point of view. This affects both the height of display and the relevance of the items offered. Too much detail, color, texture or pattern in the environment can overwhelm the child, rather than engage. Wall displays should be suitable for the toddler's interest and level of development. Rather than an alphabet or number chart, it would be more interesting to the child to hang a busy box toy at a level where it could be easily manipulated. Photos of children in the class or simple graphics of people, animals or objects should be displayed with the intention of enhancing the curriculum, rather than "decorating" to impress adults. Toddlers are coming into an age where they are pleased to see their own work on display, and when mounted under Plexiglas©, or other clear plastic cover, it is safe from enthusiastic touching. The warmth and welcoming feeling of the toddler room will be reflected in not only the furniture and arrangement, but the human touches, as well.

It is helpful, when making decisions about how to set up the toddler environment, to consider eight environmental qualities. The toddler environment should:

- ensure safety
- promote health
- provide comfort
- be convenient
- be child-sized
- maximize flexibility
- encourage movement
- allow for choice (Lally & Stewart, 1990).

Each of the eight key qualities should be analyzed for each decision made about the classroom environment, so that the choices made will provide optimal support for child growth and development and for the goals of a quality program for very young children.

Safety

The active and curious nature of toddlers makes safety a primary concern. In order to explore and experience their surroundings, they need to be free from any hazards that might impede them. When the environment is known to present no pitfalls, the caregivers are also free to relax and support the toddlers in their adventures. Childproofing the environment includes:

- Covering all electrical outlets and securing any cords to baseboard or floor. Make sure any appliances or cords are positioned out of reach.

- Using only non-toxic materials and furnishings. Toddlers explore objects by mouthing them, and it is important that not only toys are non-toxic, but other easily "tasted" items, as well.

- Testing all toys for potential choking hazard. Items smaller than a ping-pong ball could become lodged in a child's throat. Also check to see that small parts will not become detached from stuffed animals or other toys. Never allow toddlers to play with balloons,

either inflated or not. Balloons present an extreme hazard for blocking a child's airway if swallowed.

- Making sure that there is ample open, unobstructed space for crawling and walking. Any item that a child might use to pull up on must be secure and steady. Rockers or furniture with corners or sharp edges should be kept out of high traffic areas. Do not use "walkers" with toddlers as they are unstable and unsafe to pull up on for other toddlers.

- Locking up medicines, cleaning items, and other harmful substances. These should be stored in high cabinets that are out of reach for toddlers. Disinfectant and other diapering supplies should be on a high shelf out of children's reach.

- Gating any area that is off limits to the children. Check outside fences and gates to be sure that they are secure.

- Checking to see that all of the equipment and furnishings used in the classroom meet Consumer Product Safety Commission guidelines and have not been the subject of a manufacturer's recall. This information can be found online at www.cpsc.gov/

- Supervising toddlers at all times. Even the most carefully childproofed environment can present hazards where an active toddler is concerned. Caregivers must have a watchful eye at all times, and be ready to redirect a child from unsafe or inappropriate actions.

When issues of safety have been attended to early, potential problems are kept to a minimum. Continue to monitor the safety of the environment by occasionally taking a child's-eye tour of your room, looking for things that might spark curiosity and pose a hazard.

Health

Providing a setting that is clean and healthy helps to minimize the spread of illness and increases everyone's sense of physical and emotional well-being. Young children have immature immune systems, and so are highly susceptible to new bacteria or viruses that they may encounter in their child care setting. While it is not uncommon for children to become ill several times in the first few months of care, there are preventive steps that caregivers can take to reduce the spread of infection.

- Keep areas for diapering, food preparation, eating, and play separate. A sink with hot and cold water should be available in both diapering and food preparation areas and all surfaces should be easy to clean and sanitize.

- Diapers should be changed as soon as they become

wet or soiled, not according to a schedule. Caregivers must wash hands both before and after diapering, and the child's hands must be washed after a diaper change. All surfaces must be disinfected between diaper changes.

- Children should be carefully observed for signs of illness. This would include temperature, rash, ear tugging, red eyes, head scratching, listlessness, loss of appetite or unusual behavior. Parents should be contacted if a child develops symptoms of illness while at the center, and the child should not return until treatment by a physician has been obtained or the child is well.

- Toys that are shared should be regularly washed and disinfected. Toddlers are likely to put toys in their mouths, or handle toys with hands that they have had in their mouths. Regular washing should occur at nap-time or the end of the day.

- Hand washing by both caregivers and children should occur frequently throughout the day, particularly before and after eating, after toileting or diapering, and after using art or sensory materials. Caregivers must wash their hands before and after preparing food, after wiping children's noses or handling used tissues, and assisting a toddler with toileting and diapering. It is through the practice of careful and vigilant hand washing that many germs are stopped from spreading.

- All of the soft toys and surfaces in the center, such as pillows, mats, rugs and mattresses should be easily cleaned and sanitized. Removable covers that can be machine washed make this process easier. These soft elements are important to a toddler classroom, as they provide cushioning and support, as well as cozy places to play and be, so it is important that they be clean and safe.

An often overlooked aspect of the physical environment is the use of light, heat, and ventilation. It is important, even in the winter months, to have fresh air circulating in the room. Lighting should be a mix of natural and artificial, with no harsh bare bulbs or darkened corners. Heat, humidity, and circulation should be comfortable, especially at floor level where toddlers spend most of their time. Physical comfort can either enhance or reduce the desire to interact and explore, and a toddler who is "out of sorts" may be reacting to an uncomfortable environment.

Comfort

Comfort is another key element to consider when designing the toddler classroom. Children and caregivers will spend a great deal of time in this environment,

engaged in a variety of activities, and their time will be more productive and pleasant if their physical comfort is considered. There should be a mix of open spaces for active movement, and smaller, more enclosed areas for private times. Surfaces should be varied, with carpets and rugs, pillows, couches and soft chairs for children and caregivers to curl up and get cozy. Multi-level surfaces, such as platforms, steps, and lofts provide both a different point of view for the children, and an opportunity to see "eye to eye" with the caregivers. Touches of nature, such as non-toxic plants, fish, terrarium or small animals add another dimension to the toddler's experience, and can be comforting to watch. Neutral, soft colors for walls and floor and window coverings, and display items that are calming will help to set the tone in the classroom. Jarring colors, loud noises and heavy traffic through the room can disrupt the comfort of the space, and should be avoided.

Another aspect of comfort is how welcoming the environment is to children and their parents as they enter each day. Separation can be difficult for both toddlers and parents, and the tone that the center sets from the start of their day is important in easing this process. Is there a transitional area where parents can say goodbye while the caregiver can welcome the child? Are parents welcome to spend time in the center, interacting with the other children as well as their own? A sign-in area can include a message system for written communication, postings of events of interest, a calendar, photographs of the children engaged in various activities during their day, and articles or books that parents may check out. Caregivers can help parents develop a ritual of "hello" and "good bye" that can ease the transition between home and center. Daily verbal communication between parents and caregivers is very important to the well being of the child, and conveys a message of cooperation and comfort. When parents feel welcome they feel that participation and input is valued, and are more likely to trust the center and caregivers. The parents' comfort reassures the toddler and conveys to the child that this is a good place to be.

The final consideration in the area of comfort is the concept of continuity of care over time. Just as toddlers have a strong bond with their parents, they also form attachments to their caregivers. The feelings of warmth, acceptance and caring that children feel from the adults in their world are essential to their emotional development and well-being. These important relationships give toddlers the support and confidence that they need to freely explore and learn. Over time, caregivers are able to get to know the children in their care and form close relationships. Caregivers learn the child's unique personality and needs, and the child feels secure in knowing that their caregiver will take care of them and respond to their cues. This close bond can only occur if the child is with the same caregiver over a long period of time. Transitions from room to room and caregiver to caregiver undermine the child's development of comfort and trust in the caregiving situation. To provide the optimal environment for healthy emotional growth, the child should be with the same caregiver over the entire course of their first three years. This not only strengthens the connection between caregiver and toddler, but also with the child's family, as well, enhancing the comfort of all.

Convenience

When the toddler classroom is well organized and functional, it makes the caregiver's job easier, and helps to ensure health and safety, as well. The placement of caregiving areas, work and play areas, and storage spaces facilitates achievement of program goals. When the environment is organized and predictable, caregivers and children are free to focus on interactions and exploring. Toddlers need predictability and routine in their day, so that they can develop trust and feel secure to exploring and play. The room arrangement should allow for children's exploration, interaction with caregivers, and care-taking tasks. Diaper changing and feeding areas should be, self-contained and have all needed supplies within easy reach of adults, but out of reach of toddlers. Play areas should have low open shelves with baskets or tubs that make toys accessible to the children. Toy boxes or bins make it more difficult to get at the toys, and can be a safety hazard. Limit the number of toys available at any one time and rotate the collection often. This makes pick up and sanitization easier, and helps to cut down on boredom. Caregivers who are not carrying out direct caregiving tasks should position themselves on the floor or at low tables with the children, this puts them right in the action, and avoids back strain often caused by leaning over little people!

Child Size

When the environment presents toddlers with furnishings that are their own size, pictures and displays at their eye level, cubbies and shelves that they can reach and use, climbers and slides that are challenging and safe, they feel comfortable and secure and able to explore and learn. Looking at the classroom from the toddler's point of view helps the caregiver to see what they see and what would be of interest or out of sight. If the shelves are too high and the children cannot reach the materials, they loose an opportunity to practice independence and self-help skills. If the wall and floor at their level is drab and bare, an opportunity to enjoy the visual aspects

of their world is lost. Tables and chairs should be sized to the toddler's height, and should be sturdy and easy to get into and out of. Small sofas, soft chairs and mattresses on the floor provide areas for the children to rest, relax and interact with caregivers and each other. Play equipment such as home center furnishings, sensory tables, easels or climbing apparatus should be sized for toddlers, not preschoolers. The toddler versions of these items are more basic, and have been designed and constructed with the safety concerns of younger children in mind. A classroom that is just your size feels right, and is a place where you can feel at home.

Flexibility

While toddlers are creatures of habit, who seem to thrive on repetition and practice of familiar events, it is important to remain open to spontaneous events and variations in activities. Remaining flexible allows the environment and program to maintain its interest level, while not being overwhelming. Within set boundaries of the fixed parts of the classroom, there should be items and areas that can be moved and rearranged. Having easy to move equipment that offers different types of experiences, such as a climber or slide, adds new play and learning opportunities. A flexible program is one that is responsive to the varied age-related needs, abilities, and interests of the children. Flexibility in caregiving style allows adults in the toddler's world to be aware of and to adapt to children's current and changing needs and interests. Being open to surprising events such as a sudden rain shower, or an unexpected visitor, allows the children to have new experiences in a setting where they feel support and trust. Constant change can overwhelm a toddler, while occasional variations in their day can lead to interest and learning.

Time schedules in a toddler program should reflect the needs of the children rather than what is convenient for the caregivers. Young toddlers are usually transitioning from two naps a day to one, but there may be wide variations in the daytime sleep needs of individual children. A set time for caregiving tasks and activities such as eating, sleeping and toileting may not sufficiently meet the needs of individual children. When routines are flexible, each toddler's physical needs are respected and met appropriately. The schedule of the day should follow a predictable sequence to help promote security, but a rigid inflexible schedule cannot address the individual needs of children in the program.

Movement

Movement is essential to growth and development during the toddler period. New motor skills are constantly emerging, and practice is fundamental to perfecting them. The physical environment must provide children with opportunities to crawl, climb, walk, roll, jump, run, sit, stand, and simply lie down. In order to experience these activities fully, the environment must support them by being safe, clean, and challenging. Caregivers need to observe the children in their care to determine what coordinations or skills they are attempting to master, and provide opportunities to practice these skills with appropriate materials, equipment, encouragement, and support. Rather than presenting a curriculum of motor skill attainment that conforms to a prescribed ages and stages approach, each child should have a program geared directly to their own unique level of development. Children who are either ahead or behind the "typical" level for their age will be supported where they are and helped to master emerging skills. The environment should provide areas of open space, pillows and cushions, tunnels and enclosed spaces, steps and ramps, rocking boats, balance beams, risers and pits, slides, climbing ladders, push and pull toys, tumbling mats and padding, play yards with grass, sand and structures for sitting, climbing and swinging. All of these items should be safely arranged and well supervised. Not only can a caregiver provide safe play areas, but can encourage and congratulate. Group activities such as moving to music, marching with instruments, exercising, or dancing should be a part of the motor skill development program, but toddlers may not always want to participate in large groups and may prefer these pursuits on an individual basis. Making music, instruments, scarves, and singing available allows children to choose them when interested.

Choice

To effectively support the growth and development of all of the toddlers in the program, the environment should offer a wide range of developmentally appropriate choices. Toddlers should be offered a variety of activities that involve large group, small group, and individual participation, but should not be forced to participate when they are not interested. Often a toddler will feel more comfortable as an observer of an activity rather than a participant. While group stories and singing activities may be offered during the day, toddlers should not be compelled to join in unless they are ready. It may seem that a child is not paying attention, but often parents report that the child sings every song each night in his or her bed! The interests and preferences of toddlers are already becoming clear; some love language play, others are more physical, still others would rather work with their hands on pegs and beads. It is important that many different choices are available throughout the day, and

that each child is supported in his activity of choice. By observing children when they pursue activities that interest and excite them, caregivers can plan future activities that help to expand each child's experience. Rather than forcing all of the children to do the same thing at the same time, a quality program allows for individual differences and choice.

Play and Learning Activities

For toddlers, learning is an all day, every day activity. Not restricted to any particular time of the day, toddlers are exploring, examining, experiencing, and organizing their world through everything that they hear, see, do, and encounter. Interactions between caregivers and toddlers give these experiences language and a context; and anytime they are working together, whether during a diaper change or sharing a book or toy, there are opportunities to help children gain new insights. Caregivers interacting with children verbalize the activity, providing vocabulary and extending language. While the toddler environment may begin to resemble a preschool classroom, with areas organized into "centers" such as housekeeping and blocks, toddlers do their learning all over the center, fully integrating all aspects of development.

Caregivers should plan experiences, introduce new materials, direct activities and interact with children both formally and informally throughout the day. Keeping in mind the key elements of flexibility and choice, experiences should be planned and offered for: sensory or discovery play, imitation and pretending, language and word play, small and large motor play and self-help skills. These plans should reflect respect for the individual interests of the toddlers in the program, and should be sufficiently open-ended to allow children of any ability level to benefit from and enjoy them.

Sensory and Discovery Play

- A sand/water table of toddler height and size can accommodate a variety of substances for exploring. Consider beans, cornmeal or potting soil, always taking into account the age of the toddlers and providing close supervision and clean-up. A small wading pool can be used for sensory play that the children can really "get into." Paper from a shredder or Styrofoam© packing material is fun to "swim" in.

- Modeling dough, shaving cream, clay and finger paints give the toddler experience with different textures, but be aware that some young children do not like to have messy fingers. Fabrics, carpets, furs, plastic, metal, cardboard, bubble wrap, stickers, clear Contac© paper, netting, and other items provide different items for the toddlers to "feel." Some may be better felt with fingers, some may be good to walk or crawl on. Use the language of touch to label what they are feeling, e.g., hard, soft, smooth, rough, sticky, prickly, bumpy, fuzzy.

- Working with crayons or markers provides the toddler with experiences that incorporate sensory input, small motor practice and creativity. Writing and drawing materials, such as large non-toxic crayons and water-based markers, are appropriate for toddlers, who enjoy making marks and experimenting. Do not pressure children to "make something," or even to label what they have made, let them tell you about it if they wish. Their "art" may be unrecognizable to you, but it has value to them.

- Simple smelling and tasting activities help toddlers to become aware of another aspect of their environment. There are simple cooking or food assembly tasks that toddlers can perform. Spreading butter, slicing cheese, mixing batter, sprinkling cinnamon, dipping raw vegetables, scrubbing potatoes, squeezing lemons, cutting cookies, or mashing bananas provide not only sensory input, but motor skill training and pride in blossoming self-help skills. Invite parents to come and share special recipes or cooking activities that can introduce the children to new tastes. With careful planning cooking activities can become a frequent favorite.

- Toddlers are able to use paint to explore and create. Toddler sized easels, or small tables can make using paint comfortable for the children. It is not necessary to provide many colors, two or three is usually all that is needed, and be prepared to watch a creation disappear under mounds of paint! Painting with blocks, gadgets, sponges, combs, scrub brushes, rags, spools, and other items varies the experience and the result. Once again, do not ask the child to make something specific, accept what ever he is willing to share about his creation.

- Science play is a part of sensory development, also. Observing and interacting with classroom pets, watching insects, or growing plants, playing with water bottles filled with different liquid and dry items helps to develop the toddler's observation skills. Caregivers should introduce items and tell about them, then allow the children to explore and ask questions. Adults can extend language through both telling and asking about the items, or listening and reacting to what the children say.

- Listening to music, either recorded or live, is another way to provide sensory input. Tapes of environmental sounds such as vehicles, animals or weather help to increase toddler's awareness. Take listening walks, or ask children what they hear in the room. Music and sound not only provide sensory information, but can be calming, as well. Some scholars believe that music enhances early brain growth and neurological development.

Imitation and Pretending

- The ability to imitate and pretend is developed and changes over time. The first imitative behaviors start with simple games such as peek-a-boo, and progress to the child who is able to put on dress-up clothes and "go to work." Caregivers can support this development by observing behavior, providing props, and interacting and extending language.

- Dress-up clothing may consist of washable hats and purses for younger toddlers, jackets, gowns and accessories for older toddlers. Dress-up play can be an activity involving simply "trying on," or may enhance role play. Young toddlers may not be aware of their own reflection in a mirror, trying on hats and then commenting on the effect is a good way to introduce them to themselves! Provide clothes for both boys and girls, larger children's sizes are a good "fit." Do not become concerned if children of either gender try on all of the clothes. Children of this age are not yet concerned with gender roles, and often dress for the enjoyment and challenge of self-dressing and the feel of the fabric rather than the style.

- Dolls of varied size, gender, ethnicity and style are an excellent prop for dramatic and imitative play. Toddlers enjoy acting out the caregiving routines that they experience each day, casting themselves in the role of grownup. Boxes, beds, wagons, strollers and high chairs complete the care taking equipment, and blankets, spoons, bowls, bottles, and play diapers bring more real life into their play. You may observe a child acting out an emotional scene with a doll, as toddlers become more verbal they are more likely to "play through" their own fears and experiences.

- A home center provides a place to act out dramas of family life. Cooking food, rocking babies, talking on the phone, going to bed are some of the scenes that may come to life in the home center. Caregivers may want to position themselves in this center to join in the play. While you may encourage play activities, "I sure am hungry," the children should be in charge of the course of the drama. Adults can provide a model of appropriate play while continuing to allow the children to lead the way.

- Other props such as doctor kits, grocery carts and cash registers, stuffed animals and such can bring about different dramatic scenarios. Introduce the items and talk about how it is used, then let the children explore and experiment. Their use of the materials will depend on their previous experience with them. Model or demonstrate how they work and look at pictures or read books about the places you would see them.

- Set up impromptu dramatic play activities, such as a line of chairs that could be a train or bus, or a blanket draped over a table for a tent. Use large boxes to make houses, or tunnels, or cars. Often the children themselves will come up with creative uses of common items in the classroom. Many toddlers will "cook" with pegs or beads!

- Blocks, cars, people and animals are good props for dramatic play. These small scale models of the real thing can give toddlers a sense of power and mastery as they create, manipulate and, sometimes, destroy their own words.

- Imitation and pretend play can also be prop-free. Being a kitty or a puppy may be seen simply through crawling and meowing or barking. Talk with the child about the role they have taken on, pat him on the head and offer a bone, "pet" the kitty and admire his fur. As toddlers become more skilled at imitation and pretend, they are showing an increase in the symbolic function of play, and their progress toward the next stage of cognitive development.

Language and Word Play

- Toddlers are adding to their language skills at an amazing rate. Conversations and hearing a good language model enhances their ability to develop speaking and listening skills. Use complete sentences, speak clearly and use correct pronunciation and grammar. Do not use or encourage baby talk.

- Toddlers will often gesture or point to ask for something that they want. This can be a very effective communication strategy, but the response should always give them the words that they need. When toddlers use shortened "telegraphic" speech, such as "kitty go," expand their statement and repeat it, "Yes, the cat has gone away."

- Because children always understand more of what they hear (receptive language), than what they are able to speak (expressive language), caregivers should speak just a bit above the toddler's ability to speak. For example, when the child is just beginning to name things around him, use single words to label the environment. Once they are using single words, add words to describe what they see. Use questions and emphasis to elicit language.

- Be sure to give toddlers time to answer questions or form their words. It takes them time to match their needs or thoughts to the right words. Don't always second-guess what they want to say, and always ask if you don't understand what they mean.

- Successful story times with toddlers are calm, relaxed and intimate. Rather than trying to read to an entire group at one time, opt instead to read to just a few of the children, or even just one. Books should be short, well illustrated, have repetitive or rhythmic language and be about topics and characters familiar to the toddler. Read dramatically, with expression, and expect that favorites will be asked for again and again. Flannel board stories or props to go along with a story are interesting additions to toddler story time.

- Songs, poems and finger plays help to encourage language in toddlers. Simple rhymes that have hand movements, such as *Itsy-Bitsy Spider*, or *Five Monkeys on the Bed* will be favorites. Develop a collection of often-requested tunes, and identify each with a single illustration. When toddlers want to make a request, they can do so by picking out the picture of their song.

- Any time a toddler is at work exploring their world, a caregiver should be there to support and encourage language. Many toys and games will offer opportunities to play with words and stimulate communication. Telephones, dolls, puppets, photos and pictures, are items with strong language emphasis, but any toy or object a toddler encounters will offer something to talk about!

Small and Large Motor Activities

- The toddler program should promote movement, as stated previously, and activities that address large motor development should be a part of every day. But young children are also working on small motor skills. Their manipulation of small toys such as pegs, blocks, and puzzles practicing skills like sorting, stacking, nesting, stringing, banging, putting together and taking apart, helps to develop small muscles, eye hand coordination, and cause/effect awareness.

- Invest in quality materials that work, and discard items that are broken or have missing pieces. It is frustrating to try to fit together a puzzle when the pieces don't match, or to stack rings that aren't all there. Simple items with just one or two elements, such as single shape sorters, or knob puzzles provide experience without frustration.

- Dump and fill is a favorite toddler activity, and one that should be incorporated as a part of play plans.

Having tubs or baskets of soft blocks, foam balls, cups or rings give toddlers safe items with which to practice this skill. As they can go on dumping "sprees," it is important for caregivers to limit the items available, and to model the pick up part of the activity.

- There are many simple manipulative materials that can be homemade by caregivers. When making toys for young children, it is important to keep in mind the same standards of quality and safety that you would consider with commercially made items. Be sure items are too big for choking, materials are non-toxic, and assembly is sturdy and unbreakable.

- As toddlers work with manipulative materials, resist the impulse to "help." Caregivers should maintain a "hands off" policy while using language for assistance and encouragement. Select items for each child that are challenging without going beyond the toddler's capabilities, if the adults end up finishing the task for the child, valuable learning is lost and the toddler comes to feel that she is not competent.

- Many concepts such as size, shape and color are encountered in manipulative materials. Use the toddler's play with these items to put language to these ideas.

Self-Help Skills

- A major task of the toddler years is the development of independence. The routines that are established in the toddler classroom can serve to either enhance the children's feelings of autonomy or thwart them. Some of the negative behavior associated with the toddler years comes from the battle of wills that ensues when both caregiver and child want to be "in charge." Wise toddler caregivers are able to "choose their battles." They are able to identify those issues that are non-negotiable, concerning health and safety, and those that allow for more flexibility and child choice.

- At meal and snack time, offer children foods that they can easily eat themselves. Give just a bit at a time, with seconds, if wanted. Fill cups just halfway; if there are spills, there is less to clean up. Some toddlers go on food "jags" where they will only eat one or two different foods. With "picky" eaters it is best not to force the issue, but to offer only healthy choices. Work closely with the family to see that the child's nutritional needs are being met over the course of the day.

- Toilet learning is a major task in the toddler years. It is very important that the schedule and approach be coordinated between home and school, and consistency is key. Watch the child for signs of readiness and interest, there is no set schedule that all children

should follow. To encourage independence, toddlers should wear clothing that is easy to remove, such as elastic waist pants. Bathroom fixtures ideally should be child height. While praise and recognition is an important part of the learning process, toddlers should never be made to feel shamed or "bad" for accidents or missteps. The process of toilet learning is a long one, and patience is important for all involved.

- Toddlers love to be "helpers," and caregivers should recognize and encourage this behavior. Toy shelves that are accessible, hooks that are child height, small brooms, sponges and towels, all help toddlers to do grown up jobs with ease. This activity should be carried out in a positive atmosphere of encouragement and cooperation. Caregivers should model helpful behavior, and use language both to recognize behavior and encourage involvement.

- Whenever possible, toddlers should be offered choices. Being able to select the story one wants to hear or the toy one wants to play with can help toddlers feel more "in control" of their world. It is a good idea to offer a choice when attempting to assist a toddler. Asking, "Would you like me to help you with your coat, or put it on yourself?" is better than taking it from the child and proceeding to help. Only offer choices to a toddler if either one is acceptable. "Would you like to put on your coat," is not an appropriate question if you want the child to wear the coat.

- The other side of striving for independence is the desire to remain dependent. Toddlers can be conflicted in this drive for autonomy. At times they are in control and on top of things, the next moment they can dissolve in tears and frustration. This is an exciting time, but not without perils. Each choice a child makes leaves behind an option not taken. If you choose milk over juice, you may have milk, but you have lost juice! Caregivers need to be sensitive to the ups and downs of toddler life, getting to know each child in their care is the best strategy for handling the good times and the challenges.

Planning for Individuals with Special Needs

A major part of the caregiver's job is getting to know the children in her care. Each child is a unique collection of traits, abilities, and behaviors wrapped in a highly individualized personality. While the caregiver needs to be aware of "ages and stages" of development, it is important to remember that each developing skill has a "range of normal" that encompasses many months (maybe years). It is best not to compare the development of toddlers to each other, labeling some as ahead or behind, rather look at each child individually and determine if the entire scope of emerging skills is within expected norms.

Caregivers should observe and record the progress of children in their care. Making time to assess the children's development is not only helpful in getting to know them, but can aid the caregiver in planning activities. Comparing actual objective observations of children's daily behavior to developmental checklists can help a caregiver to determine how best to support the child's acquisition of new skills. When the child seems to be "stuck," or not progressing over time, the caregiver can consult with the child's parents and seek the assistance of other professionals. It is not the caregivers' responsibility to diagnose the child or to recommend a course of treatment, but to serve as a resource for the parent and a link to additional services.

The environment that is offered to toddlers should take into account the wide range of development, differing needs, varied abilities, and an assortment of interests. Materials, equipment and activities offered should be open-ended so that any toddler at any stage of development can use them effectively. Toddler care is highly individualized with caregiver, child and parents forming a team to work together to optimize each child's growth and development. The toddler's environment should convey a message of warmth, love, acceptance, and encouragement. It is a welcoming place where all children can feel supported in their quest for autonomy and unfolding of new skills and abilities.

References

Ard, L. & M. Pitts (Eds.). (1995). *Room to grow: How to create quality early childhood environments*, (Rev. ed.). Austin, TX: Texas Association for the Education of Young Children.

Bredekamp, S. & C. Copple (Eds.). (1997). *Developmentally appropriate practice in early childhood programs*, (Rev. ed.). Washington, DC: National Association for the Education of Young Children.

Dombro, A. L., L. J. Colker, & D. Trister Dodge (1997). *The creative curriculum for infants and toddlers*. Washington, D C: Teaching Strategies, Inc.

Lally, J. R. & J. Stewart (1990). *A guide to setting up environments*. Sacramento, CA: California Department of Education.

Morrison, G. S. (1988). *Education and development of infants, toddlers, and preschoolers*. Glenview, IL: Scott, Foresman, and Company.

Checklist for Evaluating the Toddler Environment

_____1. The toddler environment is free from safety hazards; outlets are covered, cords secured, appliances are out of reach.

_____2. Toys and equipment are made of nontoxic materials, are free of rough or sharp edges, are in good repair. There are no small items that can pose a choking hazard.

_____3. There is ample, unobstructed space for toddler mobility. Toddlers are supervised at all times.

_____4. Areas for food preparation, eating, toileting and play are separate from each other. All surfaces are easy to clean and sanitize.

_____5. Children are carefully observed for signs of illness. Procedures are in place for contacting parents in the event of illness or injury.

_____6. Hands of caregivers and children are washed frequently throughout the day. Toys are regularly washed and disinfected

_____7. The classroom is well lit, with both natural and artificial light, ventilated with fresh air, and temperature is controlled.

_____8. The environment offers a variety of spaces for active, small group, and individual play. There are a variety of surfaces, levels, and textures in the room.

_____9. Displays are relevant to the development and interests of toddlers, and are hung at the toddler's eye level.

_____10. Parents feel welcome in the classroom, and displays and pertinent information is provided for them.

_____11. The classroom is well organized and contributes to the physical and emotional well being of the toddlers and caregivers.

_____12. The space and furniture, fixtures and equipment are scaled for small children.

_____13. The environment provides support for movement, with opportunities to crawl, climb, walk, run, jump, sit, stand and lie down. There is flexibility in the space, with items that can be rotated to provide new experiences.

_____14. The environment supports choice by offering a variety of play and learning materials; books, toys, sensory items, blocks, art materials, pretend play items.

_____15. Caregivers serve as appropriate language mod-

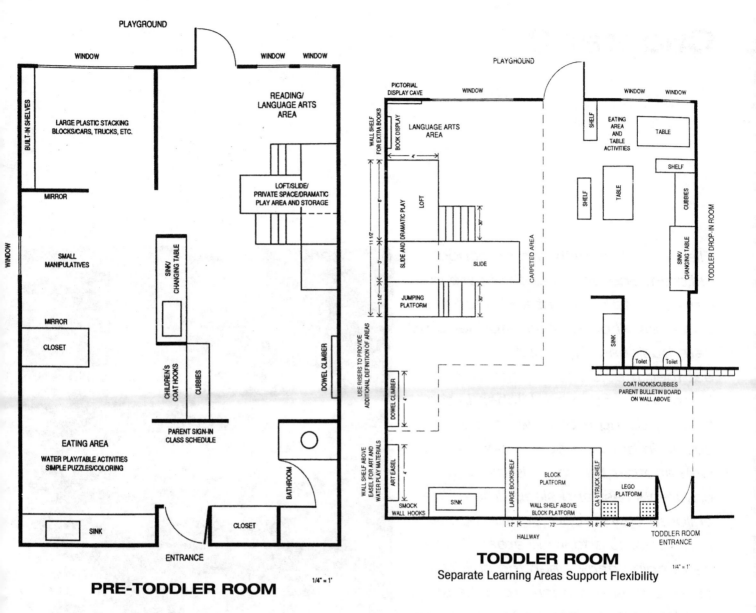

PLAYGROUND

WINDOW   WINDOW   WINDOW

BUILT-IN SHELVES

LARGE PLASTIC STACKING BLOCKS/CARS, TRUCKS, ETC.

READING/ LANGUAGE ARTS AREA

MIRROR

LOFT/SLIDE/ PRIVATE SPACE/DRAMATIC PLAY AREA AND STORAGE

WINDOW

SMALL MANIPULATIVES

SINK/ CHANGING TABLE

MIRROR

CLOSET

DOWEL CLIMBER

CHILDREN'S COAT HOOKS

CUBBIES

PARENT SIGN-IN CLASS SCHEDULE

EATING AREA

WATER PLAY/TABLE ACTIVITIES SIMPLE PUZZLES/COLORING

BATHROOM

SINK

CLOSET

ENTRANCE

PRE-TODDLER ROOM

1/4" = 1'

PLAYGROUND

PICTORIAL DISPLAY CAVE

WINDOW

WINDOW   WINDOW

WALL SHELF FOR EXTRA BOOKS

BOOK DISPLAY

LANGUAGE ARTS AREA

SHELF

EATING AREA AND TABLE ACTIVITIES

TABLE

LOFT

SHELF

SHELF

TABLE

SHELF

SLIDE AND DRAMATIC PLAY

CARPETED AREA

CUBBIES

TODDLER DROP-IN ROOM

SLIDE

SINK/ CHANGING TABLE

JUMPING PLATFORM

USE RISERS TO PROVIDE ADDITIONAL DEFINITION OF AREAS

SINK

Toilet   Toilet

DOWEL CLIMBER

COAT HOOKS/CUBBIES PARENT BULLETIN BOARD ON WALL ABOVE

WALL SHELF ABOVE EASEL FOR ART AND WATER PLAY MATERIALS

ART EASEL

LARGE BOOKSHELF

BLOCK PLATFORM

CA TRUCK SHELF

LEGO PLATFORM

SMOCK WALL HOOKS

SINK

WALL SHELF ABOVE BLOCK PLATFORM

HALLWAY

TODDLER ROOM ENTRANCE

TODDLER ROOM

Separate Learning Areas Support Flexibility

1/4" = 1'

J. Ronald Lally and Jay Stewart, 1990. *A Guide to Setting Up Environments.* Center for Child and Family Studies Far West Laboratory for Educational Research and Development, California Department of Education.

els by using complete sentences, speaking clearly, using correct pronunciation and grammar. They converse with children during play and caregiving tasks, and encourage language through poems, finger plays and stories.

_____16. Caregivers provide a program and environment that encourages the development of self-help skills in the children. Children are allowed to make appropriate choices.

_____17. Caregivers carry out regular, objective, written observations of the children's behavior and development, and share this information with parents. Caregivers make referrals to other professionals, if needed.

About the Author

Deborah Rogers has worked with young children, their parents and caregivers for 27 years. Currently teaching in public school, she has worked in a variety of settings including private preschool, campus child care, corporate child care, and as adjunct faculty in the Early Childhood Education departments of both two and four year colleges. She holds both a B.A. and M.A in Early Childhood Education, and continues to present on topics concerning the care and teaching of children under 8 to local, state and national organizations, and for the Campfire Campaign for Children Child Care Training Program.

Chapter 8

Ellen is a Mom with two preschool children. She provides child care in her home to an infant and a toddler. She uses all of her home for her child care business. The children eat their meals and snacks that have been prepared in her kitchen in the home's dining room. Her office is set up in her bedroom which, along with another bedroom is used for children's rest and sleep times. The children play throughout the house, in bedrooms and living areas. Her day begins early when the children arrive and she prepares breakfast as children help by setting the table. As the day continues the children play outdoors, draw and color with crayons, do crafts at the kitchen table, assist in folding clothes, and go with Ellen to the library, park, or shopping. Ellen provides many toys and materials and encourages the children to talk, ask questions and explore their world.

Family Child Care Environments

Sharon Hirschy

Annie always wanted to own her own business. She has always enjoyed being with children and wanted to begin a child care program. She felt that a home-based business was an affordable way to begin and believed that the warmth and casualness of a home provides a nurturing, supportive environment for children. She converted her garage into a child care facility. The room is divided into areas for centers, group work, and space for naps and meals. She added a small bathroom and kitchen area. It is cheerful, with child size equipment. She cares for 2 year olds and follows lesson plans especially designed to engage very young children and help them learn.

Judy cares for two infants and a toddler, as well as her own daughter in her home. She uses part of her home for child care. The kitchen, living room, playroom, and her daughter's bedroom are used, while other areas are "off-limits" to the children. She keeps toys and materials in storage bins and brings them out daily for the children's use. Judy has a small table and chairs that she sets up every morning in the kitchen for meals and crafts. She has a portable crib that she sets up for the infant in her care. The toddlers follow a fairly predictable schedule that includes planned daily activities, while the infant's schedule remains relatively flexible and responsive to infant needs.

Family child care is care provided for a child in a home other than that of the parent. Today, this form of child care fills a critical need particularly for families needing child care for their infants and toddlers. The examples above show that family child care has many different faces. It may be a home in which a mother or father cares for one or more children in addition to their own, one in which a caregiver or perhaps multiple caregivers care for children, or perhaps, a home of a relative caring for one or more related children.

What should family child care look like? Should all family child care look the same? Is there a best family child care environment? These questions are often asked and the answers are complex. There are no current studies that indicate that one form of family child care is better than others. However, there are key elements in family child care that are essential. High quality family child care is determined by the quality of caregiver interactions with the children, the number of children in care, and the education and training of providers (Haack, 1998: Kontos, Howes, Shinn, & Galinsky, 1995).

This chapter discusses space use and room arrangements in planning for the care and education of infants and toddlers. It is important to remember that there is no one right way. Each caregiver must determine what is most comfortable for her, her family, and the children in her care.

Characteristics essential to quality family child care programs are that they:

1. are first and foremost, safe

2. provide activities associated with each of the areas of child development: emotional, social, physical/motor, cognitive, language, and literacy development

3. allow each child opportunities to express and explore their interests

4. provide loving and supportive interactions between children and adults

5. provide appropriate guidance and structure.

Types of Family Child Care Physical Environments

The use of home space in family child care differs from one program to another. These spaces are configured to include the furnishings needed for daily routines, toys, play props, and creative materials, and space for the learning activities in which children will be engaged. Just as each home is different, so also will be the way space is used in different family child care settings. The primary types of spaces that can be provided for children in a family child care setting are:

1. Independent Child Care Rooms

One or more rooms might be exclusively used for child care and set up with child-sized equipment, toys and materials. A converted garage, such as Annie's, playroom, family room or even a room added to the house that is exclusively used for family child care, are seen in such programs. The furniture, toys, equipment and teaching materials are purchased specifically for the program to support children's play and learning.

The benefit of this arrangement is that the rooms that are used for the child care program are for that use only, and as such do not require portable materials and equipment. There is less daily preparation of the room in such a setting. However, this arrangement requires a great deal of space. This arrangement does not afford the same type of informal, home atmosphere that some providers and parents may prefer. The larger space however, does allow for a wider range of activities and the use of learning centers which will be described later.

2. Shared Family Rooms

One or more rooms that are used by the family living in the home may be used during business hours. For instance, a living room would continue to retain its furniture but additional materials and toys that could be used by the children are brought into the area during child care hours. In these programs materials and equipment are often portable, brought out by day for the children and then placed in a designated storage area when the children are not there.

3. Integrated Child Care and Home

In this plan, children use the entire home during the child care hours as in Ellen's program. The children nap in bedrooms, play in living areas, and have full use of the home. The materials provided include toys, books, games, art and music supplies or other items that would typically be found in a child's home.

Basics of Room Arrangements

There are spaces and materials all family child care rooms should have in common. The rooms should have areas for:

- quiet, calm activities such as puzzles, books, cuddly stuffed toys, tape or CD players for soft music

- small muscle activities such as Lego's© or other construction manipulatives, and sewing cards

- craft, science, and discovery activities, such as pasting, painting and drawing, magnifying glasses, collections of sea shells, sorting games, and simple age appropriate food preparations

- dramatic play activities such as dress-up, puppets, and props for role playing stories

- large motor activities such as building with blocks, dancing, walking a low balance beam, and outdoor space for running, climbing, jumping, and swinging.

A major benefit of family child care is that it provides a natural homelike setting for children. Caregivers can take advantage of this natural home arrangement by such amenities as a small basket of books next to a comfortable couch or other soft chairs to provide reading areas and areas to snuggle and rest. A craft and art area set up at the kitchen table or a small table in the kitchen can provide opportunities for the caregiver to prepare snacks and meals while maintaining supervision and conversation with children. With supervision and appropriate software and instruction, the family computer can become a learning center for young children.

The children's areas should be divided so that quieter activities are not next to more active areas. Spaces for such activities as blocks and dramatic play could be located near one another so that they do not disturb other children playing more quietly.

All of the activities do not have to be set up at the same time. But children should be provided with several choices at any one time. There should be an array of types of activities that meet children's needs to manipulate, explore, gain large and small motor control and coordination, pretend, and enjoy books, write, and create with age appropriate art media. Infants also need areas for quiet activities, small and large muscle activities, as well as baby books and opportunities to explore and experience their surroundings.

Dividing Rooms and Creating Spaces

It is often difficult to divide up a family child care home so that children have activities in different areas. The mixed-age group that is found in many family child care homes can create space problems when younger children are curious about and want to access toys and materials more appropriate for older children. Areas can be divided or separated in many different ways. Couches and chairs can be placed to form a divider between activities. The back of the couch with a piece of flannel over it with flannel board story characters, or a few puppets could easily become a storytelling and dramatic play area. On the other side of the couch a puzzle and small stack of books on a coffee table could provide a quieter place to play. Pillows can divide areas. Large pillows can be placed around an infant to keep the infant from rolling or crawling into another child's play area. Tape can be used on the carpet or floor to designate a roadway for small cars or to establish an area around blocks. Baskets, stacked milk crates, and small tables make excellent storage areas as well as natural dividers for activities. Safely designed and approved small gates and cribs can also provide barriers and designate areas for certain activities.

Family Child Care Programming

The schedules, activities, and curriculums in family child care vary. Most child care providers develop schedules and plan activities to meet children's age and developmental needs. Some caregivers follow a pre-developed and published curriculum. However, some pre-packaged curriculums are developmentally inappropriate and often do not take into consideration, the capabilities, needs and interests of individual children.

Other caregivers plan their activities and curriculum on a weekly or monthly basis, based on the cues children provide about their capabilities and interests. Often these activities are planned around themes, such as holidays or current community events (circus, rodeo, zoo week, springfests, and so on). These programs are usually eclectic, taking activities and ideas from many sources to build on the interests and prior experiences of the children. For example, if the children find a dead bird outdoors, this becomes an opportunity to learn more about birds through activities such as writing a story about the bird, looking at a bird's nest through a magnifying glass, learning about how birds learn to fly, and taking a trip to the local library to select books about birds.

Some caregivers prefer more spontaneous programming, in which informal interactions and conversations lead to topics and ideas for learning activities.

Caregivers observe and interact with children in a manner that provides them cues as to children's emerging abilities and special interests. These programs have the benefit of being most homelike in that they imitate the typical atmosphere of informal give and take/share and interact that characterizes adult-child relationships in supportive home settings. Such programs can be quite beneficial to children so long as they provide opportunities and activities that enrich growth, development, and learning in all of the developmental areas: emotional, social, cognitive, language, and literacy.

Those caring for infants also plan curriculum, albeit quite spontaneous and informal. The curriculum is planned with the individual needs of each infant in mind. For instance, cold weather could provide an opportunity to feel and compare warm and cool things, to share simple picture books about winter, to try on and name different types of cold weather clothing, and to sing winter songs. The caregiver is the source of this curriculum as she provides not only appropriate infant activities, but also social interaction and conversation through which infants learn language and many different concepts. These interactions encourage infants to observe and explore their surroundings.

Guidelines for Programming in Family Child Care

1. Establish a Schedule

All children do better with a schedule. Infants need predictable yet, flexible schedules that are geared to their individual rhythms and needs. Both the caregiver's day and the child's day will go better when children can expect the same time schedule each day for meals, naps, and play. A predictable schedule helps children gain knowledge of time, and also helps them to anticipate and self-manage transitions from one routine to another. Some family child caregivers set up very general schedules, while others are more specific.

Ellen's Schedule

8:00-10:00	Children arrive, breakfast, free play
10:00-12:00	Story time, art activity, meal preparation, outdoor time
12:00-3:00	Lunch, reading, nap
3:00-5:00	Library or outdoor time, free play

Annie's Schedule

7:00-8:00	Children arrive; breakfast
8:00-9:30	Center play
9:30-10:00	Group time and handwashing
10:00-10:30	Snack and storytime
10:30-11:15	Outdoor play
11:15-11:30	Small group time
11:30-12:15	Preparation for lunch and lunch
12:15-2:30	Naptime
2:30-3:00	Put away nap linens; snack
3:00-3:30	Craft
3:30-3:45	Small group time
3:45-5:00	Centers or outdoor time

2. Plan Ahead for Activities

Planning ahead for activities provides caregivers with the reassurance of having the necessary and appropriate materials and supplies ready for children's use. Caregivers should plan activities on a weekly or monthly basis, and can do so by creating weekly or monthly charts and lists of activities with their required supplies and materials. For example, a craft project scheduled for next week might require glue, flour, paint, and sequins. The necessary materials can then be purchased well ahead of time during the caregiver's next trip to the shopping center. When a field trip is planned, permission forms can be distributed to parents, a list of items to take on the trip, a schedule and perhaps travel route established, and extra chaperones or other people who need to be contacted can all be carried out well in advance.

3. Plan Storage Areas for Materials and Equipment

Family child care programs often have limited space. Some child care programs use portable storage containers such as stacking bins, rolling carts, and plastic bins with wheels to hold supplies and materials. These can be stored in closets or a designated garage area and brought out each day. They can also be labeled for the different types of materials they hold. For instance, two plastic shoe boxes may hold art and craft materials and can be placed on a child's table in the dining room when the children are in care. A bin containing blocks can be placed in the living room next to an open area for building, while a bin of books can be put on the couch for a reading area.

Dividing materials according to activity and placing them in labeled containers can create organization and help maintain order. Organizing materials in this way helps caregivers to select materials to promote specific types of learning experiences. Placing these containers in different parts of the room creates specific areas for each type of play and helps to define learning or activity centers for children. Such containers are easily moved and stored when the child care day ends.

4. Create Learning Centers

Centers are designated spaces created to encourage a particular type of concept learning or skill development. Each learning center is supplied with the appropriate toys and materials to promote learning. Some of the most common learning centers that caregivers use are: books, art and creative activities, language arts, manipulatives, puzzles, blocks, dramatic play, science, water play. While some programs create physical areas for learning centers, the learning center can be the place where for example, a bin of books is placed for reading and sharing stories or the most practical place for children to carry out a particular activity or task. Centers can be very informal, such as a couch with some books, or can be more formalized such as a playroom with a kitchen area, large block area, and puzzle area. Caregivers who use their family space for child care often find that creating mobile centers is effective. Using the containers mentioned above, an art center can be set up quickly and effectively in an available space, and the supplies later stored in a closet when the day ends.

Guidelines for Mobile Learning Centers

- Use easily portable materials. Small containers with lids, canvas bags with handles, or containers with wheels are good investments that allow materials to be kept together and easily moved.

- Place quiet centers next to other quiet centers and more active next to active. For instance, blocks can be placed near the dramatic play center, while books can be next to a puzzle area.

- Place centers that could be messy on a tile or vinyl floor near a water source for easy clean-up. If the area is carpeted, placing a plastic table cover under the activity reduces frustration over spills and facilitates clean-up. Art and water play can take place in a kitchen area.

- Divide areas of the room by using tape, pillows, baskets, tables and furniture. As mentioned earlier, the reading area can be effectively divided from more active play areas by placing the books on a couch and the blocks behind the couch. Tape on the floor can define the space for a dramatic play area and keep it from running into the blocks. Designating areas in this manner helps children to focus on their activities and minimizes interferences with other children's work. Safety is easier to maintain since large areas that can temp indoor running are eliminated.

- Provide centers that offer a variety of choices. Have areas set up daily that provide opportunities for quiet calm activities, structured activities (such as blocks, games, and crafts) science and discovery activities, dramatic play, and large motor activities.

Activities for Children in Family Child Care Settings

Art Centers

Art encourages creativity and enhances small motor controls including eye-hand coordination. Art activities encourage children to explore and experiment with many types of media: crayons, finger paint, play dough, glue and clay. To facilitate the child's creative attempts, the caregiver can provide different sizes of paint brushes and a variety of objects and materials with which to paint. Use materials readily found around the house, such as small sections cut from window screens, cotton balls and swabs, straws, twigs, sandpaper, as objects with which to spread paint. Mix different types of materials into paint and playdough, such as salt, rice, cinnamon, or vanilla. Items found around the house, such as toilet paper and paper towel tubes can be assembled and glued into unique sculptures. Wrapping paper tubes, boxes of all sizes and shapes, (e.g., oatmeal boxes), and stickers, stamps and envelopes can all be used to create interesting works of art!

Water and Sand

Many family child care programs offer sand and water play indoors. Water and sand play should be conducted in an area where the flooring is easily swept, mopped, and cleaned, preferably in the kitchen. A plastic baby bathtub or large plastic container with low sides placed on a plastic tablecloth provides an excellent space for water or sand play. Kitchen tools such as measuring cups, funnels, plastic spoons, straws, basters work well in both sand and water. Consider adding food coloring to the water.

Manipulatives

Puzzles, Legos© Lincoln Logs© are good choices for manipulatives. Puzzles can be made by gluing large colorful pictures (e.g., calendar pictures) to cardboard, and then cutting them into several parts. (The younger the child, the fewer should be the number of puzzles parts). Sometimes puzzles with all of their parts can be found at garage sales. Puzzles can be stored in plastic boxes and should be rotated so that children do not become bored with them. In addition, young children can use coffee cans, baby food jar lids, milk cartons with their tops flattened, and boxes for stacking, picking up, and other manipulative activities. Manipulatives can be placed on a coffee table or the smooth surface of the floor. If there is carpeting in the play area, a large piece of cardboard or pegboard can provide a flat, stable surface.

Books

Books are probably one of the most important items that a child care program can offer a child. Books provide many opportunities to develop a variety of concepts and early literacy skills. Turning pages develops hand-eye coordination. Language development, emotional development and social skills are enhanced as a caregiver reads to children and discusses stories, as well as involves the children in retelling and role playing the stories. Books are available through many sources such as, local public libraries, school library sales, book fairs, garage sales, and the children's own books. Choose books that are age-appropriate, sturdy, colorful and easy for a child to handle. Many caregivers choose books based on popular movies or TV shows. While some of these books can be appropriate, age appropriate themes and language accompanied by attractive and meaningful illustrations are qualities to look for in children's books. Ask your local librarian or check the Internet at http://www.ala.org/booklist/v96/002.html or http://www.nypl.org/branch/kids/gloria.html for booklists. These locations can offer lists of age-appropriate books for infants, toddlers, and preschoolers.

Dramatic Play

Dramatic play is important to children's social and emotional growth. It provides opportunities to interact socially with playmates learning to communicate, share, cooperate, and negotiate, to try on adult roles, experiment with play themes and engage in fantasy, and to use language to express ideas. Infants and toddlers can enjoy dramatic play as well as preschoolers. A large unbreakable mirror at floor height gives children a chance to see themselves in their dress-up clothes and to experiment with facial and body expressions. Toddlers and preschoolers enjoy dressing up in adult clothing. Young children enjoy such simple props as hats, purses, briefcases, and different types of shoes for dramatic play. For safety and ease of dressing, the clothing should be shortened to prevent tripping and should have large neck holes and elastic waists with no loose strings, buttons, snaps, or other objects that could get caught on furniture, strangle, or cause choking.

A large box, such as a box for a washing machine provides infinite possibilities for dramatic play. The bottom and one side can be cut out and the box can be painted by the children. Cut a window in one side and you have a store, fast food restuarant, a puppet theater, bank, or a variety of other pretend play settings. When out of use, it can be easily folded and stored. Smaller boxes can become cars, boats, and trains. Plastic plates, spoons, and leftover party napkins can provide table settings for a tea party.

Language Arts
Children need to develop language skills in a variety of ways. Social and verbal interactions that children have with their caregivers and other children contribute to their language development. Conversation and dialogue are extremely important to this development. With infants, these interactions include point and name activities, talking about routines such as diaper changing, warming the bottle, holding and hugging a teddy bear. As children get older they can be engaged in conversations that include "what if," "why," and "how" questions. Questions posed to children should be open-ended; that is, the child's response should not be simply "yes" or "no." Rather, a question might begin with, "Tell me about___, or "What do you see under that magnifying glass?" "What do you think we should do about that?" Encourage children to talk with one another: "Tell Jamie about the way you made the sand go through the sifter."

Provide tape recorders and tapes for listening activities and to record and tape or video children in their daily activities. (These recordings are wonderful ways to communicate and share with parents the activities and skills of their children.) Children are natural performers and such activities encourage their facility with language. Use stories in many ways. Read stories, act out stories, provide puppets to enact stories, have children retell stories.

Allow children to dictate stories and ideas to you and write what they say as they watch. If they tell you something about a picture they draw, write it in a place on the picture designated by the child or on a separate paper that can be clipped to the drawing if they do not want you to write on their drawing. Make books using children's own dictated words. Write a story about a field trip from children's comments and post it in the room or send it home for parents to read with their child. Make writing materials available in the dramatic play area or on a table.

Infants need to hear lots of conversation. Look into a baby's eyes and talk to them about what they are doing. Tell them about your day and theirs. Give them words for things they see or do. Share baby books with them often. Use puppets and dolls to add interest to stories and interactions. Sing and sway or "dance" with the infant often. All of these activities help infants develop concepts and language skills. Moreover, positive and nurturing social interactions with infants builds their sense of trust and confidence in their caregivers and in themselves.

Science and Discovery
Children are naturally curious about their world. A home can offer many opportunities to explore and learn. For example, purchase an 81/2 by 11 magnifying sheet at a dollar store or office supply. This is large enough for young children to see into and they can carry it about and hold it over objects to make them larger to see. Provide a box of varied interesting items that children can touch, explore, and discuss. Such items as sea shells, leaves, and rocks build concepts and encourage discussion, helping children to learn more about the world around them. Purchase large, inexpensive magnets at a hardware store and invite children to explore what appliances and other objects in the home attract the magnets. If thematic units are used, expand the themes with many different types of materials. For example, a theme unit on animals could be enriched with pictures of animals, prints or photographs of animals, selected animal stories, pretending with plastic animals, building block "homes" for animals, talking about where animals sleep and what they eat, making lists of animals we have seen, and sorting card pictures of animals into two classifications such as pets or zoo animals. These items and activities can take place in the discovery center.

Safety Issues in Family Child Care Environments

A good program and interesting spaces for children mean nothing if the environment is unsafe. Family child care providers must be particularly diligent in preparing and maintaining safe surroundings, furnishings, equipment, toys, and sanitary conditions for children. In a home where older children and adults live, many potentially hazardous items (such as tools, electrical appliances, personal hygiene items, medicines, sporting equipment) can be inadvertently left where children can obtain them. The following precautions can help to establish a safe family child care environment:

1. Do a daily walk around the home. Every morning before the children arrive do a safety check of both the indoor and outdoor areas. Use the Family Child Care Safety Checklist below to focus your inspection.

2. Have an escape route planned for emergencies. Plan fire or other emergency escape routes for every room. Also, plan how you will assemble the children and where you will go, and how parents can contact you in case of a serious emergency or disaster.

3. Practice fire and weather drills with the children on a regular basis and repeat the practice when new enrollees enter the program. (Preferably not on their first day or during their first week, as this could be frightening to children new to this setting.) This way you and the children will be prepared and not as likely to panic should a need to follow the drill arise.

4. Have someone else do a safety check in your home on a semi-annual basis. Ask another professional or perhaps a parent to inspect your home for you. They may find hazards you do not notice because you are so used to your environment.

There may be other safety precautions required by individual state licensing or regulatory standards. Providers should become well acquainted with such standards and apply them conscientiously in their programs.

Family Child Care Safety Checklist

_____1. Are there any cords or appliances where children can reach them or trip over them, and are all electrical outlets covered?

_____2. Is the floor clean and clear of spills, food, and small objects?

_____3. Are all plants out of children's reach?

_____4. Is the furniture sturdy and in good repair with no protruding nails, parts, or rough edges?

_____5. Are bumpers secure around hazardous corners and edges of furniture?

_____6. Are all medications, toiletries, cleaning supplies, and other hazardous items out of reach of children? Are safety locks for cabinets and drawers in place?

_____7. Are bathrooms and the kitchen clean and sanitized?

_____8. Is furniture placed to provide safe and easy access for children who want to climb onto it?

_____9. Is furniture so arranged that the caregiver can see and supervise what children are doing at all times?

_____10. Are all toys sanitized and free of broken or loose parts or sharp edges?

_____11. Are crayons, paints, and other materials used by children non-toxic and properly stored when not in use.

_____12. Are house and furniture paints lead-free?

Family Child Care Environments for Children with Special Needs

Can a family child care program accommodate children with special needs? Indeed, it can. In fact, many child care providers do care for young children with special needs and feel that these children and the other children benefit from their interactions with one another and from what the program can offer them.

Caregivers should be aware that, according to federal law, they cannot exclude a child from their care because the child has a disability. According to the United States Department of Justice (1997) "Centers cannot exclude children with disabilities from their programs unless their presence would pose a *direct threat* to the health or safety of others or require a *fundamental alteration* of the program." Therefore, most children with special needs can be accommodated within a family child care setting. There is help for child care providers. Federal law provides for services to children with special needs that are administered through state agencies. Every state offers information and referral services; for example, in Texas, the Early Childhood Intervention (ECI) program provides: information to caregivers about specific disabilities; screening and assessment services; collaborative planning with families and caregivers for needed services; and guidance on adapting activities and materials to accommodate a child with special needs. Such agencies can be located by contacting your pediatrician or local school district, or your state education or human services agency. How can you structure your program so that it meets the needs of all children?

1. Look at your physical environment. Are there materials or furniture that need to be rearranged to accommodate equipment such as a walker, wheelchair, or breathing machine?

2. Check your schedule. Are meals and nap times appropriate for the child with special needs? It may be necessary to schedule a separate meal time when the other children are playing or sleeping that provides additional time for the child with special dietary or feeding needs. If the child needs special rest or sleeping accommodations can they be arranged in an easily maintained and supervised area?

3. Provide appropriate materials. The child with special needs may require different types of physical equipment. Garage and toy sales can be good sources for equipment such as small slides, riding toys, and infant exercisers. Make certain such items are safe, washable, and in good repair. (*Note: The Consumer Product Safety Commission advises that many garage sale items for children may be items that have been recalled for the hazards they have posed. Make certain that you are not purchasing a recalled item.*)

4. Enlist outside help. If the child's disabilities are complex, it may be necessary to have additional help during meals and other high need times, such as special projects or outings. A parent or college student may be available to volunteer or perhaps work part-time for a small wage. Organizations such as early childhood intervention agencies, Easter Seals, the March of Dimes and other social service agencies can assist with locating volunteers, adaptive and assistive equipment, and planning engaging and meaningful activities for children with disabilities.

5. Talk to the children and parents in your program about the child's disability and how you will be able to care for all the children in your program in a supportive and nurturing way. Parents may worry that because of another child's special needs their child will receive less attention. Assure parents that no child's needs will be overlooked. Point out the benefits to children and adults of learning to accept differences among people.

Working with Specific Disabilities

Many professional organizations and health care professionals can provide specific information on the care and education of children with specific disabilities. The following are some general suggestions that might be helpful for initial planning.

Children with retardation Children with retardation often progress developmentally at a slower pace. Toilet learning often takes longer, language may be delayed, and they may be slower in gaining large and small motor coordination and skills. Provide activities and materials for the child's developmental level, not the child's age level. Select materials to encourage growth, development, and learning in all of the developmental areas. Recognize that the behaviors of children with retardation can pose the same types of risks as younger children, such as putting things in their mouths on which they could choke. Take special precautions to protect them from small objects and other hazardous toys and items in the household.

Children with Attention Deficit Disorders and Hyperactive Behaviors Provide a child care environment where adults can easily see and supervise the children. Open rooms or rooms with gates keep the child within sight. Provide ample opportunity for outdoor and large motor activities. Small toddler climbing equipment indoors will encourage large motor development. At the same time, it is important to provide calming activities as the hyperactive child is readily overstimulated and frustrated. Speak directly to the child (do not shout across the room) using a soft, calming voice with them. Give only one or two directions at a time. Too many directions confuse and cannot be followed. Be prepared to repeat instructions and requests often. Play soothing music, invite the child to sing songs with you, and adjust the environment to include soft colors and an uncluttered simple décor. Hyperactive children do better with limited choices and tasks that have been broken into small simple steps to make them more achievable. Offer only a few toys at a time and rotate toys and materials when interest decreases.

Children with Asthma and Allergies Vacuum and dust daily to keep the rooms free of allergens. Consider using a hypoallergenic filter in the heating and air conditioning systems. During rest and nap times give the child clean washable pillows and blankets, and launder them frequently. Be sure the child is not allergic to any pets that you may have in the home. Have the parents demonstrate for you how to use the child's asthma equipment. Request a spirometer that will allow you to know when the child is having breathing problems. This is a small device that a child can blow into that will give you an idea as to how much breathing difficulty the child may be having. The spirometer is inexpensive and available by prescription. Ask the parents for specific instructions on what to do if the child is in difficulty, and make certain that the child's medications are available and you know how to administer them. The child's physician should be given the name of the child's caregiver, and with the parent's written permission, in the event of an emergency, the caregiver can contact the child's physician or health care professional.

Children with Physical Disabilities Make sure that the environment is arranged for the child's needs. If the child requires special equipment, ask the parents or physical therapist to demonstrate their appropriate use. If adaptive devices are needed for eating and toileting, be sure that you understand their use and ask that you be

given instructions on how to teach or help the child to use the equipment. Inspect the home to make certain that there are clear pathways and clear away objects that can tumble easily from shelves or table tops. Tables, couches and chairs may need to be rearranged to accommodate the child and loose area rugs and other small furnishings may need to be removed to minimize risks and avoid accidents.

Quality Family Child Care Environments

Caregivers who take the time to plan and consider all aspects of their family child care environment find that they can provide a family child care setting that is efficient and affordable, and can meet the developmental needs of children. Well planned family child care can support positive behaviors in children, encourage positive social interactions, and stimulate children intellectually. There is not one best family child care environment. Quality exists in all types of homes and in all types of child care settings. In planning, caregivers make

A Family Child Care Home Space Use Plan

How might you arrange your child care program?

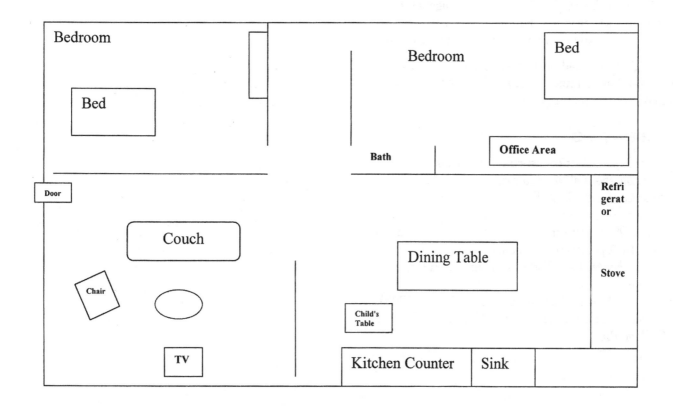

decisions about what serves the best interests of their own families and the children in their care, deciding what interactions and materials will facilitate and enhance each individual child's growth, development and learning.

Planning for a Quality Family Home Child Care Environment

1. Decide how you will arrange your space. Draw a diagram of your space and how it will be used. How will you maintain it?

2. Decide on how you will plan activities and the type of activities and materials you will use. Will you have a formal curriculum, one that you and the children generate, one that you follow from a book?

3. Check the safety of your home. Develop a plan for fire drills, weather emergencies, and daily safety checks.

4. Prepare a schedule. Plan your day and week so that you and the children know what to expect and when.

5. Obtain age-appropriate equipment and materials that are easy to store and maintain. Make certain that used equipment and toys are washable, safe, sturdy, in good repair, and are not items that the manufacturer has recalled. Check with local social service agencies and state child care agencies that may have special programs that provide equipment and caregiver training.

6. Plan activities ahead of time. Keep a running list of materials that you need to buy and contacts you need to make for the planned activities.

References

American Department of Justice (1997). *Commonly asked questions about child care centers and the Americans with Disabilities Act.* www.usdoj.gov/crt/ada/adahom1.htm

Haack, P. (1998). Defining high-quality family child care. In A *policy briefing: Family child care peer-to-peer exchange.* New York: Ms. Foundation for Women, pp.10-13.

Kontos, S., C. Howes, M. Shinn. & E. Galinsky (1995). *Quality in care and relative care.* New York: Teachers College Press.

About the Author

Sharon Elizabeth Hirschy has been involved in family child care for over 20 years. She has been an accredited family child care provider, has taught providers and assisted them in becoming accredited, and has written several manuals for family child care. She has taught college courses in child development and holds a Master's Degree in Child Development and Family Science. Sharon has been very active in local, state, and national organizations dealing with children and families and is currently teaching special education in public school while completing her doctorate in Early Childhood Education.

Environments for 3-, 4-, and 5-Year-Olds

Chapter 9

"How about we make a ship?" asks Derrick after seeing Tameisha's three hollow blocks placed haphazardly in a pile. Derrick and Tameisha began placing the blocks side by side. "Don't put no blocks right here!" he orders, pointing to an open area in the center of the ship. "That's where we sit!"

James joins in the construction, which now measures 4 by 6 feet. He and Derrick load the "cargo" by placing trucks and other small toys inside the open sides of the hollow blocks that form the ship's outer edges.

Tameisha throws some toys into the open area, and Derrick immediately pulls them out, saying emphatically. "Don't put toys in there!" This leads to his idea of covering the hole with long building boards, placed carefully side-by-side. "This is going to be our basement," he says. "Everyone is going to sit right here," which they do. Derrick calls to the teacher seated on the floor nearby. "Look how we made it," he says, recounting the experience to the teacher who had stopped by the block center.

Derrick and James joined by Tim, resume loading the ship, which requires much movement. James frequently lies on his stomach as he pushes unit blocks into the remaining hollow blocks. Derrick points out the "elevator" he has just built on one side. "I'm going up in the elevator. Going upstairs." "Bye, bye." "I'm going down."

Blocks

Katie Best Butler

The Value of Block Play

These 4-and-5-year-old children are fortunate to have a teacher who values blocks for their contribution to child growth and development. A supply of blocks and accessories, adequate space, time, and a supportive teacher who stops by frequently and sits near enough to listen, provide a learning environment in which many types of learning can occur.

The following are quotations from scholars who cite the many benefits of block play during childhood:

Children have always built, testing their theories about the physical world. They stack units, knock them down, enclose spaces, bridge gaps, and repeat and refine ideas—often without the intervention of adults or the introduction of commercial materials (Hewitt, 2001).

For the preschool child *"who works in painstaking fashion to create an elaborate structure, block play is exciting, inspiring, and greatly satisfying. As structures are built block upon block, they take on a life and story that interests and motivates the child. These structures may reflect a child's recent experience or adventure, a wildly imaginative idea, or an issue or event that may be of concern to him or her"* (Church and Miller, 1990).

Blocks provide experiences that can be—all at the same time—visual, aural, tactile, kinesthetic, and conceptual" (Robison, 1977). *(Blocks) present a hundred puzzling questions to the child but do not dictate answers. The child's resourcefulness and imagination are endlessly challenged but never rigidly channeled. Building among the children is varied and free with no preset standards"* (Cartwright, 1974).

Block play contributes to growth, development and

learning in all domains, physical/motor, social, emotional, cognitive, language, and literacy. Opportunities for language development and other aspects of literacy development abound in block play. Derrick was especially vocal as he engaged in activities with the ship.

Based on observations of spontaneous block play in naturalistic classroom settings a literacy enriched block-play center appears to be promising in the development and practice of emergent reading and writing skills. By adding literacy props to their collection of traditional block play accessories, teachers can expand the realm of constructive block play into the world of reading and writing. In this type of enriched block play center, young children will have an opportunity to build not only houses and highways but also a foundation for literacy" (Stroud, 1995).

Feelings, both pleasant and unpleasant, can find expression through play with blocks.
In the benign world of the block corner, the child can build, destroy, and repair to his heart's content—until he has had his fill…. Blocks are so totally indestructible that a child feels safe in playing out his fears of disaster from without and his destructive impulses from within. Projecting his feelings on something so real and concrete, a child is able to rob them of their power and possible threat. Whether constructive or destructive, the dramatic play which building blocks help to implement serves to round out the personality of a child" (Caplan and Caplan, 1973).

Block play helps children grow in their own estimation as they discover they can build and do things that are valued by others as well as themselves. As Derrick and his friends played with the hollow blocks, they stretched high to reach the ones on the top shelf and lifted them down to carry to the building site. They often tugged, pushed, and pulled them into the desired position. While they worked, their bodies bent and straightened. Stowing the unit blocks inside the hollow blocks involved the eyes and hands as well as the larger muscles. These and similar motor movements release energy, develop coordination and strength, enhance hand-hand and eye-hand coordinations, and develop visual perception.

Play with blocks meets the needs of children at different levels of social development as a child can work alone, beside someone, or in cooperation with others. If the classroom environment is favorable, most 4- and 5-year-old children gradually begin to work together in cooperative efforts.

As children engage in block play, they make mathematical and scientific discoveries, such as the change of speed of a vehicle when it rolls down a steep ramp made from blocks or a ramp placed at a near-level angle. As children play with blocks they engage in such cognitive tasks as observing, comparing, classifying, and predicting. These tasks contribute to concept development. Interactions with objects and feedback from playmates and adults during block play facilitate ideas, concepts, and progress toward abstract thinking. Even the process of putting away blocks provides an occasion for sorting, classifying, counting, ordering, and practicing with equivalent sets (Leeb-Lumberg, 1984).

> *For children to increase the conceptual knowledge, they must have the time and opportunity to explore, try out, make mistakes and develop solutions with blocks again and again. To learn they must do it themselves* (Charney, Clayton, and Wood, 1990).

When children play with blocks on a regular basis they acquire numerous concepts associated with math and science. This repertoire of concepts is profound in its possibilities. Concepts that children may acquire as they handle blocks, engage in the building process, and play with their constructions in the company of other children include the following:

•area	•classification	•topology	•space
•conservation	•mapping	•size	•representation
•number	•shape	•discrimination	•stability
•depth	•equivalence	•surface	•balance
•reversibility	•fractions	•distance	•measurement
•bridging	•gravity	•relationships	•matching
•value	•patterning	•seriation	•weight
•directionality	•cause and effect	•symmetry	•effect
•three-dimensionality	•one-to-one correspondence		• position

As with concept development, the ability to solve problems is an important component of cognitive development. Problem-solving engages creative thinking processes. Play is an important medium for developing problem-solving skills, and block play is particularly suitable. Children need an atmosphere that provides flexibility, freedom of choice, support, and encouragement in order to enjoy and become engaged in exploration and experimentation. In such an environment, opportunities to enlist problem-solving thinking and social interaction skills are provided. Success in problem-solving builds confidence and strengthens the child's ability to tackle other challenges. As Church advises, "Listen as children build with blocks and you will hear them dealing daily with problems of construction and design as well as social problems. Comments such as, 'This won't stay up!' 'I need more blocks to finish my tower,' and, 'Your house is in my road!' are all exclamations of problem-solvers at work" (Church, 1993). Though block building is perceived by many as "just playing," and indeed, children will say they are "playing," in actuality, the children are learning math, science, literacy and other important academic concepts and skills when working with blocks (Alexander, 2000).

The Adult's Role

For children to gain the greatest benefit from block play, it is important that the teacher understand and recognize its value and benefits. The teacher must also know how to create an atmosphere that maximizes the experience for children. This involves allowing children to self-direct their activities while the adult provides the space, props, and assistance as needed. As with pretend play in other centers, the adult can interject play suggestions or ask questions that extend imagination, thinking, and learning. However, the adult's role should be as non-interfering as possible and should support children's constructive play rather than attempting to direct it (Church and Miller, 1990).

Stages in Block Play Development

It is believed that children go through developmental stages in their use of and construction with blocks. One study has described four stages beginning at about 18 months of age: 1) carrying blocks, 2) piling blocks and laying them on the floor, 3) connecting blocks to create structure, and 4) making elaborate constructions (Dodge, Goldhammer & Colker, 1988). Most children go through these stages beginning with the first stage regardless of the age of first introduction to blocks. However, older children progress through the stages more rapidly. Block play is unique in that all ages of children enjoy constructing with blocks and will do so with varying levels of sophistication and complexity depending on their prior opportunities to experience block play.

Materials and Accessories for Block Construction

Blocks

There are a variety of teaching materials that are called "blocks," but many are more appropriate for the manipulative or table toys learning center because of their size. The type of blocks most suitable for the block center are called *unit blocks* and *hollow blocks*. Made from solid hardwood, both unit and hollow blocks are clean, firm, heavy, and indestructible. They are natural in color, smooth, squarely cut and unstructured. These characteristics make blocks adaptable for a variety of uses. Children enjoy their size, shape, smoothness, and infinite possibilities for use.

If the classroom is large enough, it is helpful to have two block centers: one for unit blocks and one for hollow blocks. Most of the accessories are different for both, and the type of building and play is different. When unit and hollow blocks are located together, the unit blocks are often used for decorations or accessories for the hollow blocks rather than for construction. If classroom space is limited, it is better to have both together in one center than to have one center of either unit or hollow blocks only.

Hardwood unit blocks and hollow blocks represent a sizable investment. However, well-constructed blocks outlast almost any other teaching material. Depending on their usage and care, hardwood blocks can last twenty years or more. Starting small with affordable starter sets is a way to begin to bring blocks and children together. Additional blocks can be added from time to time as budgets allow until a full set and accessories have been acquired.

Unit Blocks

Unit blocks have been a staple in school rooms for almost a century. An educator often profiled in early childhood education history books, Carolyn Pratt, is credited with developing the unit block system in 1913. Carolyn Pratt was an educator who had received woodworking training in Sweden and developed the blocks for her experimental classroom at Harley House and at the City and Country School that she helped found in New York City (Hewitt, 2001). Pratt designed the blocks to be incremental units of larger blocks. Today these unit blocks are available in a variety of shapes and sizes. The basic unit block measures $1\frac{3}{8}$ inches by $2\frac{3}{4}$ inches by $5\frac{1}{2}$ inches. The rectangular, square, and triangular blocks which come in various sizes, are either a multiple or division of the basic unit block so that each will fit together in any configuration. A set of blocks also includes such shapes as pillars, cylinders, arches, curves, switches, and boards. All are scaled to the unit block in one or more dimensions. Some companies sell blocks individually so that added shapes or sizes not included in the original set can be purchased.

Unit block sets are available from school supply companies in a variety of sizes ranging from a basic set of 85 blocks in 11 to 15 shapes to a set with 644 blocks in 19 shapes. These hardwood blocks are usually of excellent quality, smooth, and rounded and are most often cut from solid northern maple, a wood that does not splinter or dent easily. A classroom of 15 children should have a minimum of 100 blocks, preferably 300 or more. There should be at least 15 different shapes for four- and five-year-old children (Moore, 1997).

If the blocks are locally made, they should be cut uniformly so that all the units of a particular size are the same in thickness and are of uniform length and width. Each block should represent multiples or divisions of the width or length of a standard unit. All of the edges and corners should be rounded and smooth. Locally made blocks are often made of softwood and tend to split and splinter. They may lack many of the pleasing qualities of well-made commercial hardwood blocks.

Hollow Blocks

Hollow blocks are much larger than unit blocks and have fewer pieces and shapes in the set. These blocks are rectangular, square, and triangular in shape. Boards of two lengths are included. The square block is the basic unit and measures 11 by 11 by $5\frac{1}{2}$ inches. The other block shapes are multiples or divisions of the square block. The basic unit block, which is also $5\frac{1}{2}$ inches in one dimension and other unit blocks can be used with the hollow blocks.

Hollow blocks come in sets that contain from 12 to 80 blocks of different sizes and shapes. Some companies sell individual blocks. Most hollow blocks are open on two sides for ease of handling and added play value. Children playing together have been observed to lie on their stomachs on each side of a hollow block talking through the opening. They have "sailed" boats through the opening as if it were a bridge over a stream of water and "driven" cars and trucks through the "underpass." Enough hollow blocks should be available for children to build a structure large enough for two to four children to fit inside.

Hollow blocks can be used on playgrounds when indoor space is limited. Children can build large structures without being crowded. A flat surface is needed so the blocks will balance, and a non-abrasive surface keeps the blocks from getting scratched. A dry storage area is required if hollow blocks are kept outdoors.

In addition to hardwood hollow blocks, other large blocks are commercially available. They may be made of cardboard, plastic or dense foam that is covered with plastic material. These are less expensive than hardwood hollow blocks and will show wear more quickly. Their lighter weight may make them more practical for two- and three-year-old children.

Accessories to Use with Unit Blocks

Block play can be enhanced through a variety of accessories or props. There should be enough props and accessories for four children engaged in block play at the same time. The accessories should be scaled to the size of the blocks. They should be sturdy and safe with no sharp edges, loose or broken parts. Some rough areas on wooden accessories can be smoothed with sandpaper. Wheeled vehicles should roll easily and quietly on securely fastened wheels. All props and accessories should be continually checked for potential hazards or needed repairs, and unsafe items discarded.

All accessories, books, pictures, puppets, and family and community figures should reflect diverse cultures, abilities, and ages of people as well as nonsexist standards. A world globe can be located on top of a block shelf for easy access and examination. Discussion about the globe can include information about ways people travel, particularly when they must cross large bodies of water. Significant locations on the globe can be identified such as children's own country, state, and city, that of their grandparents or other relatives, and places they have heard or read about or perhaps visited.

To create a literacy-enriched block center, props and accessories might include such items as a telephone, books, magazines, and pictures or photographs depicting variety of construction activities, e.g., children playing with blocks, buildings, construction sites, construction equipment and various types of vehicles. Writing supplies such as pencils, markers, and crayons with post-it pads, rolls of adding machine paper, calculator tape and masking tape may be used for making signs or for other purposes created by the children. House plans or blueprints of small buildings may be displayed on the wall or spread out on the floor. A sheet of easel paper can be made available to draw plans for use in constructing a block building. A road map or travel atlas might inspire the building of a network of roads traveled by small vehicles. Books about the current block building play theme or of special interest can be placed strategically in or near the block center.

Accessories may be displayed on or inside a block shelf. Small items of similar type (such as small vehicles) may be stored together in one container. Affix symbols of the accessories, such as pictures, photographs, or drawn outlines beneath the accessory where each is located and returned for storage. This facilitates clean-up and provides opportunities for children to match objects to symbols. School supply catalogs are good sources for these pictures. The pictures or symbols should be laminated or covered with clear adhesive paper and attached to the shelf with masking tape. Create a file of the symbols and continue to add to them until there are symbols for all the accessories you use. Large vehicles can be "parked" in slots marked off with colored plastic tape on the floor next to a wall of the block center. Smaller vehicles may be stored on the block shelves.

Prop boxes are separate boxes that contain materials related to themes that enhance dramatic play in the block and/or sociodramatic play center. Prop boxes include items related to themes such as camping, circus, health, safety, taking a trip, travel in space, and various occupations. Materials can be added to the boxes as new items are found. The contents of prop boxes can be used with either unit or hollow blocks.

Miniature people and animal figures contribute to and support constructive play with blocks. Family figures are available from school supply companies in a variety of ethnic groups. The most frequently found ethnic groups are: White, Asian, Black, Latino, and Native American. These figures may be made of wood or soft pliable plastic. Community helper figures should reflect a variety careers and should avoid gender or culture stereotypes. In the same manner, individuals with disabilities can be portrayed participating in a variety of activities and careers through the use of miniature people with disabilities available from some school supply companies.

Animal figure sets are also available in categorical sets such as, farm, wild, forest/woods, sea, and shore, arctic, prehistoric, and endangered animals. Stuffed animals of various types may also be used to enhance play in the block center.

Land transportation vehicles can include small cars, trucks of all types, buses, tractors, motor homes, motorcycles, bicycles, construction machines, and health and safety vehicles such as police, fire, emergency and garbage vehicles. The addition of a double-decker bus, dog sleigh, and other land vehicles found primarily in other regions or countries enlarges children's awareness of various modes of transportation.

Small airplanes, helicopters, space-related vehicles, blimps, and hot-air balloons may be made available for use with themes related to air transportation. Several airplanes of different sizes or types are more typical of what is seen at a real airport.

A variety of boats and ships contribute to water travel play themes. There are few boats available from school supply companies, but they are sometimes available in toy stores, thrift shops or garage sales. They must be sturdy with few parts and no hazardous features. A canoe and kayak are water transportation vehicles that have a multicultural history.

Small blocks, such as colored inch cubes or colored parquetry blocks, spools, empty film cans, and large beads are examples of items that can be made available for decorating buildings, hauling in trucks, and other creative uses. Doll house furniture; small dollhouses and other small buildings and train and track sets also extend dramatic play and construction. Other props and accessories that can be made available from time to time include: small trees made of wood and painted, small traffic signs, rainbow blocks, unusual block shapes, acorns, nuts, and pine cones gathered by the children, sea shells, discarded door keys, small pulley with string or thin rope, yarn, foil, paper and cloth swatches.

Small finger-size or larger sturdy branches that have fallen from trees may be gathered by the children and sawn into uniform lengths in the woodworking center. The ends should be sanded so that they are smooth. These can be used for hauling and for building a log house or other ideas generated by the children.

Rotating accessories occasionally brings novelty to block play. New or additional props and accessories can be used to enhance and support a specific play or construction themes or to build upon and support a particular interest of a child or the playgroup.

Accessories to Use with Hollow Blocks

Fewer accessories are needed with hollow block play because the children become the characters themselves. However, they do need props to elaborate their play.

Accessories for use with hollow blocks may include any of the literacy material listed earlier, hats and other dress-up clothes, large wooden or sturdy vehicles, puppets, a colorful bed sheet, blanket or quilt, empty electrical vinyl tubing spools (about 12' high; found in hardware stores), steering wheel, and large traffic signs.

Children use the spaces they create with hollow blocks to incorporate props in creative ways. For example, one child used a wall of the block center as one side of a long u-shaped building he had constructed. He put a few hollow blocks horizontally on the floor in rows at one end, and placed a toy TV on a block at the other end. When it was completed, he invited his teacher to come see the movies at his theater. The two of them watched the pictures move on the toy TV.

Space Requirements

The block center is usually the largest learning center in the classroom because of the nature of the activity. A space of 9 by 12 feet provides an area where children can build and use props without being crowded. It is preferable to use this space only for activity with blocks and accessories so that children can leave their buildings in place until the next day for further construction if they so desire. Sometimes classroom space does not allow for this. Group activities may have to take place in this space and possibly the placement of cots during rest time. The space can be enlarged for movement activities by spreading shelves outward.

The block center should be located away from the flow of classroom traffic to minimize interference and mishaps. An enclosure with three sides provides this protection. When the center is located in a corner of the room, the walls provide two sides of the enclosure. The third side can be made from block shelves placed at a right angle to the wall. The backside of shelves of an adjoining center or the rear of the home center kitchen equipment may be used as dividers. If more shelves or dividers are available, part of the fourth side can be enclosed.

Block play is noisy and should be strategically located to minimize its interference with other classroom activities. A location adjoining the home center is a good choice because of the potential for shared dramatic play between the two centers. For example, a small group of playmates borrowed nearly every dish from the home center to equip the elaborate restaurant they had constructed with hollow blocks and empty electrical wire spools. They took turns being the "cook" who got to wear the colorful chef's apron. The spools were used as tables for the "customers."

The floor of the block center should be covered with low-pile carpeting that is flat enough for standing a quadruple unit block on its thin side or on end. Indoor/outdoor and commercial carpeting are good choices. The carpet should lie flat with no curling edges and should not wrinkle. The carpet helps muffle noise, absorbs other room sounds, and provides a soft and warm surface for children as they sit, lie, or crawl on the floor. Plastic tape can be used to define an area one foot in front of the block shelf to prevent children from building too close to the shelves. This space allows children to obtain blocks from the shelves without interfering with constructions in progress.

Store the blocks and accessories on low open shelves where children can access them easily. Shelf storage is orderly and less hazardous than piling blocks in a bin or box. The shelves should have sturdy, securely attached backs to prevent blocks and accessories from falling through the backside. School supply companies sell free-standing open shelves with two shelves that are compartmentalized for sturdiness. Shelves can also be built locally. Block shelves should measure 4 feet wide, 2 or 2½ feet high and eleven or twelve inches deep. Most block shelves have casters on the bottom. Hollow blocks can be stacked on the floor beside a block shelf or next to a wall if shelf space is limited.

To facilitate order and safety, there is a recommended system for shelving blocks. The smaller unit blocks should be placed in the upper left hand corner of the shelf. Place the next larger sizes to the right until the top shelf is filled. Store the longest and heaviest blocks on the bottom shelves for stability and safety. Place all straight edge blocks so that the children can see the blocks' full length from the front of the shelf. Cylinders and odd shapes such as the large arch blocks may stand upright (Church and Miller, 1990).

As with the accessories, to help children replace blocks on the shelf after use, affix matching symbols to the shelves where each block shape belongs. Draw around one block of each shape on the backside of colorful adhesive backed paper, cut each out, and then attach each to the shelf where that particular shape is stored. Not only does this keep the block shelves in order, it provides opportunities for the development of mathematical concepts as the children match shapes to symbols when the blocks are put away.

Planning for Children with Special Needs

Children with special needs have the same needs of all children in addition to those related to their individual

challenges. They need to be included in block play activities. In order for children with special needs to participate fully the physical arrangement of the block center may need to be adjusted (Church, 1993). Many children with special needs are able to sit or lie on the floor, where blocks can be made more accessible to them. Some may need to use special assistive equipment. They may need help accessing blocks from the shelf. Visually impaired children need accessories that have conspicuous textures, shapes, and sounds. Some of the unit blocks could be covered with a pleasing texture of thin material using tape to hold it in place. Children with hearing impairments may need pictures that interpret procedures for using and storing the blocks. Children with learning disabilities or developmental delays may require longer periods for hands-on activities to become engaged and constructive. Generally, it is helpful to start with fewer blocks and add to the number as the children become more skilled and interested in block play.

Help children with special needs to interact successfully with others by teaching them how to share and how to follow the rules of the block area. You may also need to help a child with special needs respond to the overtures of others. Children with special needs often fail to acknowledge peers who approach them. When this happens consistently, the other children may give up trying to be friendly. Show or tell a child what to do: 'Mario wants to join us. Is this OK?' (Church and Miller, 1990).

Often children with special needs need help communicating and interacting with others. By the same token, classmates may need coaching in how to communicate and interact effectively with children with special needs. Adults should observe children's interactions with one another and in sensitive, supportive ways assist children in forming positive friendships and helpful behaviors. Avoid causing any child to feel singled out or embarrassed (Church and Miller, 1990).

Activities

Houses and Furniture
(3 years and older)

Objective: To become more aware of houses for people, the furnishings inside houses, and how families make their homes comfortable and functional.

Materials needed: Unit and/or hollow blocks, miniature family figures, small dollhouses, doll house furniture, pet figures, cars, pictures of houses and furniture, a furniture catalog, and one or two children's books about houses and furniture, including *Building a House* (Barton, 1981).

What to do:

1. Take a walking field trip to see houses in the neighborhood. Note the different types: house, apartment building, mobile home, and so on.

2. Visit inside a house and note the types of furniture in one or more rooms.

3. Provide materials in the block center and encourage children to explore them. They may choose to put the furniture in the dollhouse or build enclosures to represent houses with furniture inside.

4. Engage children in a dialogue about houses; ask questions such as: "How do people go in and out of your house?" "Why do most houses have front and back doors?" "Where would you sit if you did not have chairs, stools or sofas?" "What makes a house a home?"

And still more:

1. Help children learn about different types of houses/homes, (e.g., single dwelling, duplex, apartment complexes, condominiums, mobile homes, one story, two or more story houses, etc.) and where people get furniture, (e.g., craftspersons/carpenters, furniture stores, build it themselves, antique sales, garage sales, improvise, etc.).

2. Invite family participation with activities such as taking their child on a tour of their house or living quarters to count the windows, doors, light fixtures, or other architectural features. They can note what types of furniture are used to carry out various tasks or activities at home; (e.g., eating, watching TV, doing homework, sleeping, folding clothes, storing clothes, linens, and playthings, and so on).

Building a Home for a Pet Dog
(3 years and older)

Objective: To expand knowledge of how dogs are housed if they do not live indoors with people.

Materials needed: Unit or hollow blocks, family figures, dog figures. If plastic or wooden dog figures are not available, use stuffed animals or make some figures by cutting out pictures of dogs from magazines or drawing outlines of dogs, laminating them and using tape to

attach them to a unit block that is of comparable size. Other materials include fabric scraps to use for a bed or dog blanket, pictures of dogs in doghouses, books about dogs that include a picture of a doghouse.

What to do:

1. Poll parents to learn who owns a dog and doghouse. Engage the children with pet dogs to talk about their dog's use of the doghouse.

2. Give the children time to explore the props.

3. Talk about what a dog does during the day. Ask what happens to a dog at night or when it is tired and/or sleepy. Invite those who have dogs to share information about their dogs.

4. Point out the fabric scraps and ask how these might be helpful to a dog.

5. Examine and discuss pictures and share books about dogs.

6. Suggest that the blocks be used to build a house for the dog figures and/or make a block fenced-in back yard where dogs can play without getting in the street. Streets and sidewalks may be built for taking dogs on walks.

And still more:

1. Visit someone in the neighborhood with a friendly dog and doghouse.

2. Invite a parent or friend to bring a pet dog to visit for about 10 to 15 minutes at the beginning or end of the day.

3. Invite parents who have dogs with doghouses to send photos of both. Ask the parents of children who do not have a dog with a doghouse to take their child to visit someone who does.

Recognize and Name Three Shapes
(3 years and older)

Objective: to identify a circle, square, and triangle

Materials needed: The book, *Circles, Triangles and Squares* (Hoban, 1974) and other books about square, triangular, and round cylinder shapes, blocks of these shapes, traffic signs that have these three shapes, paper cut the same size as the block shapes; other props and pictures depicting these three shapes.

What to do:

1. As the children build and play with the blocks and accessories, look for opportunities to ask which shapes they are using.

2. Read *Circles, Triangles, and Squares* and examine pictures depicting these shapes. Invite the children to identify the different shapes.

3. Match the paper shapes to the blocks and name the shapes

4. Have children visually search for the shapes in or on objects around the block center and classroom (e.g., wheels, lights on vehicles, triangles in signs, and so on).

5. Engage children in a discussion about shapes: "If you were going to roll a block, which one would you choose?" Invite the children to try to roll a square block, triangular block, then a round block. Predict in advance what will happen and talk about the results.

6. Place a triangular block on top of a square block that is standing on its edge. "See my little house? What shape is the roof? What is the other shape?" "What can you build with these three shapes?"

And still more:

1. Take a shape walk around the school or center. Make a graph of the items of each shape located during the walk.

2. Invite parents to participate by having them point out street and traffic signs as they travel to and from school with their children. Have them encourage children to name the shapes.

3. Review the book *Circles, Triangles and Squares* with the children inviting them to describe any of the items pictured in the book that they see when they are traveling to the school or center.

4. Encourage parents to ask their child to look for round, square, and triangle shapes around their home.

Heavy or Light
(4 years and older)

Objective: to distinguish between heavy and light.

Materials needed: A square shaped unit block and square shaped hollow block, a lightweight truck and a heavy truck, two identical boxes or pans large enough to

carry several blocks at a time, pictures of people carrying loads, and a pulley, rope with two sand buckets or another type of container with a handle.

What to do:

1. Encourage the children to lift both the unit and hollow block squares, one after the other, and tell which is heavy or light.

2. Invite children to look at both trucks and predict which one is heavier. Invite a child to lift the lightweight truck and carry it to you. Then ask the child to carry the heavy truck. Have them load the trucks with blocks and compare the weights.

3. Draw children's attention to how their bodies must adjust to lift heavier weights.

4. Hang a pulley from a swing frame on the playground or a hook from the ceiling. Fill one bucket with more blocks than the other. Invite the children to predict which bucket will be heavier and which can be pulled upward faster. They may then pull the rope to make the bucket with the light load go up. Repeat the action with the heavier bucket load. Talk about the difference in weight and the effort required to lift and pull heavy and light loads.

5. Again, note the way a person in a picture is carrying a load and decide whether it is heavy or light by calling attention to their posture and other body language. Ask, "What kind of load makes you bend over a little when you carry it?" "What kind of load is easiest for you to carry?" "How should you lift heavy things?" "How can really heavy things (furniture, appliances) be moved from one place to another?"

6. When putting the blocks away, ask a child to bring two blocks to you and ask which is heavy and which is light. Load children's arms with blocks and ask them to describe whether the load is heavy or light.

And still more:

1. Take a walk to look for people carrying things and try to guess from body language whether their loads are heavy or light.

2. Invite children to pack the two suitcases or bags with loads of different items. Ask them to predict which is heavy and which is light; lift each, perhaps at the same time, and determine which is heavy and which is light.

3. Talk about how very large items require the strength

of more than one person to be lifted or moved, and some heavy loads are lifted by equipment and machines, e.g., dolly, fork-lift.

References

Alexander, N. F. (2000, Winter). Blocks and basics. *Dimensions of Early Childhood*, 28(1), 29-30.

Barton, B. (1981). *Building a house*. New York, NY: Greenwillow Books.

Caplan, F. & T. Caplan (1973). *The power of play*. Garden City, NY: Anchor Press.

Cartwright, S. (March, 1974). Blocks and learning. *Young Children*, 29(3), 141-146.

Charney, R., M. K. Clayton, & C. Wood (1990). Bringing blocks back to the classroom. *A newsletter for teachers: A resource for developmental educators* 2(1), 1-4. Greenfield, MA: Northeast Foundation for Children, Inc.

Church, E. B. (1993). *Learning through play: Problem solving*. NY: Scholastic Inc.

Church, E. B. & K. Miller (1990). *Learning through play: Blocks*. NY: Scholastic, Inc.

Dodge, D. T. with M. Goldhammer & L. J. Colker (1988). *The creative curriculum for early childhood*. Washington, DC: Creative Associates International, Inc.

Hewitt, K. (January, 2001). Blocks as a tool for learning: Historical and contemporary perspectives. *Young Children*, 56(1), 6-13.

Hoban, T. (1974). *Circles, triangles and squares*. NY: Macmillan Publishing Co., Inc.

Leeb-Lumberg, K. (1984). The block builder mathematician. In E. S. Hirsch (Ed.). *The block book* (Rev. ed.). Washington DC: National Association for the Education of Young Children.

Moore, Gary T. (1997, May). A place for block play. *Child Care Information Exchange*, pp.73-77.

Robison, H.F. (1977). Exploring teaching in early childhood education. Boston: Allyn and Bacon.

Checklist for Evaluating the Block Center

Rate the following items on a scale of 1 to 4 with "needing improvement" as 1 and "outstanding" as 4.

_____1. The block center is strategically located to minimize noise and interference.

_____2. The block center is located away from classroom traffic pathways and enclosed on three sides to encourage focused play and minimize interference.

_____3. The blocks are stored in low open shelves in a safe and orderly way.

_____4. Block symbols are placed on shelves according to shapes for orderly replacement and symbol learning.

_____5. The blocks are available daily.

_____6. The children are free to use the blocks in their own way as long as it is constructive.

_____7. Accessories are provided and rotated frequently.

_____8. The play setting changes occasionally, reflecting children's ideas and interests.

_____9. Children are encouraged to explore, experiment and be creative with blocks.

_____10. Imagination and creativity is evident in the engaged play of children in the block center.

About the Author

Katie Best Butler, Ed.D. is retired from College of the Mainland, Texas City, Texas, where she directed the NAEYC Nationally Accredited Child Development Laboratory School during its first thirteen years. She was also an adjunct instructor in the Child Development Program there for twenty-three years. Dr. Butler has worked with children and their teachers in public school, churches, Head Start, and Title XX centers. She has presented workshops for various national, regional, state, and local organizations. Dr. Butler has served on the boards of TAEYC, HAAEYC, and GCAEYC and other professional organizations. She was honored with the TAEYC Susan Hargrave Trainer of the Year Award in 2001.

Chapter 10

Four children are working in the art
center in pre-kindergarten classroom.
Sarah paints a variety of circular forms
in red. When the teacher, Ms. Jane,
comes over to observe, Sarah says,
"These are flowers." Ms. Jane writes
Sarah's statement on the picture and
says, "You used red, curved lines to
make your flowers."

Another child, Jason, is sitting at
a table cutting small pieces of construction paper and gluing them
onto a piece of newsprint.

Meanwhile, Michael and Allison
are using playdough at another table.
Michael flattens a ball of playdough
with his hand and uses his fingers to
make indentations in the dough.
"Look," he says, "I made my toes."

Art

Liz Vaughan

Art experiences contribute to all aspects of the young child's development – cognitive, motor, social, emotional, language/literacy as well as aesthetic. A variety of art activities and media can encourage the development of many skills and concepts.

Cognitive. Cognitive development is stimulated through activities that involve thinking processes of observing, recalling, classifying, inferring, predicting, and creating. For example, children observe and discriminate visual characteristics of color and shape in such activities as easel painting and weaving. They discriminate tactile features through collage activities, finger painting, and modeling. They recall past experiences and represent them symbolically in drawing pictures. They classify properties of materials and designs-rough or smooth, straight or curved. They also make inferences and predictions about their work as they engage in the artistic process: "When I mix the blue paint and the yellow paint, it will make green."

Art experiences should engage the children in creative activity, focusing on the process rather than the product. Children should be encouraged to do the thinking and decision-making in the activity rather than copying a teacher model or using predrawn, precut forms.

Motor Skills. Children develop fine motor skills through the manipulation of tools and materials such as brushes, scissors, crayons, and clay. They develop eye-hand coordination and pincer-grasp control as they move from a scribbling stage to representational and then schematic drawing.

Their earliest scribbles are vertical and horizontal lines. They demonstrate increased motor skill and control as they begin to draw circular forms and lines. When they begin to represent persons and objects symbolically and label their drawings, which usually occurs around age 3 or 4, they have moved into the represen-

tational or preschematic stage. In the schematic stage, which often begins around age 6 or 7, their art work exhibits greater order and structure with the use of a baseline and an increasing understanding of perspective. Parents often need information about these stages to understand and appreciate their importance.

Social and Emotional Skills. Art provides an opportunity for emotional expression. When someone values their unique creations, children develop feelings of pride. They develop a sense of autonomy as they work independently. They also develop social skills of sharing, turn-taking, and cooperation as they work with others.

Language/Literacy. Art encourages language development as children clarify color, shape, size, and other concepts while talking about their art work. Conversations with the teacher or other children may be part of the experience, and children may also dictate statements or stories related to their pictures. The use of symbol charts develops reading readiness skills of directionality (left to right) and the connection of print with meaning. As fine motor skill develops children begin to write on their paper. They may write letters in their name, letter-like forms, or scribble writing.

Aesthetics. Art activities also give children an opportunity to learn about art elements and principles of design.

Art elements include:
- **line**- the path traced by a moving point,
- **form** - the external appearance of shapes,
- **space** -the distance or area between forms,
- **color** - the hue and its shade and intensity, and
- **texture** - the degree of roughness or smoothness of a material.

Principles of design include:

- **rhythm** - the controlled movement found in designs creating a flow or beat,
- **balance** -the attraction of the eye to all parts of the picture,
- **proportion** - the use of size relationships, and
- **unity** - the integration of all elements of a picture into a coherent oneness.

Through exposure to quality art work, children develop an appreciation for art and begin to recognize art's cultural and historical significance. Using art prints and art postcards in the classroom allows children the opportunity to recognize the work of individual artists and styles representing different periods. Children should become aware of natural and man-made forms of art in the world around them and learn to use art media creatively. Children need opportunities to explore a variety of art media and techniques (Bredekamp & Rosegrant, 1995; Edwards, 1997; Jackman, 1997; Kostelnik, Soderman, & Whiren, 1999; Pattillo & Vaughan, 1992; Wolf, 1984).

Curriculum Integration

Art experiences can be integrated into all curriculum/ center areas. In the library center discussions of illustrations can occur. Children can become aware of styles and techniques used by different artists. In the writing center children can illustrate their own stories or books or decorate cards. Art elements and principles of design are used in children's block and woodworking constructions.

Educators using the Reggio Emilia Approach have demonstrated ways in which art can be used to symbolize the learning occurring in various classroom projects. As children investigate and study different topics, they use a variety of media and materials to construct a graphic representation of their feelings, ideas, and understandings ((Bredekamp & Rosegrant, 1995; Hendrick, 1997; Kostelnik, Soderman, & Whiren, 1999).

Space Requirements

The art center should be located in a large, quiet area of the classroom. A sink or access to water should be available. If a water source is not close by, then a bucket or dishpan of water or wet paper towels should be set up daily.

Since art activities are often messy, the floor surface should be of linoleum or covered with plastic drop cloths. Any work surfaces or adjacent walls that are hard to clean should be protected with paper or plastic. Newspapers on tables provide for quick and easy

cleanup. Cleaning supplies such as paper towels, sponges, mops, brooms, and dustpans should be readily available.

The area should be well-lighted. Children will need a drying rack or area to place wet pictures and a storage area for dry pictures. A few activities may require electricity, so a nearby outlet is desirable (Jackman, 1997, Pattillo & Vaughan, 1992).

Basic Equipment and Materials

Equipment needs include:

- **Tables and chairs** - Provide adequate work space for children. Rectangular tables work best to accommodate larger paper sizes.
- **Display areas** - Bulletin board or tack strips are needed for displaying children's art work. Windows, walls, and the backs and sides of shelves and furniture may also be used. Some teachers hang art work from the ceilings or from mobiles.

Children may not want to display their art work in the room; their wishes should be respected. When art work is displayed, it should be hung at the children's eye level in a manner that adds to the room's attractiveness. The decision to display certain art work should never be based on which pieces are best or prettiest.

Labeling the art work with the children's names should begin when the children are toddlers. Teachers should print the child's name correctly in the upper left-hand corner. Such labeling helps children learn to recognize their names and understand that we read print from left to right.

- **Rebus charts** - For many art activities, teachers can post charts that give children directions for the use of materials. Use file folders and draw symbols and pictures for each activity step. Do not provide a model for children to copy.
- **Easel** - Set up an easel on the floor or on a table top so that children may stand and paint.
- **Shelves** - Plenty of shelf space should be provided for equipment and materials. Shelves should be low so that children can easily obtain and return items without teacher assistance.
- **Scissors** - Provide blunt-end or safety scissors.
- **Scissor holders** - Commercial or homemade holders may be used.
- **Brushes and applicators** - Provide a variety of sizes and types of paintbrushes. Other utensils may be

used to apply paints. For example, toothbrushes, combs, and feathers may be dipped in paint and then applied to paper. Spray bottles and roll-on deodorant bottles can be filled with paint and then sprayed or rolled onto paper. Eye droppers can also be used to drip paint onto paper.

- **Printmaking media** - Provide various objects for printing such as rubber stamps, cookie cutters, wood blocks, sponges, kitchen utensils, and spools.
- **Paint containers** - Commercial holders may be used, although muffin tins, butter tubs, and other household items work equally well.
- **Glue bottles** - Provide squeeze bottles of various types.
- **Other containers** - A variety of bowls, cans, tubs, and trays may be used to hold crayons, modeling dough, and collage materials.
- **Smocks** - Provide protection for clothing with paint smocks, aprons, or old adult shirts.
- **Additional equipment** - ruler, hole punch, salt shakers, stamp pad, and plastic yam needles (Jackman, 1997; Kostelnik, Soderman, & Whiren, 1999; Pattillo & Vaughan, 1992).

Materials include:

- **Paper** - Use papers that represent a variety of sizes, shapes, and textures such as construction paper, manila paper, white drawing paper, newsprint, finger paint paper, butcher paper, posterboard, foil, sandpaper, paper towels, tagboard, wrapping paper, tissue paper, paper plates, crepe paper, coffee filters, and corrugated cardboard.
- **Drawing and marking media** - Provide a variety of drawing crayons, water-based markers, chalk, and pencils.
- **Paints** - Provide tempera paints, water colors, and finger paints in a variety of colors and textures. Tempera can be varied by adding small amounts of flour, sand, sawdust, sugar, and thickened liquid soap.
- **Adhesives** - White paste, white glue, and glue sticks may be used.
- **Modeling materials** - Vary modeling materials to provide tactile experiences. Clay, play dough, and homemade dough recipes work well. Try this recipe for play dough: Mix 1 cup flour, 1 cup water, 1/2 cup salt, 2 tablespoons oil, 2 teaspoons cream of tartar, and food coloring (optional). Cook in skillet over medium heat, stirring continually. Dough is ready when it forms a ball

and is not sticky to the touch. After cooling, store in an airtight container.

- **Additional materials** - Other materials include tape, paper clips, brads, straws, burlap, yarn, Styrofoam©, cotton balls, tongue depressors, cotton-tipped swabs, pipe cleaners, food coloring, and liquid starch.
- **Found materials** - Many inexpensive materials may be collected to use for collages or other activities. These materials include boxes of all shapes and sizes, cloth scraps, lace and ribbon scraps, magazines, greeting cards, newspapers, wallpaper samples, buttons, beads from old jewelry, paper bags, catalogs, and paper tubes (Jackman, 1997; Kostelnik, Soderman, & Whiren, 1999; Pattillo & Vaughan, 1992).

Safety

Safety should always be considered when planning art activities for young children. Problems may arise from inhalation, ingestion, absorption, electrocution, and burns. Consider the appropriateness of materials for the children's ages. If electrical appliances are used for some activities, a teacher should always be responsible for handling them. Discuss rules for the use of materials with children beforehand.

Check labels of commercial art materials and appropriate substitutes. Materials should have a CP or AP label, which is a certification of nontoxicity by The Art and Craft Materials Institute, Inc. A partial list of toxic materials includes lead-pigmented paints, printmaking inks, enamels fired onto metals, lead glazes, ceramic glaze chemicals, instant papier maches, vermiculite, aerosol sprays (unless used outdoors), all solvents, oil paints, and wallpaper paste (Kostelnik, Soderman, & Whiren, 1999). The Center for Safety in the Arts (http://artswire.org:70/1/csa) has publications available related to hazardous materials.

Outdoor Area

Art activities can easily be transferred to the outdoor area. Having natural light, added space, and more freedom to be messy allows for new explorations and creativity. Tables and easels can be placed on the playground or porch. Chalk can be used on sidewalks. Pictures can be hung with clothespins on chain link fences to dry. Nature materials collected on the playground can be used for collages (Jackman, 1997; Miller, 1989).

Anti-Bias Considerations

Encourage anti-bias attitudes in the art center by providing appropriate materials. Provide paper, paints, playdough, and crayons in a variety of skin-tone shades from light to dark brown (Derman-Sparks, 1989). Certain colors may have cultural connotations and can be used to enhance art activities. Activities representing arts and crafts of various cultures may also be provided such as weaving and pottery activities. Display prints and images of artwork from various cultures throughout the classroom (Edwards, 1997).

Planning for Children with Special Needs

Children with various special needs should be encouraged to participate in art experiences. Teachers can motivate children by focusing on the process rather than the product and not overemphasizing realistic drawing.

Some education suppliers sell adaptive materials such as nonloop scissors, knob crayons, and hand grips for children with physical/motor impairments. Felt-tipped pens or water-based markers require less pressure than crayons to produce a strong line. Easels and workspaces should be wheelchair accessible. Use larger-sized materials, such as, butcher paper, poster markers, and large brushes. Tape down paper to hold it in place or use trays to define workspace. Children with visual impairments need tactile activities such as collages, modeling, and the use of textured surfaces. Gluing yarn on paper can be a substitute for drawing. Outlining the border of the paper with a black marker, or making a border of tape or dried glue may aid the child with visual difficulty. Art activities also may provide a therapeutic release for children with emotional/behavioral problems. Working with modeling doughs may relieve stress and anxiety. Use a tray or cookie sheet to define boundaries for children who need additional limits set (Deiner, 1999; Gould & Sullivan, 1999; Miller, 1996).

Skill Activities

Car Track Painting
(3 years and older)

Objective: To develop pincer control (fine motor); identify terms related to direction (cognitive); discover line, color, and shape (language/cognitive/aesthetic); and experiment informally with media (aesthetic)

Materials Needed: 8½- inch by 11 -inch construction paper (various colors), small rubber cars and trucks, tempera paint (several colors), shallow bowls, smocks

What to Do:

1. Mix tempera paint and place a small amount of each color in bowls.

2. Provide construction paper and smocks.

3. Post the chart shown in Figure 1.

4. Ask: How are the cars alike? ...different? Which directions can your car go? What happens when you drive the car on the paper? What happens when the colors mix?

Figure 1

Car Track Painting

1. Dip car in paint.

2. Drive on paper.

Glurch
(3 years and older)

Objective: To express thoughts and feelings through modeling (emotional/aesthetic), discover shape and texture (language/cognitive/aesthetic), and use senses to gain information (cognitive)

Materials Needed: white glue, water, borax, large plastic container with lid, individual trays or table covering, spoon and measuring cup to mix

What to Do:

1. Mix 1 cup white glue and 3/4 cup of water together. Mix 2/3 cup cold water and 4 teaspoons borax. Add to first mixture. Stir until solid.

2. Place in container and cover. Children may use the glurch to model on trays or on a covered table.

3. Ask: How does the glurch feel? What happened when you stretched it? What else can you make with the glurch?

And Still More:

Add tempera to water before mixing to color the glurch.

Glued Yarn Design
(5 years and older)

Objective: To discover line, color, shape, and texture (language/cognitive/aesthetic), experiment informally with media (aesthetic), and develop pincer control (fine motor)

Materials needed: 81/2- inch by 11-inch construction paper (various colors), white

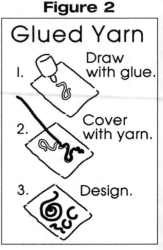

Figure 2

Glued Yarn

1. Draw with glue.

2. Cover with yarn.

3. Design.

glue, glue bottles, yarn (different lengths and colors), container for yarn

What to Do:

1. Place glue in bottles and yarn in container.

2. Place in the art center with construction paper.

3. Post the chart shown in Figure 2.

4. Ask: How did you make your design? How does the yarn feel? How are the pieces of yarn different?

Theme Activities
Theme: Shapes
Sponge Painting

Objective: To discover line, color, shape, and texture (language/cognitive/aesthetic), experiment informally with media (aesthetic, develop pincer control (fine motor), and compare objects for similarities and differences (cognitive)

Materials Needed:
Sponges (cut into various shapes such as triangles and circles), thick tempera, shallow containers for paint, clothespins, smocks, tray for sponges, sponge for washing table

Figure 3
Sponge Painting

1. Dip sponge in paint.

2. Print on papers.

3. Design.

What to Do:

1. Cut two slits in the top of each sponge shape and attach a clothespin.

2. Place the sponges on a tray in the art center.

3. Pour paint in containers.

4. Provide smocks and sponge.

5. Post the chart shown in Figure 3.

6. Ask: How are the shapes different? ...alike? What happens when the colors mix? Where have you seen these shapes before?

And Still More:

Print sponges directly onto table. Place paper on top of design, press, and lift before washing to produce monoprint.

Theme: Colors
Coffee Filter Drip

Objective: To discover color (language/cognitive/aesthetic), experiment informally with media (aesthetic), develop pincer control (fine motor), use the senses to gain information (cognitive), and describe phenomena in the environment (cognitive)

Figure 4
Coffee Filter Drip

1. Get water.

2. Drip on filter.

3. Design.

Materials Needed:

Coffee filters, food coloring, water, small bowls or containers, eye-droppers

What to Do:

1. Cover the table.

2. Place small amounts of water in each bowl. Add food coloring to each.

3. Place one or two eyedroppers in each bowl.

4. Provide coffee filters.

5. Post the chart shown in Figure 4.

6. Ask: What happens when you drip the water on the filter? What happens when the colors mix?

And Still More:

Use paper towels instead of filters.

Theme: Five Senses
Sand Painting

Objective: To discover line, color, shape, and texture (language/cognitive/aesthetic), experiment informally with media (aesthetic), develop pincer control (fine motor), and use the senses to gain information (cognitive)

Materials Needed: Sand, powdered tempera (several colors), salt shakers, spoon, 8 1/2-inch by 11-inch construction paper (various colors), white glue, glue bottles, table covering.

Figure 5
Sand Painting

1. Glue.

2. Sprinkle Sand.

3. Design.

What to Do:

1. Cover the table.

2. Place sand in salt shakers. Add one teaspoonful of powdered tempera to each, stir, and replace lids.

3. Fill glue bottles.

4. Place shakers and glue bottles in the art center and provide paper.

5. Post the chart shown in Figure 5.

6. Ask: What happens when you shake the colored sand on the glue? What will happen when it dries? How will it feel?

And Still More:

Substitute salt or cornmeal for the sand, or use various spices to add a sense of smell.

References

Bredekamp, S. & Rosegrant, T. (Eds.). (1995). *Reaching potentials: Transforming early childhood curriculum and assessment* (vol. 2). Washington, DC: National Association for the Education of Young Children.

Deiner, P. L. (1999). *Resources for educating children with diverse abilities: Birth through eight* (3rd ed.). Fort Worth, TX: Harcourt Brace.

Derman-Sparks, L. & ABC Task Force (1989). *Anti-bias curriculum: Tools for empowering Young children*. Washington, D.C.: National Association for the Education of Young Children.

Edwards, L. C. (1997). *The creative arts: A process approach for teachers and children* (2nd ed.). Upper Saddle River, NJ: Merrill/Prentice Hall.

Gould, P. & J. Sullivan (1999). *The inclusive early childhood Classroom: Easy ways to adapt learning centers for all children*. Beltsville, MD: Gryphon House.

Hendrick, J. (Ed.). (1997). *First steps toward teaching the Reggio way*. Upper Saddle River, NJ: Merrill/Prentice Hall.

Jackman, H. L. (1997). *Early education curriculum: A child's connection to the world*. Albany, NY: Delmar.

Kostelnik, M. J., A. K. Soderman, & A. P. Whiren (1999). *Developmentally appropriate curriculum: Best practices in early childhood education*. Upper Saddle River, NJ: Merrill.

Miller, K. (1989). *The outside play and learning book: Activities for young children*. Mt. Rainier, MD: Gryphon House.

Miller, R. (1996). *The developmentally appropriate inclusive classroom in early education*. Albany, NY: Delmar.

Pattillo, J. & Vaughan, E. (1992). *Learning centers for child-centered classrooms*. Washington, DC: National Education Association.

Wolf, A. D. (1984). *Mommy, It's a Renoir!* Altoona, PA: Parent Child Press.

Checklist for Evaluating the Art Center

Rate the items below on a scale of 1 to 4 with "needing improvement" as 1 and "outstanding" as 4.

_____1. Adequate and well-lighted space is provided for art activities. The floor is linoleum or covered with newspapers or plastic drop cloths.

_____2. Basic equipment – tables, chairs, shelves, easel, sink or dishpan of water, containers for art materials such as paints and glue – are provided.

_____3. A variety of art experiences and materials are provided – painting, modeling with clay or play dough, drawing, collage, and printing.

_____4. Smocks or other protective clothing are provided for children.

_____5. The area has adequate space to dry and store art work.

_____6. Children's art work is displayed at their eye level, and the children choose when to display it.

_____7. Children work independently. They can get materials themselves, they are encouraged to clean up, and activities are self-directing.

_____8. The creative process is emphasized rather than a final product.

_____9. Anti-bias materials and multicultural activities are provided. Examples include paper, paints, or fabrics of various shades to represent skin tones.

_____10. Nontoxic materials are used and safety hazards are minimized.

About the Author

Liz Vaughan is an associate professor of teacher education at Shippensburg University of Pennsylvania. Her classroom experience includes public school, child care, and university lab school programs. She holds a doctorate from the University of South Florida and master's and bachelor's degrees from Stephen F. Austin State University.

Chapter 11

Science

Irma C. Woods

During outdoor play on a bright sunny day in a preschool program, a preschool teacher notices two of her four-year-olds sitting on the ground under a tree. The children appear to be silently absorbed in something. Walking closer, the teacher observes the two children digging intently with wooden spoons.

"Paul and Evan, looks like you are working hard," the teacher says. "Yeah," replies Evan. "We have to. We gotta find out what's at the bottom." "At the bottom?" asks the teacher. "The bottom of the dirt," replies Paul. "We know there's something. We're gonna find out." "How do you know there's something at the bottom of the dirt?" continues the teacher. Without looking up and continuing to dig, Paul replies, "Because the dirt is on top of something."

eeking to understand their world Paul and Evan are engaged in wondering, investigating, and experimenting to find answers to their questions. Filled with curiosity, Paul and Evan use the tools, wooden spoons, to explore and test their ideas. They display a rudimentary understanding of the earth's crust by concluding that if dirt is on top of the earth, there must be something beneath the dirt. Like all scientists, Paul and

Evan ask questions, problem-solve, and have ideas for finding answers to their questions. Science is natural to children because it requires those characteristics typical in childhood: curiosity, wonder, active involvement, persistence, and experimentation.

What is Science?

This question often leaves teachers of young children perplexed because the subject of science if often equated with their own school experiences in specific content areas such as biology, chemistry, and physics. Teachers may view science as factual information that needs to be memorized and therefore, too difficult for young children to comprehend. Science, however, is a process of understanding the world through active involvement with that world. In defining science, Kilmer and Hofman (1995) identify three components: (1) knowledge of scientific phenomena, (2) processes of observation, collection, and analysis of information, and (3) application of science technology to everyday life situations. Science is an active process whose goal is to discover "…that all things and events in the universe occur in consistent patterns that are comprehensible through careful, systematic study, …that through the use of the intellect, and with the aids of instruments that extend the senses, people can discern patterns in all of nature" (American Association for the Advancement of Science, 1989, p. 25).

Natural phenomena need to be accurately presented and scientifically correct. Its presentation to children must be based on children's ages, developmental levels, and explained within the contexts experienced by the children. When adults explain a scientific phenomenon as "magic," children are deprived of the opportunity to process information and gain understanding. When inaccurately explained, natural phenomena such as rain or flooding, for example, may continue to be unexplained mysteries, generating fear rather than knowledge. Equipped with authentic information, children are better able to apply scientific information in in their lives. For example, in the event of inclement weather, children can learn to choose proper clothing and to take necessary precautions to protect themselves and their property.

Science in Early Childhood Settings

The *National Science Education Standards* of the National Research Council (1996) and the *Benchmarks for Science Literacy* of the American Association for the Advancement of Science (1993) emphasize that all children have the ability to increase their knowledge

and understanding of the world around them and becoming scientifically literate should begin at an early age. Early childhood programs have the opportunity to create environments that foster science inquiry and exploration.

Children naturally begin to explore the world around them from birth. Using their senses, infants discover the properties of objects (size, shape, texture, weight, and others), by touching objects, putting objects in their mouths, moving objects around, holding objects in their hands, and by moving their bodies in space. Infants learn that objects also occupy space and sometime they can go under an object or around an object or over an object depending on the properties of the objects. Infants attend to the sounds, smells, movement, textures, and sights in the environment.

Toddlers ask, "Whazz-it?" countless times in an effort to satisfy their curiosity about the world. They carry objects around, poke things to find out how those things work, look in bags, boxes, and purses to find out what is inside of them, and check things out in their surroundings.

Preschoolers display a more organized system of observation. They classify by sorting and grouping. They count and compare. They notice and comment that "Marisa got more chicken nuggets. You're only suppose to get four!" They make the observation that the plant is drooping because "It needs water." As children interact with the world around them in everyday events and activities, they are developing concepts about how the world works. Concepts are "…the building blocks of knowledge; they allow people to organize and categorize information" (Lind, 1999, p.74). However, concepts also allow children to do more than organize and categorize. Concept formation allows children to predict, analyze, identify relationships, and extend their knowledge. For example, when a child notices one plant in the classroom is drooping and another plant is not, the child may draw the conclusion that the drooping plant may need water, thereby identifying the possible relationship of water to plant survival. Early science education needs to challenge children's thinking and be based on an understanding of concept development in young children.

Theoretical Base for Science

One of the most influential theories supporting science and concept development in early childhood education is Jean Piaget's theory of cognitive development. This theory proposes that children construct their own knowledge of how the world works by interacting with the environment directly rather than by being told by someone else how things work. By manipulating objects and "acting on" the objects children develop concepts or knowledge of objects.

Piaget identified three types of knowledge: physical knowledge, logico-mathematical knowledge, and social conventional knowledge (1952). Physical knowledge involves developing an understanding of the physical world by manipulating objects in the environment, exploring the properties of the objects, and learning how objects work. For example, by playing with water in its liquid form, a child learns the properties of water: it is odorless, colorless, and flows; it takes the shape of its container, is wet, and can be absorbed with a variety of materials. In its solid form, the properties of water are different. Properties of objects and substances are best learned as inherent in the objects. To isolate properties from objects, as is often done in early childhood activity and resource books through such themes as "Color" or "Shape," circumvent the child's opportunities to construct and acquire physical knowledge specific to the objects and substances that they might explore. Objects and their properties are part of children's daily everyday experiences, and concept development takes place through hands-on activities in a rich environment that is further supported by adults who guide and respond to children's inquiries.

Logico-mathematical knowledge is knowledge based on the child's ability to identify relationships between and among objects. Properties of objects are relative because it depends on what objects are being compared. An orange is bigger than a grape but smaller than a watermelon. As children manipulate objects they construct their knowledge of the relationships between and among objects.

Social conventional knowledge is transmitted to children through social interactions. Social knowledge cannot be constructed by children through hands-on activities. Rather, it is learned through their social interaction experiences in which conventions and values of the family and community are conveyed. This includes culture, traditions, customs, and rules for socially accepted behavior.

Piaget's cognitive theory of constructivism supports science education as providing opportunities for children to construct knowledge by exploring and manipulating real and concrete objects in their environment. The use of workbooks, worksheets, and science demonstrations by the adult do not support this acquisition of physical and logical-mathematical knowledge. Adults support children's construction of knowledge by the guiding questions they ask to further children's thinking.

Value of the Science Center

In an early childhood program, the science center may be referred to as the discovery center, the sensory center, or the "Let's Find Out" center. Regardless of the name used, the science center is one of the basic centers found in most early childhood environments. Activities in the science center influence all the domains of child development.

Cognitive Development: Materials and activities in the science center give children opportunities to develop physical knowledge by manipulating and learning about the properties of real objects. Children also develop logico-mathematical knowledge by comparing, classifying, sequencing, observing, analyzing, and describing. Adults can guide children's thinking by asking questions that will generate experimentation: "What do you think will happen if…?" "How can you make it change?"

Physical Development: Children use fine and gross motor skills as they manipulate and experiment with objects and substances. They also use their own bodies as they experience the use of space, motion, and force.

Language Development: Children learn scientific vocabulary, names of tools used in science activities, and can describe observations and draw conclusions. The wide range of science topics appropriate for young children affords numerous opportunities to extend concepts and vocabulary. Children can dictate data and keep records which they can then "read."

Social Development: the science center encourages children to work together as they observe and experiment with objects. Children share materials, ideas, and develop cooperation skills.

Emotional Development: Activities in the science center can empower children by gaining knowledge about the physical world. Correct scientific knowledge helps children develop confidence and competence by correcting misperceptions and dispelling fears. Authentic information helps children plan and use scientific knowledge appropriately in their own lives, giving them a sense of control of otherwise unfamiliar or perhaps, frightening phenomena. Scientific knowledge also helps children to develop an appreciation for living things and natural beauty that help create an inner sense of order and peace.

Space and Location

In organizing a science center, a teacher must consider the physical elements needed. Sufficient space should be provided for the number of children who will be using the center at a given time. The space should be easily identifiable by the children. Dividers can define the space, such a low panels or shelves. Although it is not necessary to label the center, labeling is one way to expose children to printed word forms. Correct printscript should be used with upper and lower case letters. Labels are also useful for parents.

The science center should be in a quiet area of the room that is conducive to observation, experimentation, and sharing of information. However, avoid placing the science center in an uninviting, obscure area of the room that minimizes its use. Sometimes the science center is the last center to be set up and thus is given leftover space that may not be appropriate.

Plan the location of science materials according to the types of materials used. For example, plants may be located in various parts of the room and not just in the science center. Animals in different habitats can also be placed in different parts of the room.

Other consideration when setting up the science center include the following:

Lighting: If possible, locate the science center near a window for natural light. This is especially important when growing plants or caring for animals. Indeed, natural light is an important consideration for most scientific experiments and activities.

Electrical outlets: Usually at least one electrical outlet is needed for equipment such as tape players and a light table. Outlets not in use should be properly covered to assure safety, and all electrical equipment supervised when in use.

Water: Locate the science center close to a water source. Many science activities such as growing plants require water. If a water source is not readily available, consider having two large containers, such as five-gallon buckets, in the science center or close to it. One container can hold clean water needed for science activities throughout the day. The second container can store used water after activities have been completed. At the end of the day, the water can be discarded, preferably outdoors on grass, trees, or other plants. For health and safety reasons, use a tight-fitting lid on each container.

Appropriate floor covering: Active participation of children often means accidental spills, which are easier to clean when the area is not carpeted. However, carpet squares may be stored in a corner of the science center for children to sit on while engaged in science activities. In a fully carpeted room, the floor in the science area can be covered with a sheet of plastic.

Wall space: At least one wall is needed for displaying pictures or posters. It may be a room wall or one created by the back of a shelf or a low panel defining the science center. Realistic pictures pertinent to concepts being studied should be used and displayed at the children's eye level.

Equipment and Materials

In setting up the science center, some basic equipment and materials are necessary. Use shelves appropriate for the children's height when organizing the materials and activities. If shelves are not available, use a low table to display the materials. A child-size table with chairs may be placed in the science center for individual or small group activities, but the floor may work as well. Avoid materials that simply "collect dust" such as rocks that simply sit on a shelf. Provide materials for exploration and experimentation.

Some equipment and materials may need to be purchased or donated. Other supplies may be readily available in the school or center. Equipment and supplies for the science center can take time to collect.

Bought or donated materials include:
- tripod magnifier stand
- outdoor-indoor thermometer
- magnets (horseshoe and bar)
- hand magnifier
- pocorn popper
- hot plate
- balance scale
- tape recorder
- prism
- rain gauge
- aquarium
- flashlight

Consumable materials include:
- masking tape, transparent tape
- batteries
- paper bags
- cotton balls
- string
- paper cups
- spices
- fruits and vegetables
- wax paper
- paper towels
- yarn
- potting soil
- popsicle sticks
- sandpaper

Readily available materials include:
- plastic glasses, cups, bowls
- eye droppers
- measuring cups

- measuring spoons
- bulb baster
- eggbeater
- funnel
- sifter
- suction gadgets
- ramp
- lock and key

- tongs
- sponges
- spoons
- dishpans
- spatulas
- plastic spray bottles
- pulley
- lever

Items found in the natural environment include:

- feathers
- leaves
- twigs
- rocks
- soil samples
- nonpoisonous plants

- mosses
- shells
- bark
- live insects
- empty nests

When collecting natural items, children need to be guided in searching carefully with as little disturbance to the environment as possible. Show children how to handle animals and plants with care and respect. Show children how to turn over rocks and logs and carefully replace them when searching for specimens.

Children will frequently bring items to the classroom that can be incorporated into the science curriculum. Show interest in what the children bring, and develop science experiences using the items. This will not only generate continued interest in the science center and keep the science center alive and stimulating, but also will enrich the supply of science materials.

Realistic pictures to support themes or concepts presented to the children are a must. The pictures should be mounted on lightweight cardboard and laminated for longer use. Some magazines that are excellent sources for pictures are state highway, parks and wildlife publications, *Ranger Rick*, *National Geographic World*, and *National Audubon*. State tourist promotional magazines also provide pictures that are culturally relevant and sensitive to children and their geographic environments. (See Resources section at the end of this book.)

Children's health and safety are important elements in science experiences. Appliances such as a hot plate or corn popper need to be used under an adult's direct supervision. Avoid hazards such as candles, balloons and matches. Containers for science materials and supplies should be plastic rather than glass, and only safe, non-toxic materials and supplies should be used in any activities with young children.

Locate water activities away from electrical outlets. When not in use, ensure that all outlets are covered with protective plugs. When water play activities are set up indoors, have a mop or sponge handy to clean up spills. Be knowledgeable about the plant life in your area. Check all plants in your facility to ensure that they are safe for children. A good resource is the book, *Healthy Young Children: A Manual for Early Childhood Programs*, published by the National Association for the Education of Young Children. Other sources of advice are the local poison control center, and the local county extension agent. In conducting cooking activities, make sure the children have washed their hands and the cooking utensils and food preparation area are clean.

Science Curriculum and Children with Special Needs

Children with special needs also enjoy and benefit from hands-on activities to gain physical skills and develop concepts. The following are some suggestions for adapting the science center for children with special needs.

Children with motor impairments

Locate the science center in an area easily accessible to children in wheelchairs or with braces or other adaptive or assistive equipment

Provide sufficient space and uncluttered pathways for children who have difficulty moving around.

Provide nonskid pads on the shelves to prevent materials from slipping or falling.

Use containers that can be easily grasped such as cups with two handles, and baskets with handles for transporting materials.

Children with visual impairments

Locate the science center in an area with good lighting.

Provide clearly stated, logically sequenced verbal instructions.

Pair the child with a helpful partner.

Provide tactile cues and arrange materials in the order in which they will be used to carry out an activity.

Use tactile dividers or placemats to separate different activities on the shelf or table.

Provide large bold print books and clearly illustrated rebus charts.

Children with hearing impairments

Provide instructions through signing communications and/or well articulated speech.

Provide well designed rebus and other visual materials to guide the activity.

Pair the child with a helpful partner.

Demonstrate the steps and the use of the materials, prior to the activity.

Provide simple, well-sequenced instructions on an audio tape and provide head-set listening devices for amplification.

Children with mental retardation

Match activities and expectations to the child's developmental level.

Organize materials in clear and easy to follow steps. Keep steps and instructions to a minimum.

Demonstrate the use of materials before placing them on the shelf or table.

Pair the child with a helpful partner.

Reinforce concepts being taught by providing meaningful follow-up activities.

Children with behavior problems

Provide clearly stated specific and ordered steps for the activity.

Control the number of children at the science center.

Provide activities that bring about a "soothing" effect, such as certain water activities.

Clearly explain the activity and use of materials, but avoid too many instructions at once.

Reduce distractions from adjacent learning centers.

Integrated Curriculum

Science can easily be integrated into all other areas of the curriculum. Mathematical thinking is used in science as children classify objects, make comparisons, organize objects in sequence, notice likenesses and differences in objects, count, and record observational data. Children's literature on science can effectively be used to extend the scientific concepts presented in the science center. The adult needs to select children's science books that are scientifically correct. Many such books are found in the non-fiction sections of the public library. An excellent example of a scientifically cor-

rect book is *Monarch Butterfly* (Gibbons, 1989). This book accurately presents factual information about the monarch butterfly. In creative movement, children can represent the movements of animals with the bodies. Songs and fingerplays can focus on natural phenomena such a rain, apples falling from trees, and birds flying. In the art center children can use paint, crayon, markers, and chalk to draw or paint their representations of the world around them. Cooking activities give children experiences in investigating the physical properties of food and changes that take place when heat is used to cook the food. Children can compare raw apples and cooked apples. What are the differences in color, taste, texture, and size? In the manipulative center, children can sequence a set of picture cards on the life cycle of a butterfly. Children can complete puzzles depicting realistic representations of animals, flowers, and other natural phenomena found in the environment. While one learning center may be labeled "Science," science activities can be included in all the learning centers and throughout the curriculum.

Taking Science Outdoors

Science is already outdoors! The children's playground and the outdoors in general offer countless opportunities to explore, investigate, analyze, and experiment. Children can learn about plants, animals, soil, climate, weather, and characteristics of many living things. They engage all of the senses of sight, touch, smell, taste, and movement in their scientific explorations. The outdoors also offers opportunities to strengthen cultural meanings. An herb garden can evoke the images of home and family when a child recognizes an herb used at home for cooking or for seasoning tea. A vegetable garden teaches children scientific information of how seeds sprout and grow into plants to produce food we need to sustain life. Flower gardens help children develop appreciation for natural beauty and contribute to aesthetic awareness and affective development.

The outdoor environment is an environment that supports children's natural sense of wonder and curiosity. The trees, plants, flowers, and animal life found outdoors supports children's need to know about the world and how we live harmoniously with nature. First hand experiences with nature as children hold a caterpillar in their hands, chase butterflies, investigate openings in tree trunks, examine dry leaves on the ground, or splash on water puddles, contribute to concept development and greater understanding of the world in which we live and our role in it.

Activities

Observing Roly-Polys
(3 years and older)

Objective: To observe and describe the movement of roly-polys

Materials needed: Outdoor area with roly-poly, magnifying glasses

What to do:

1. In small groups, guide the children in observing the small animals.

2. Use a magnifying glass for closer observation. Ask open-ended questions to expand children's thinking: "How does the roly-poly move?" "How/Why does it make itself into a ball?"

3. Allow the children to gently pick up a roly-poly and hold it. Guide the children in describing how the movement of the roly-poly feels on their hands. Return roly-polys to their environment.

4. Look up the scientific name for roly-polys.

Examining Leaves
(4 years and older)

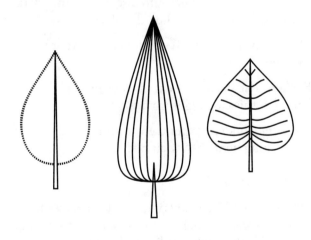

Objective: To observe and compare leaves

Materials needed: Paper bags, one for each child in the group; 8 inch by 10 inch sheets of paper, one for each child in the group; a magnifying glass; a tray to organize the materials.

What to do:

1. Have the children collect leaves outdoors and place them in their paper bags. Remind children to pick only leaves that have fallen and are on the ground.

2. Have the children place their leaves on their sheet of paper.

3. Have the children observe and compare their leaves.

4. Engage children in a dialogue about what they see.

And still more:

1. Using a magnifying glass, have the children note the colors, edges, shapes, and lines on the leaves.

2. Ask which things are the same in the leaves and which are different

3. Have the children sort the leaves according to different properties such as size, color, and shape.

4. Make a graph of the leaves found by the children. Place the graph in the science center.

5. Write an experience story with the children to share with parents.

6. Read a book about trees and determine the names of trees from which the leaves fell.

7. Sort leaves by tree name.

Earthworms
(5 years and older)

Objective: To observe and describe how an earthworm moves

Materials needed: A digging place, shovels, clean Styrofoam© trays, magnifying glass

What to do:

1. Encourage the children to dig for earthworms in an area where they can be found. (If you do not have such an area, contact a local bait shop that can supply some earthworms for observation.)

2. Place a few earthworms on the trays for the children to observe. Use a magnifying glass for closer observation.

3. Ask the children "How does an earthworm move?" "How does it know where it is going?" "What do you

think earthworms eat?" "Have you ever seen earthworms on sidewalks or driveways after a rain?"

4. Read a book about earthworms to clarify information and concepts.

And still more:

1. Set up an earthworm farm where children can observe the movements and tunneling of the earthworms.

2. Discuss with children how earthworms aerate and enrich the soil and help plants to grow.

3. Encourage the children to dictate a story about what they have learned about earthworms to share with parents.

Theme Activities
Theme: Soil
Mud Balls
(3 years and older)

Objective: To observe and feel change in soil

Materials needed: Small, individual containers with soil, one for each child in the group; premeasured water individual containers, one for each child in the group; aprons or old shirts; popsicle sticks for mixing

What to do:

1. Encourage the children to touch and handle the dry soil.

2. Provide premeasured water and popsicle sticks to stir the mixture.

3. When the soil and water are well blended, have the children form a ball.

4. Allow the children to experience the mud by rolling, patting, and mashing it.

5. When the activity is finished, have children wash their hands.

6. Discuss with parents what children are learning from working with mud.

And still more:

1. Engage children in conversation about mud, its composition, texture, color, smell, and uses. Use this

opportunity to extend vocabulary. Ask, "How does mud feel?" "What else can you do with mud?" "What do you think will happen if we add more water to the mud?"

2. Provide additional dry soil. Have the children observe and feel the dry soil. Ask, "What will happen if the mud ball is rolled in the dry soil?" Engage children in a discussion of the differences between the dry and wet soils.

3. Encourage the children to form shapes with their mud. Allow the shapes to dry. Guide the children's observations and dialogue about what happens when mud dries.

Theme: Light
Shadow Play
(4 years and older)

Objective: To experiment with how shadows are formed

Materials needed: A sunny day is all that is required for this activity

What to do:

1. On a sunny day, take the children outdoors and have them locate and name objects and equipment on the playground. Guide them into discovering the "dark spots" beside or surrounding the objects.

2. Elicit conversation with children about what those spots are.

3. Explain that shadows are formed by objects that block light, (in this case, light from the sun).

4. Have the children experiment with forming shadows by blocking light with their bodies.

And still more:

1. Have the children experiment with shadows by using a variety of objects to block light, for example, boxes, blocks, sticks, balls, and brooms.

2. Trace the children's shadows on paper.

3. Take the children outdoors to see their shadows at different times of the day. Have children examine the shadows for size, shape, and direction. Ask, "Do shadows look different at different times of the day?" "What makes shadows look different?"

Theme: Birds

Investigating Birds' Nests
(5 years and older)

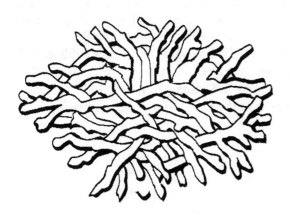

Objective: To investigate what birds use to build their nests

Materials needed: empty birds' nest, plastic tweezers, popsicle sticks, tray for organizing the materials, collection of realistic pictures of a variety of birds' nests, chart paper (*Note: Collect only birds' nests you know birds will not return to in the spring to use again.*)

What to do:

1. Engage the children in conversation about their observations of birds and their nests.

2. Ask open-ended questions to encourage thinking and dialogue: "Where do birds build their nests?" Use the pictures to stimulate meaningful conversation: "Why do you think birds choose different places to build their nests?" Accept the children's responses, but tactfully add clarity to avoid misperceptions as necessary.

3. Display the tray with the materials. Have the children observe the nest and talk about it. Ask, "What (materials, objects) do you think a bird used to build this nest?" Create a chart on which the children's responses are recorded.

4. Have the children use the tweezers and popsicle sticks to investigate what materials were used to build the nest.

5. Classify the materials and graph the results: paper, twigs, string, ribbon, and so on. By graphing, determine which materials were used most and least often.

6. Have children wash hands thoroughly after the activity.

And still more:

1. Compare the children's original predictions with the results of their investigations. How accurate were the predictions?

2. Look for and observe birds' nests outdoors or observe birds building nests. Read the book *Birds' Nests* by Eileen Curran.

References

American Association for the Advancement of Science (1989). *Science for all Americans: Project 2061 report on literacy goals in science, mathematics, and technology.* Washington, DC: Author.

American Association for the Advancement of Science (1993). *Benchmarks for science literacy.* Washington, DC: Author.

Curran, E. (1985). *Birds' nests.* Mahwah, NJ: Troll Associates.

Gibbons, G. (1989). *Monarch butterfly.* NY: Holiday House.

Kendrick, A.S., R. Kaufman, R., & K.P. Messenger (1993). *Healthy young children: A manual for early childhood programs.* Washington, DC: National Association for the Education of Young Children.

Kilmer, S.J. & H. Hofman (1995). Transforming science curriculum. In S. Bredekamp & T. Rosegrant (Eds.). *Reaching potentials: Transforming early childhood curriculum and assessment* (Vol. 2, pp. 43-63). Washington, DC: National Association for the Education for Young Children.

Lind, K.K. (1999). Science in early childhood: Developing and acquiring fundamental concepts and skills. In American Association for the Advancement of Science. *Dialogue on early childhood science, mathematics, and technology education* (pp. 73-77). Washington, DC: American Association for the Advancement of Science.

National Research Council (1996). *National science education standards.* Washington, DC: National Academy Press.

Piaget, J. (1952). *The origins of intelligence in children.* NY: International University Press.

Checklist for Evaluating the Science Center

Rate the items below on a scale of 1 to 4 with "needing improvement" as 1 and "outstanding" as 4.

_____1. The intended use of the science center is readily apparent to children.

_____2. Boundaries between areas effectively communicate where areas begin and end.

_____3. Activities are designed to develop specific scientific concepts or skills.

_____4. Materials are easily accessible to the children.

_____5. Each science activity is self-contained and organized on trays, in buckets, pans, or baskets.

_____6. Materials are real, concrete, and relevant to children's experiences.

_____7. Activities are organized in such a manner that children can use them independently.

_____8. A variety of science activities are available from which to choose.

_____9. Materials and activities are designed for active exploration and experimentation.

_____10. Materials and activities are changed on a regular basis.

_____11. Realistic illustrations and accurate literature is used to convey concepts.

_____12. Illustrative materials are displayed at the children's eye level.

_____13. All living things are cared for appropriately and with respect.

About the Author

Irma Cantu Woods, PhD is an associate professor of Child Development/Early Childhood Education at Del Mar College in Corpus Christi and a former child development specialist with the Texas Department of Human Services. She is an active member of the Bay Area Association for the Education of Young Children and a frequent presenter at local, state, and national conferences. She holds a doctorate in Early Childhood Education from the University of Texas at Austin.

Chapter 12

Music

Kathy Morrison

Music is and always has been an integral part of human experience. Music is central to comprehensive learning and includes organizing, attending, problem solving, and creativity (Carlton, 1994). Music in a preschool classroom can be used throughout the day for signaling routines and transitions, to focus attention, for relieving stress, to support and enrich curriculum themes, to reinforce skills, to encourage creative expression, and simply for enjoyment. As we all know, children learn best by "doing," that is, they learn through play, experimentation, exploration, and discovery. A high quality preschool classroom provides varied opportunities for children to explore, discover, and experiment with music.

Music is thought to enhance brain growth and neurological development by engaging a number of cognitive processes. In her book, *Start Smart*, Pam Schillar (1999) states that all early sounds, including music and rhythms, play a role in shaping the brain's neurological structures. This author further asserts that there is evidence that listening to music can boost memory, attention, motivation, and learning.

Scartelli (1984) has reported that music is a mood enhancer. It is believed that listening to favorite songs or types of music boosts certain chemicals in the brain called endorphins that, among other benefits, boost attention and memory. Others have found that music rhythms, patterns, contrasts, and varying tonalities help children to remember new information Webb and Webb (1990). This means that music may well be a powerful way to present information to learners.

Transitions

Music can be used to help children transition from one activity to the next. Songs such as *The Clean-up Song* instruct and engage children in routine tasks during the day. Instructional (or transition) songs sung to familiar tunes can signal children to line-up, sit in the circle, come to group time, or put on their jackets. (See examples below.) Often transition times become unorganized and even chaotic. Music can help children anticipate and focus on what they are expected to do and enlists cooperation. Routines guided by music afford a certain level of self-direction for children and make routine tasks more enjoyable.

Focus Attention

Music is also an effective tool for helping children to focus their attention. When we begin a whole group or small group lesson with music, the musical activity allows the brain to "settle," to get the "lay of the land," to focus on the task at hand. For example, a teacher might begin a lesson on frogs by singing *Three Green and Freckled Frogs*. As the teacher sings and demonstrates the movements, the children redirect their attention and begin to focus on the ensuing activity. Their attention is directed toward the teacher and soon all members of the group are beginning to participate in the song and fingerplay. When the song is completed, the children are attending to the teacher and the lesson can begin.

Relives Stress

Music and rhythms relieve stress in children by providing an outlet for energetic movement or a pleasant listening experience that calms and soothes. Vigorous rhythm and movement activities increase heart rate that in turn increases oxygen to the brain, a biological phenomenon that helps learners to focus and think more clearly.

Music provides motivation and a backdrop for movement. Singing and moving to music is fun and relaxing for people of all ages. As children dance, march, skip, wiggle, turn, stomp, clap, and so on, they engage and coordinate large motor controls and skills. Singing, humming, swaying, whistling, and just listening to pleasing music is comforting to most children and can relieve tension, stress, and anxiety. In addition, most children enjoy moving to music, and this enjoyment contributes to stress relief. These benefits suggest that children should have opportunities to listen to, sing and move to the sounds and rhythms of music throughout the day.

Creative Expression

Many children are uninhibited and feel free to express themselves in response to music. Howard Gardner, a Harvard University psychologist and research scholar has identified several types of intelligence (Gardner, 1983, 1993). Among the multiple intelligences that he has studied are musical intelligence and bodily kinesthetic intelligence. Gardner believes that individuals exhibit strengths in one or a combination of the eight (and possibly more) intelligences that he has identified. Children who have musical intelligence are able to sing on key, to learn words to songs easily, have a good sense of rhythm and tempo, and are sensitive to the sounds around them. They particularly enjoy exploring and learning to play musical instruments. Children with bodily kinesthetic intelligence have excellent control and coordination of body motion and movements and skilled fine motor controls. They manipulate objects and use space in skillful and creative ways. They are expressive and creative in their response to music and effectively express emotion and ideas through body movements. A rich music and movement curriculum can meet the cognitive and emotional needs of these children while encouraging and building musical and bodily kinesthetic intelligence in children who are less musically inclined.

Enjoyment

Music and movement bring playfulness and good humor into the classroom. Teachers who model a love for music and enjoy creative and expressive rhythm and movements encourage children to use their bodies to express themselves and to have fun. The teacher and children share the enjoyment through smiles and laughter as they move and respond together to music. When an activity is enjoyable and fun, children are intrinsically motivated to participate. Teachers should be observant and sensitive to children's interest in and desired to participate in musical experiences. While not common, there are some children who do not find pleasure in music and rhythms or feel timid about participating. Children should be given time to feel comfortable participating in group music activities and not be pressured to participate. For the most part, children choose to participate and join an activity when they realize that there is fun to be had.

Integrating Music into Other Curriculum Areas

Music can link specific concepts or skills to curriculum units or themes. There are many sources of professionally recorded music from which to obtain music of all genre. Recordings often address preschool curriculum concepts: colors, shapes, days of the week, months of the year, counting, and so on. These recording can be played daily to reinforce learning and to allow children to practice selected skills in an engaging and enjoyable way.

Music can easily be used to enhance the reading and writing curriculum. Many children's songs have now been made into storybooks or big books. These books can be read and sung with the children. This enables children to "read" the book as they sing their favorite tune. Charts with the songs and fingerplays printed on them allow children to see the words as they are sung or recited. When teachers also point to the words as the song is sung, children become aware of the left to right progression of print and begin to match words that they know to their print forms.

Math concepts are also readily integrated into children's music experiences. As children keep a steady beat while moving to music, they begin to both feel and count the music's beats per measure. Children moving to a marching rhythm feel and count four beats per measure, and when moving to a waltz, they respond to three beats per measure. Teachers can call attention to the number of beats by counting and clapping the beats as children move: "1-2-3, 1-2-3, 1-2-3." Many songs and fingerplays are about numbers and include simple math concepts, for example, *The Number Rock* and *Five Little Pumpkins*.

Music and Children with Special Needs

A goal of bringing music and children together is to assure that all children have opportunities to fully participate to the extent that that can and want to do so. Some children with developmental delays or mental retardation may find learning and remembering the words to songs challenging and frustrating. Imitating rhythmic patterns and maintaining tempo and an appro-

priate volume level may also be difficult to do. These children may need more time and repetition with the expected skills to become comfortable with music activities. Providing simple songs that have repetitive refrains, and engaging in movement activities that can be segmented into one or two coordinations at a time, help children master some of the skills needed to respond to music in a satisfying way.

When children with hearing impairments have some residual hearing, (that is, their hearing loss is not total), they often can hear and/or feel rhythmic patterns and respond to them. However, depending on the amount of hearing loss, the child may not be able to hear melody and harmony in music. Teachers can use appropriate amplifiers, sign language to teach the words and rhythms of songs, visual aids such as charts with the lyrics and rhythms printed on them, and use low frequency instruments (cello, bass violin, lower octaves on the piano, or keyboard) which are easier to hear. Instruments such as a guitar, drums, or piano that vibrate and can be touched to feel the music are good choices. When singing, adults or classroom partners can remember to face the child who relies on lip movements, facial expressions, and body language for cues.

Children with visual impairments benefit from partner activities where they can be verbally guided through songs and movement activities. An adult or partner can hold the hand of the visually impaired child while dancing and moving to prevent falls and bumps. The auditory and tactile experience of using rhythm instruments is particularly enjoyable for these children. Adults will need to read aloud and demonstrate an activity with the child who is unable to see charts and observe the actions of other children.

Children with physical/motor disabilities may need assistance with holding rhythm instruments, scarves, and other props. Improvising ways to make this easier helps these children to become full participants. Such improvisation might include securely sewing bells to the fingers of a pair of gloves; securely sewing scarves to a bangle bracelet; wrapping foam rubber around the handles of rhythm instruments such as rhythm sticks and mallets to make them easier to grasp; and using Velcro© strips to attach instruments to the wrist. A child in a wheel chair can be brought into movement activities if rolled and pushed gently to the beat of the music, and depending on the type of disability, the child may be encouraged to use upper body movement to respond to music. Children with physical/motor disabilities who use adaptive or assistive equipment need more space and clear pathways in order to participate safely.

Sensitive and creative adults find many ways to bring children with disabilities into the full range of music learning and participation. When open-ended materials and activities are provided, children of all abilities can be successful. Because there is no right or wrong way to express oneself creatively, children with special needs can feel successful and competent when they play and participate in the music area.

Providing Multicultural Music Experiences

The music center is a perfect place to add a variety of multicultural materials. Children should be given opportunities to learn songs, chants, rhythms, and dance of many cultures, particularly those cultures represented in their class, school or center. There are many multicultural musical instruments on the market that reflect a variety of forms of music. There are sound making toys and instruments from cultures and countries around the world. Music stores and specialty stores often have sound toys, rhythm instruments, and other musical items from countries such as Mexico, Africa, and Asia and cultures such as Native American and Hawaiian. Music can be selected to represent the cultures and heritages of children in the class, perhaps, Scottish, Irish, German, or Caribbean music is appropriate. Recorded music from many cultures and ethnic groups is available through music stores and school supply companies. Children's families can be invited to share traditional music and dance routines with the children and to demonstrate musical instruments that they play and enjoy in their homes and social events. What better way to bring diverse cultures into the classroom than through music?

The music center in a preschool classroom should be available to children every day. The area should contain rhythm instruments, props, favorite recordings, song books, instructional pictures, rebus charts, listening equipment and other materials, all displayed and stored in a manner that makes them accessable to the children. The area might also include a keyboard or a piano. Some children might extend their music play into the puppet center, the home area, or the block area. For example, a child might use puppets to mime a song, or the dress-up clothes in the home area to serve as a costume for a performance, or use the hollow blocks for a stage. When teachers provide children with opportunities to be musically creative, to improvise, and to respond to music in their own unique ways, music appreciation and learning are enhanced.

Planning Spaces for Music

The music center should be located near the whole group or circle time area in the room to allow ample space for rhythms and movement. Children are able to take advantage of the carpeted area designated for circle time for creative movements, marching, dancing, or performing with the whole group, in small groups, or individually. The space should be near a plug to allow for the use of a DVD, CD, or audio tape player, and should include a low shelf or table for this equipment.

Equipment and Materials

Audioplayer and headsets: A DVD, CD, or audiotape player should be available for daily use. After the children have been taught how to safely operate the player they should be able to use it independently. Some school supply companies provide audioplayers that are especially manufactured for classroom use. As well, there are many high quality recordings in various formats (DVD, CD, audiotape) that are appropriate for young children. These are available through school supply catalogues, teacher stores, book and music stores and toy stores. Many varieties of music should be incorporated into children's music experiences and music should be a part of every day. Children should have opportunities to enjoy classical, folk, country, nursery rhymes, action songs, exercise tapes, and music from many cultures and ethnic groups.

Listening station: Most audioplayers for classrooms have a jack into which headphones can be connected. Providing headphones in the music area allows children to listen quietly to favorite music.

Low open shelves, table, pegboard: Low shelving, a table, and a pegboard stand or pegboard mounted on the wall provide places to display and store the music equipment and materials. Labels (words or picture symbols) on the shelves and pegboard, or trays or baskets on the table help children to use materials and equipment and return them to their proper place when not in use.

Rhythm instruments: A variety of well-constructed rhythm instruments such as small tambourines, bells, sandpaper blocks, drums, maracas, rhythm sticks, triangles, xylophones should be available. There are a variety of rhythm instruments available for purchase to enrich the music area and to represent the cultural backgrounds of the children in the group. Soundmakers can be included such as aluminum pans, metal and wooden spoons, and metal pots and pans.

Keyboard: A keyboard with earphones or headsets allows children to experiment with making and composing music Songbooks with simple tunes that are color coded provide an engaging music challenge. These books allow children to practice playing simple tunes such as "Row, Row, Row Your Boat," while enhancing reading skills and following directions.

Rebus song cards: Teacher-made song cards with songs and fingerplays that the children know allow children to practice reading while singing their favorite songs.

Creative props: Large and small scarves, ribbons, and crepe paper streamers in a variety of colors encourage children to move creatively with music.

Dramatic play props: Ballerina tutu's, tights, drum major outfits, and other music-related costumes encourage dramatic play with movement and music.

Activities for the Music Area

Open ended activities should be the focus of the music area. Teachers can change the music and props to encourage different types of creative activities each week. The music area should provide children an opportunity to experiment, explore, and discover music and movement.

Moving to Music

Each week provide a different type of music to listen to and to move to in the music area. Place a selection of recordings that focus on one type of music for the children to explore. One week provide classical music, the next week provide folk music, and so on. Explain to the children what type of music will be highlighted in that area and invite them to compare how the different types of music sound and how the sound and rhythm of the music changes the way they move and dance.

Enhancing Curriculum Themes

Provide music and props in the music area that coordinate with the current curriculum theme, topic, or project. This is easy to do around holiday themes, however, music can enhance other curriculum themes, for example teach songs, dances, chants, and fingerplays that support concepts relating to such themes as rain forests, pets and other animals, farm life and farm animals, space travel, and so on. Many curriculum guides on such themes suggest coordinated songs and musical experiences. Introduce the center and its theme related props each week to help children understand the connection between the music, the props, and the theme.

Musical Instruments

Encourage children to compose their own music with the musical instruments. Play along with the children as they move to music with their instruments. Using songs such as the *Barnyard Song*, children can use musical instruments to represent the sounds of farm animals. They might use the instruments to make sounds from nature such as rain, thunder, or wind. Encourage children to experiment with the instruments to make new sounds and to cooperate with each other to form a pretend band.

Examples of Transition Songs for Preschool Children

Clean up Song

Clean up, clean up
Everybody do their share.
Clean up, clean up,
Everybody everywhere.

Lining Up *(Insert your own children's names)*
(Tune: London Bridge)
Jason, Carrie, and Tyrone
Please line up. Please line up.
Jeff, and Michael, and Susan
Line up by the door.

Sit in the Circle
(Tune: Mary Had A Little Lamb)
We all need to sit in the circle,
Sit in the circle,
Sit in the circle,
We all need to sit in the circle,
So we can read our book!

Three Green and Speckled Frogs

Three green and speckled frogs
Sat on a speckled log,
Eating some most delicious bugs.
One jumped into the pool,
Where it was nice and cool,
Then there were two green speckled frogs.

Checklist for Evaluating the Music Center

_____1. The music center is in a space that facilitates freedom of movement.

_____2. Compact disk, DVD, and/or tape player with a variety of recorded music are available.

_____3. An assortment of musical and rhythm instruments is available for children's use.

_____4. Teacher-made and/or commercial charts and other visuals depict words to songs, rhythms, musical instruments, musicians, and other music-related information.

_____5. Props such as scarves, ribbons, crepe paper streamers, and costumes that can enrich and encourage creative movement are available.

_____6. Music and musical instruments representing diverse cultures and traditions are included.

_____7. Musical and rhythm instruments are carefully and properly stored in their own cases, hung on a pegboard, placed on a labeled shelf or in other appropriate and protective places.

_____8. Music, songbooks and music related storybooks are easily accessed by the children.

_____9. Sensitive and appropriate music experiences are provided for children with special needs.

_____10. Music and music experiences are integrated into routines, transitions, and curriculum activities throughout the day.

References

Carlton, E. & P. Weikart (1994). *Foundations in elementary education: Music*. Ypsilanti, MI: High/Scope Educational Research Foundation.

Gardner, H. (1983). *Frames of mind: The theory of multiple intelligences*. NY: Basic Books.

Gardner, H. (1993). Multiple intelligences: The theory in practice. NY: Basic Books.

Schiller, P. (1999). *Start Smart!* Beltsville, MD: Gryphon House.

Scartelli, J. (1984). The learning brain. *Journal of Music Therapy 21*, 67-78, 341.

Webb, Douglas & Webb, Terry (1990). Accelerated learning with music: A trainer's manual. Norcross, GA: Accelerated Learning Systems, 334.

About the Author

Kathy Morrison, Ed.D. is an Assistant Professor of Early Childhood Education in the School of Education at the University of Texas at Tyler. She is a national consultant for the High/Scope Educational Research Foundation and is the co-editor of *Family Friendly Communications* published by NAEYC.

Nobody Else in the World Like Me

No – body else in the world like ME –, ME –, ME –, ME –, ME –!

Ever has been or ever will be – ME –, ME –, ME –, ME –!

Look at ME, oh, look at ME –! I'm so glad that I am ME –,

and that I will al–ways be – ME –, ME –, ME –, ME, ME !

Make a Circle in the Air

Make a cir - cle in the air, in the air – – .

Make a cir - cle in the air, in the air – – .

Make a cir - cle in the air, and leave it right there.

Make a cir - cle in the air, in the air – – .

Lift Your Arm, Put it Down

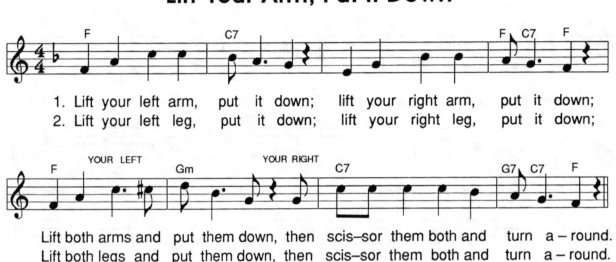

1. Lift your left arm, put it down; lift your right arm, put it down;
2. Lift your left leg, put it down; lift your right leg, put it down;

Lift both arms and put them down, then scis-sor them both and turn a – round.
Lift both legs and put them down, then scis-sor them both and turn a – round.

Clap Your Hands and March Forward

Clap your hands and march for – ward! Clap your hands, march a – way!

(children need not follow one behind the other as in regular marching)

Clap your hands. Keep on march – ing! Clap your hands, then stop and say, "Hooray!"

Now march back – ward same as for – ward. Clap your hands all the way!

Keep on march – ing, march– ing, march– ing, then stop and say, "Hoo–ray!"

Chapter 13

Dramatic Play

Kathy Morrison

One of the most important areas in a preschool room is the dramatic play area. This area serves as the cornerstone for all creative dramatics in the classroom. Research has shown that children who have had many opportunities for dramatic play in early childhood have larger vocabularies, use more varied language, and eventually become better readers and writers. Dramatic play activities provide opportunities for children to practice using lan-

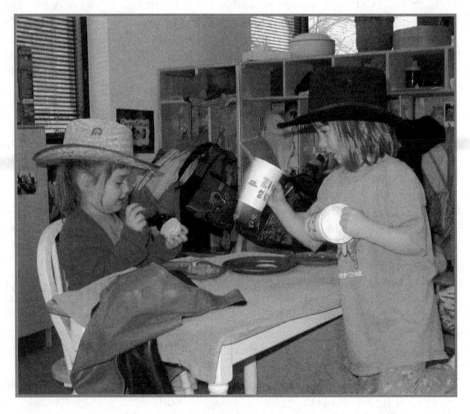

guage in a variety of contextual situations. Children need regular opportunities for dramatic play. From these repeated opportunities, children gradually begin to elaborate upon the dialogues and interactions within their dramatic play setting (Otto, 2001).

Benefits of Dramatic Play

The benefits of dramatic play are numerous and span all of the developmental areas of physical/motor, emotional, social, cognitive, language, and literacy. Among the many contributions to child development is its influence on language development. Children's vocabularies are increased as children act out roles and events that they have experienced in their lives. For example, a child who has recently been to see the dentist will attempt to recreate the experience through pretend play. He might pretend to look into a doll's mouth and say, "Open wide," or "Mmm, you have two cavities!" He might pretend to fill the cavity and ask the "patient" to rinse, or role play other dentist office experiences using the language of dentistry as he understood it. Vocabulary development undergirds a child's successes in comprehending both the spoken and written word. As such vocabulary development contributes significantly to learning to read. It is interesting to note that during dramatic play, children tend to behave in actions and in words beyond their age. The more children use new words, expressions, and ideas, the sooner they become a part of the child's thinking and speaking repertoire.

As children role play, they begin to gain understanding of social interactions, to synthesize experiences, and to explore their feelings and ideas about their experiences. Dramatic play then contributes to children's expression and understanding of emotions, their own and those of others. The whole range of emotions that children experience in their lives (joy, humor, sadness, fear, anger, and others) can find expression in a safe and constructive context. For example something as simple as a birthday party can cause stress and anxiety in a child. By role playing events surrounding the birthday party the child gains familiarity and a sense of control. Dramatic play gives children important opportunities to gain emotional intelligence and self-regulation of emotions through acting out, talking about, and pretending in a variety of roles and play scenarios.

Through the social interactions that evolve through pretend play, children practice their social skills of making and maintaining friends, negotiating play preferences, sharing and cooperating, and dealing with others' points of view. While very young children enjoy pretend play with objects, as children get older, their desire for and enjoyment of playmates adds depth and breadth to their play experiences. A creative and well designed dramatic play area invites playmates to enjoy their associations with one another.

The dramatic play area is often misperceived as contributing little to a child's cognitive development or academic preparation. Quite the contrary is true. Piaget's stages of cognitive development are profoundly exampled in children's sociodramatic play: sensorimotor activities, symbolism, sorting, classifying, ordering, extending and elaborating on existing concepts, testing one's own perceptions and adapting to new perspectives (Piaget, 1963). Dramatic play requires children to think diver-

gently as pretend and fantasy take them into unknown and unexperienced realms. The thinking required to participate in group pretend play is imaginative, creative, and divergent. It engages higher-order processes, more so than such activities as working a puzzle or filling in blanks on a work sheet. This thinking must manipulate objects, negotiate play assignments, create a character or role and carry it out, think forward to next actions within the scenario, tap prior knowledge and experience to guide behaviors and play themes, integrate one's ideas with those of others, formulate language to communicate effectively with playmates, and improvise props and scenery necessary to support the play. All of this thinking and decision-making must take place within a very short span of time, and involves rather sophisticated problem-solving challenges.

Play scenarios generally have all of the elements of a good story: place, characters, plot, climax, and conclusion; or more simply stated, these scenarios like stories have a beginning, middle, and end. Along with the language development that naturally evolves through these elaborate and extended play events, dramatic play contributes richly to literacy development. Indeed, literacy, math, science, music, art, social studies, even physical education can all be integrated into the dramatic play areas in ways that enrich the curriculum for children and broaden children's knowledge and skills.

Types of Play

Sara Smilansky (1968) divides play into four types: 1) functional, 2) constructive, 3) dramatic, and 4) games with rules. Functional play begins in infancy with simple, repetitive behaviors. This play begins when the child is no longer content to simply watch people or objects, but begins to interact with them. Interactions at this level are repetitive and enjoyed at the simplest level, e.g., a child pouring and dumping objects from a small bucket enjoys the activity for its own sake and finds repeating the activity enchanting. Functional play is not limited however to infancy, but continues as children get older. Constructive play occurs when children use objects to create and interact with playmates, and, playing alone or with others, pretend and create a role. This play is more symbolic in that children can use objects in a representational way, e.g., a unit block pushed along a "roadway" is used to represent a truck. 3) Dramatic play is a more sophisticated form of symbolic play and involves more elaborated pretending and make-believe. Dramatic play represents a higher level of play behavior and is observable when two or more children take on related roles and interact with one another (Jackman, 1997).

Cooperative play spans both dramatic play and games with rules. This type of play requires children to communicate and cooperate to be successful. When children are involved in cooperative play, they adopt a single, coordinated play theme, and plan, negotiate, and differentiate roles in pursuit of their shared goal. (Trawick-Smith, 2000). That is, children assign roles and cooperate to carry out a play theme: "You be the mommy, and I'll be the baby." As children work together to create a dramatic play experience, they are moving into a higher level of play. Cooperative play represents the most complex form of social participation. During cooperative play, conflicts often occur as children attempt to define and assign roles and organize or carry out a play theme or scenario. These conflicts among children can be beneficial, as they require children to make adjustments, cooperate, negotiate, and solve their problems or disagreements. While children may need adult coaching or assistance in these conflicts, the dramatic play area provides a perfect venue for problem solving and learning to take the perspective of others.

Dramatic Play Spaces

Ample space should be provided for the dramatic play area. The space should be carpeted and must be flexible. Space must be available for the dramatic play area to be enlarged or made smaller as play themes dictate. The space should be located near or next to the block area to facilitate interactions between the two areas. For example, children in the block area may be pretending to change the oil under a car built from blocks. This play might expand into the home area as children come into the "house" from the "garage." Both the dramatic play area and the block area are excellent areas for dramatic play and both areas are typically noisy.

The dramatic play area can easily change into a variety of settings by changing the theme and props. The dramatic play area can be a cafe one week, a doctor's office the next, and a shoe store the next. The dramatic play area can be made to appear more "homelike" by adding occasional lighting (a small table lamp), area rugs, or pillows. All that is required is for the teacher and/or the children to change a few props and for the children to use their imaginations. Teachers can develop prop boxes for reoccurring play themes, and develop additional prop boxes to meet the unique interests and play themes of children. Ideas for prop boxes are derived from cues provided by children, and the age, interests,

and capabilities of the children. The possibilities for prop box themes are limitless and teachers are limited only by their imaginations.

Ample space should be provided for this essential area of the room. Because the dramatic play area can be anything from an alligator swamp to a zoo, the space must be flexible enough to accommodate a variety of props and configurations. Some weeks the space might be smaller to reflect a small cozy bear's cave, another week it might be much larger to accommodate the creation of a sailing ship. The teacher must arrange the space to meet the needs and interests of the children in the classroom. As needs and interests change, the space may need to be adapted.

Equipping the Dramatic Play Area

There are some basic equipment and materials needed to arrange and supply an inviting dramatic play area. While not all of these items would be placed in the dramatic play center at once, building an inventory to support whatever types of play scenarios evolve is an important goal. The following are some of the more common items used in sociodramatic play:

- Low shelves
- Child size refrigerator, sink, cooking range, hutch or other small cabinet to hold dishes and supplies
- Child size dishes, cooking utensils, pots and pans
- Doll bed and washable bedding
- Clean, washable throw pillows, floor pillow(s) and one or two stuffed toys
- Small table and chairs
- Child size soft chair or love seat
- Full length mirror
- Hooks or other storage for dress up clothes
- Dolls and doll clothes representing both male and female gender and different ethnicities
- Assorted dress-up clothes and costumes (again, representing both male and female gender and different ethnicities)
- Brooms, mops, dustpans
- Telephones, phone book, small address book and pencil
- Clock, timer, scales, cash register

- Food replicas and clean discarded food cartons
- Small trays, baskets, canvas totes
- Small magazine holder for books, catalogs, and children's periodicals
- Writing tools: note pads, telephone books, menus, grocery ads, pencils
- Small bulletin board for messages; wall space for visual materials, such as pictures associated with the play theme or for rebus charts of recipes or tasks to be completed
- Aesthetic items: small flower arrangement, window curtain, framed art
- Selected prop box items displayed attractively to support a play theme

Integrating Other Curriculum Areas into Dramatic Play

The dramatic play area can encourage reading and writing. Including pencils and paper, note pads, telephone books, menus, white erase boards, grocery ads, magnetic letters, and so on, can encourage early literacy learning. Children can write grocery lists, telephone messages, make a menu for supper, leave instructions for a baby sitter or any number of writing activities that they might have experienced in their homes. By providing tools for reading and writing in the dramatic play area children are encouraged to practice reading and writing skills as they play.

Mathematics is easily integrated into the dramatic play center. Children use numbers and counting while participating in a variety of play scenarios. They might use a calculator to pretend to add up the cost of their groceries, or attempt to count play money, or pretend to tell time as they play in this area.

Props and materials in the dramatic play area should be logically placed and organized storage provided for them when they are not in use. Items to be stored in prop boxes and on shelves should each have a clearly labeled place on the shelf. This allows children to replace all the materials they have used to their proper storage location. An added benefit to organized and labeled storage is the development of sorting and classifying concepts and skills. For example, as children place the canisters or measuring cups in their correct order, they are seriating, i.e., arranging objects sequentially from smallest to largest, another important mathematics concept.

Multicultural Materials

The dramatic play area is also a logical place to include a variety of multicultural materials. Dolls that reflect different ethnicities and genders convey the message that we are all alike, and yet we are different. A variety of swatches of fabrics or scarves that reflect different cultures can be used as clothing, capes, headdresses, dresses, blankets, and table clothes. Pictures and books depicting people of varying cultures can be placed in the dramatic play center. In addition, a variety of cooking utensils used in various cultures can be included such as a wok and a tortilla press. Well chosen culturally responsive dramatic play props help children gain authentic knowledge about families and people of cultures other than their own.

Planning for Children with Special Needs

The dramatic play area can easily be adapted for children with special needs. The area can be arranged with pathways that accommodate children in wheel chairs or on crutches. Materials should be displayed in such a way as to invite and facilitate independence and use. Materials can be placed on shelves where they are easy to reach by children who use wheel chairs or other assistive equipment. It is helpful to children with special needs if materials are logically placed to convey their intended use. Specific storage areas for props and materials must be clearly designated with print and/or symbols to represent the item to be stored. Following individual cues, interests, and capabilities, props can be included that are used by, and particular to the experiences of children with special needs. This should be done in a very sensitive manner to help children feel included while building empathy and acceptance among other children in an inclusive environment. Adults must be most careful not to cause a child to feel singled out, embarrassed, or uncomfortably different. Visuals and books can be provided in the dramatic play center that depict people with special needs participating fully in a stimulating and inclusive setting.

Extending Dramatic Play into the Outdoor Environment

Dramatic play can easily be extended to the outdoor play area. Providing children with dolls and buggies, dishes, pots and pans to take outdoors extends dramatic play to another setting. Children's play themes may change as dramatic play props are put to additional creative uses.

Children might play picnic or taking the baby for a walk. They may pretend to hang clothes on a clothesline. A few props brought outdoors from the dramatic play area enriches and expands dramatic play throughout the day. "Playing house" is a natural choice for preschool children. Children love to try on different roles and activities experienced in their families and different occupations in the community.

Activities

Each of the examples of prop boxes listed below can be used to encourage creative dramatic play. The activities in this area should be open-ended, allowing children to explore the materials and create their own roles and experiences. The prop boxes serve to facilitate creative dramatic play in a variety of ways.

Prop Boxes

Note: Items placed in prop boxes should be carefully selected for the age and capabilities of children who will use them. Adults should follow the same rules and precautions for selecting age- and individually-appropriate items as are followed in selecting other toys, play items, and teaching materials.

Café: menus from local restaurants, pads and pencils, aprons, dishes, chef hats, play money, cash registers, and play food. Children can pretend to cook, to order from the menu, or to be a server. Providing a simple real food recipe for the cook to prepare enhances this activity. Select foods that are nutritious and that do not cause allergies.

Doctor's Office: white jackets, stethoscopes, nurses uniform, pretend thermometers, rubber gloves, gauze, tape, masks, eye droppers, tongue depressors, eye chart, cot, blankets, pencil and paper, empty and small clean plastic bottles, a scale. This prop box can be used in a variety of ways. In addition to a doctor's office, these materials might be used as veterinarian props when stuffed animals are included in the prop box.

Ophthalmologist or Eye Doctor Office:

typewriter or computer (working or not), keyboard, telephones, writing paper, old stationary, paper clips, staplers, file folders, and so on. Arrange the furniture similar to an office at home. Include a small children's desk, or school desk for children to sit at and work. Old discarded computers and printers can be added to the dramatic play area to simulate an office.

Camping: back packs, tent, play shovels and tools, sleeping bags, logs or long blocks to represent a campfire, tin coffee pot and pan, stick horses, a picnic basket, and a quilt. Children can pretend to go on a camping trip with the family. They might build their own tent using quilts and tables in the room if a small tent is not available. As play progresses, children might include bears or other wild animals found in the woods, so stuffed toys or puppets could be included in this prop box. Flashlights to turn on in the tent add great interest to the play.

Shoe store: old pairs of shoes (a variety of types) , shoe boxes, shoe sizing device, cash register, play credit card machine, chairs, etc. Set up a few chairs in the dramatic play area for shoe customers. Help the children to set up the cash register and the counter to pay for shoes. Children enjoy measuring each other's feet using either a real shoe sizing device, or a ruler. The size of the shoes can be marked in large numerals on the shoe boxes. Children can write the size of their friend's foot, and pretend to find shoes that are that size. Children can take turns being the customer trying on different types of shoes or the shoe sales person. Children enjoy pretending to take money.

Nursery Rhyme and Fairy Tale Prop Boxes

The following ideas from prop boxes are based on fairy tales or nursery rhymes. Prop boxes associated with other familiar children's books and stories are also enriching. After reading the book or telling the story several times, children become very familiar with the sequence of the story or rhyme. By providing prop boxes that relate to children's literature, literacy development is enhanced.

Little Red Riding Hood: cape with a hood, baskets, food, a wolf costume or puppet, a grandma's cap, a logging cap and flannel shirt for the woodsman. Children can take turns acting out the story and improvising the words and actions. Observe the children while they are playing with the prop box materials, and record how they changed the story. Tell the story to the whole group the way that the children have changed it during dramatic play. Engage them in a discussion about how the stories differ.

The Three Billy Goats Gruff: paper horns stapled to tag board to form 3 headbands for the goats, a mask for the troll that lived under the bridge. Provide a small table for the goats to walk over, and for the troll to crouch under. Encourage the children to act out the story using the words that are repeated in the book. Observe to see if they can come up with a different ending to the story. Encourage them to take turns role playing each of the characters.

Mary Had a Little Lamb: A large stick or walking cane to serve as a staff, some stuffed lambs, glasses and a long dress for the teacher, and so on. Make sure you sing the song frequently throughout the week. Encourage the children to sing the song as they act out the story. Have pictures of the sequence of the nursery rhyme displayed on the wall in the dramatic play area. These will give the children cues on the sequence of the song.

Checklist for Evaluating the Dramatic Play Center

Rate the items below on a scale of 1 to 4 with "needing improvement" as 1 and "outstanding" as 4.

_____1. There is ample space for a variety of play themes.

_____ 2. The dramatic play center is well equipped with basic furnishings to invite and enrich pretend play.

_____ 3. A variety of materials and props are available to extend and enhance dramatic play.

_____4. Dolls, clothes, and other artifacts reflect a variety of ethnic backgrounds, and gender.

_____5. The play area provides many opportunities to learn about diverse cultures.

_____6. Dress up clothes (men's and women's) are easy to self-manage and do not have hazardous features such as loose buttons, strings that could choke or catch on something, belts that bind, lengths that trip.

_____7. Literacy development materials are available including books, pictures, environmental print, note pads, pencils, grocery ads, telephone books, and so on.

_____8. Some real materials are included, e.g., telephone, typewriter, real pots and pans.

_____9. Low shelves are available to display and store materials and shelves and storage spaces are clearly labeled.

_____10. The dramatic play area is available on a daily basis.

References

Otto, B. (2001). *Language development in early childhood.* Columbus, OH: Merrill/Prentice Hall.

Smilansky, S. (1968). *The effects of sociodramatic play on disadvantaged pre-school children.* NY: John Wiley & Sons.

Jackman, H. (1997). *Early education curriculum: A child's connection to the world.* NY: Delmar Publishers.

Piaget, J. (1963). *The origins of intelligence in children.* (M. Cook, Trans.). NY: Norton.

Trawick-Smith, J. (1992). The classroom environment affects children's play and development. *Dimensions of Early Childhood, 20* (2), 27-30.

About the Author

Kathy Morrison, Ed.D. is an Assistant Professor of Early Childhood Education in the School of Education at the University of Texas at Tyler. She is a national consultant for the High/Scope Educational Research Foundation and is the co-editor of Family Friendly Communications published by NAEYC.

Chapter 14

Library

Mary Ann Waldon

Marisa and Lori are lying on their stomachs on the carpeted floor discussing a book. "My dad has a truck like that," Lori says. On a soft pillow nearby, Jose looks at a book, turning each page slowly.

At the table, Clairise and Jena have finished creating stick puppets and begin having their puppets speak to each other. "What are you going to do today, Sam?" says one. "I'm going swimming," replies the other.

anguage development occurs in all centers throughout the early childhood room as children interact with materials and engage in activities. Such experiences enable children to discover through all their senses and then interact with others about what they are learning. Using language is of key importance in language development (Morrow, 1997).

However, the library center (also referred to as the language arts center or book area), emphasizes activities that encourage language and attention to the printed word. This center becomes part of the literate environment that encourages literacy. Children who have stories read to them become interested in messages that can be attained through books. In addition, brain cells are triggered; many existing connections are strengthened and new brain cell connections are formed (White House Conference, 1996). Children will be more easily led into reading because they have already been immersed in print and the printed word (Jewell & Zintz, 1986; Newman, Copple & Bredekamp, 1999).

Language is closely related to thinking, although the precise nature of that relationship is not known (Machado, 1995). As children interact with the environment, they form concepts and need names for objects and experiences. By providing enriching experiences, labels and dialogue, adults can encourage both language and intellectual growth. Social and verbal interaction, with other children and adults, within a variety of contexts expands a child's sentence structure, which along with vocabulary growth are measures of the child's language development.

Space Requirement

The library center is most effective when it occupies a quite area with little traffic. It should be large enough to accommodate children lying down to read as well as sitting at a table to explore language enhancing materials and activities.

The library center invites more involvement of the children when it is a soft environment that promotes a feeling of quiet relaxation. One can make the environment soft by covering the floor with a rug or carpet,

adding large pillows or bean bag chairs, and supplying several stuffed animals. A book nook or cozy spot can be made from an oversized cardboard box, covered with contact paper, and tipped on its side with a pillow inside.

A table where children can dictate their own stories into a tape recorder, for example, or listen to a tape as they follow along in a book is desirable. Video cassettes of familiar stories, children's plays and musicals may be viewed by children as well. An easily accessible electric outlet will allow for the use of tape recorders, record players and other equipment. Of course, safety precautions must be followed. Adults should set up the electrical connections though children can be taught to safely operate equipment.

A display book stand displaying the full front covers of books will encourage children to self-select and examine books of interest. There should be a book case to store additional books that are not on display allowing for rotation of books and easy access when special interests or topics arise.

In addition to the book display stand, furniture should include a child-size table with two to three chairs as well as a child-size rocking chair, floor pillows or other cozy furnishings and places to enjoy books.

Materials

It is recommended that there be approximately 100 books to allow for rotation into the library center with about 15 to 20 books on display at one time. Books from the local public library can augment the supply of facility owned books.

When selecting books, adults should consider the characteristics of preschool children. Read (1993) has identified the following language and literacy characteristics of young children and suggests considerations for book selection:

Rapid acquisition of language	Books with language slightly more complex than the children use, with some new words, repetition and rhyming
Relatively short attention span	Book length matched to the child's ability to attend
Curiosity about the world	Books about people with experiences similar to their own and reflecting the daily lives of children and their parents
Imagination	Stories that personify animals or inanimate objects
Need for warmth, affection, and secure relationships	Stories that have happy or just endings that portray mastery or heroic action
Greater sense of autonomy	Stories that portray other children, animals, or people who are coping with the stresses of growing up to lessen the feeling of dependency
Beginning distinction between	Make-believe stories that portray danger, death, strife, generosity, and kindness but that end with a sensible resolution to help children distinguish reality from fantasy.

With these characteristics in mind, teachers should aim for variety in selecting children's books. Literature for children can be classified into many different genres (Edwards, 2002) and should include:

- concept books, such as those about shapes, colors, sizes, direction, and objects and their functions

- Mother Goose rhymes and poetry books, which enable children to hear rhyme and have fun with words

- nonsense books, which help children develop humor

- wordless picture books, which promote speech, imagination, and creativity

- predictable books which contain a simple repetitive story line that enables children to participate in the story reading or telling

- classics which have been loved by children over the ages such as *The Three Bears*.

It is worth noting here that fantasy and fairy tales for very young children should be selected carefully. Although some stories and books such as *Where the Wild Things Are* by Maurice Sendak, help children handle their fears, other books might be too violent (for example, gobbling the grandmother in *Little Red Riding Hood*) or contain negative stereotypes such as the portrayal of women as wicked stepmothers and witches).

In addition to striving for variety, teachers should consider some general criteria in selecting books.

- Stories have high literary and artistic value leading children to request that they be read over and over again.

- Stories have simple, definite plots.

- Stories have a climax that leaves children feeling satisfied.

- Stories have action, suspense, engaging characters, and repetition.

- The vocabulary and comprehension level matches the ages and interests of children. Books for 3-year-olds have more pictures and less print than books for 5-year-olds.

- Stories depict various ages and ethnic groups in positive ways. Depiction of various ages enable children to see models of all generations, that is, grandmother and grandfather figures, parent figures, and children.

Multicultural books give children opportunities to see and value many cultures, including their own.

- Stories are free of gender bias. They depict girls and boys equally engaged in a variety of roles and displaying a variety of emotions and attitudes (for example, girls can be brave and boys can exhibit tenderness and nurturing behavior).

- Books about special needs topics should be available.

- Illustrations are large, realistic, and colorful and photographic images are crisp and clear.

- Books are easily held by a child. Children prefer a book with one story rather than an anthology. Cloth and board books are types of books more easily handled by very young children.

- Books are sturdy and well constructed.

Books selected according to these considerations enable children to enjoy their early literacy experiences, and begin to develop more positive concepts about others. Stories that portray prosocial themes and anti-bias perspectives help children develop concepts and attitudes essential to participation in a democratic society.

In addition to books, a library center can be stocked with other materials that promote language development. These materials include a flannel board and flannel board stories, story cards to sequence, puppets, teaching pictures and pertinent objects, which can be rotated into and out of the center as needed. Selection of these materials is based on the same criteria for selecting books.

A flannel board can be made by covering heavy cardboard or wood with flannel or felt. Felt, flannel, or interfacing fabric such as Pellon© can be used for the characters and other figures or objects in a story. The lighter weight interfacing fabric is transparent enough to trace the characters directly from a book and then color them.

Placing characters on a flannel board as one tells the story engages attention and listening. Later children can use the story characters to retell the stories to each other.

Many of the furnishings and materials for the library center such as a rug, pillow, puppets, bookcases, and books may be purchased in garage sales. In addition, pillows and puppets can be made easily from household items. A soft stuffing for pillows is clean discarded nylon hose. Puppets can be made from a variety of materials such as socks, popsicle sticks and paper sacks.

Teaching pictures on a variety of topics can be purchased in educational materials stores and through catalogs. However, pictures that promote discussion and language development are readily available from magazines and catalogs. Pictures should be large and selected according the children's interests. They can be mounted on colored construction paper and covered with clear contact paper or laminated. Pictures should depict various ages and ethnic groups in positive ways. They can be stored by topic in file folders.

Planning for Children with Special Needs

Few adaptations in book selections will be needed for children with special needs because book titles can cover a range of topics and reading levels. It is important to select books that help all children understand special needs and challenges. Two examples of such books are *See You Tomorrow Charles* by Miriam Cohen and *I have a Sister, My Sister is Deaf* by Jean Whitehouse Peterson. Be aware of the special sensitivity of any child; select a book dealing with that sensitivity and read it with the child and share it with the group.

The physical space in the library center may need to be arranged to accommodate children with physical/motor, visual or auditory challenges. For example a child in a wheelchair or walker assisted will need a space to navigate among the book display and table areas. Books and other material should be placed on upper shelves within easy reach rather than on shelves near the floor. Children with visual impairments may need books with large bold print. Or perhaps stories can be enjoyed through the use of cassette tapes and head sets for listening. Children with auditory impairments benefit from stories that are signed to them by someone skilled in signing. Creating an inclusive environment is essential. Design the library/language arts center so that no child can be left out and children with special needs can enjoy as much independence as possible.

Outdoor Extensions

Expanding the library center to the outdoors is a simple extension of the indoor library center. Guiddemi and Eriksen suggest five "zones" of outdoor activities: nature, adventure play, active play, quiet learning, and quiet play (Rivkin, 1995), p. 22). Two of these zones of play for children, quiet play and quiet learning, can happen anywhere on the playground and can be adopted for use for the literature environment outdoor (Rivkin, 1995).

One of the most appropriate would be a shady spot perhaps under a tree. A tray with a handle often used for cleaning supplies can be a simple carrier for books. A blanket can be carried out for sitting.

The outdoor environment is a very suitable place for the dramatic play extension of book reading. Simple props can be provided for the dramatic play. Dramatic play provides opportunities for movement both outdoors and indoors. Studies suggest that there is a strong relationship between dramatic and pretend play and early brain growth and neurological development (Jensen, 1998).

Activities

Book related activities help children develop early literacy skills and can support curriculum themes or topics. The activities may reinforce a concept presented in a group activity or may be geared to particular needs of children in the class.

An adult should be available in the center for two types of activities: 1) to read stories to a group of two or three children, and 2) to write titles or stories that children dictate after an activity. Reading to children leaves them with positive feelings about books and reading, especially when they sit with a nurturing caregiver. Research suggests that engaging positive emotions during literacy experiences may produce chemical changes in the brain that are beneficial (Jensen, 1998).

Dictation, often referred to as a "language experience story," should be taken in print script form. Language dictation serves several purposes. First, it helps children learn that ideas can be read from the printed page. This implies that the teacher reads back with the child what the child has dictated. Second, it provides an opportunity for children to see their language in printed form and learn to follow the printed word from right to left on the page. Third, it promotes respect for the child's language and expression of ideas. Several selections of children's dictation and drawings on the same topic may be combined into a book, which is placed in the library center. Having books that are dictated by the children increases their appreciation and enjoyment of language and books.

Caps for Sale (*Age 3 and up*)

Objective: to attend for five minutes while a story is read.

Materials needed: *Caps for Sale* by Esphyr Slobodkina, caps to be worn by the teacher and children.

What to do:

1. Place all the caps upon your head and begin reading *Caps for Sale* to three or four children. As the story proceeds, use the caps to dramatize what happens with them. Encourage the children to participate in the story by taking the caps at the appropriate times in the story. Have them throw down the caps when the peddler tricks the monkeys into throwing down the caps so that he can pick them up.

2. Place the book and caps in the library center. Children will pick up the book to tell the story to each other and use the caps to dramatize the story as they tell it.

And still more:

1. Encourage the children to tell the story to their parents.

2. Continue reading many different types of stories to children in the center on other days. Use simple props and use your voice as the means of conveying the message.

Find the Pairs *(Age 4)*

Objective: To identify a pair of objects/pictures on request.

Materials needed: Container such as box or basket; pairs of items such as earrings, doll shoes, mittens, shoe laces, stockings, and other items that are readily available in pairs; pictures of paired items such as hands, feet, shoes, roller skates, and socks.

What to do:

1. Place the box or basket of objects in front of the children and have two children try to pair the objects.

2. Have children point out the paired items in the pictures to each other, naming the pairs as they work.

And still more:

1. Encourage children to design their own pair of mittens by tracing around another child's hands with fingers placed close together. Later have the children share their mittens in a group and tell about their designs.

2. Encourage parents to point out pairs and discuss them with children.

My Story *(Age 5)*

Objective: To sequence a story consisting of three to five parts

Materials needed: A wordless picture book such as *One Frog Too Many* by Mercer and Marianne Mayer; a tape recorder and cassette tape

What to do:

1. Place the wordless book in the library center.

2. Demonstrate how to operate the tape recorder. Have a child tell his or her story into the tape recorder and play it back to listen. Children's versions will vary according to their interpretations.

3. If you wish, play back the story to a group of children as they observe the pictures.

And still more:

1. Allow each child to use a separate tape and play it back for the child's parents.

2. Cut up an old book to create a picture sequence story. Place the story in an envelope with the title on the outside. Encourage children to place the pictures in sequence and tell the story into a tape recorder.

Theme Activities
Theme: Community Workers
What I Want to Be

Objective: To develop vocabulary and language related to various careers

Materials needed: Wordless books on careers such as *What I Want to Be When I Grow Up* by Carol Burnett, George Mendoza, and Sheldon Secunda, tape player, cassette tape, listening post with headset that plugs into the tape player (optional)

What to do:

1. Make a tape to accompany the book. Begin with an introduction such as "This book is about some of the things you can do when you grow up. In this book Carol Burnett, a TV actress pretends to be many things so you can see the different clothes people wear and what they do. Let's look at the book together. Find the page that has the star (placed on the page where you want to begin). We will start there."

2. Talk about the career depicted on each page. For example, on the page showing Carol Burnett as a deep sea diver, you might say: "Do you see the special mask she is wearing that helps her breathe under water? Deep-sea divers explore the oceans, which have deep water. They find many kinds of plants and animals. Would you like to be a deep sea diver?"

3. Continue through the entire book. Call attention to important features in the illustrations and invite children to talk about them. Give clear directions about turning the pages so children can look at the pictures about which you are speaking.

4. Have children listen to the tape and look at the book individually or in a small group. A listening post will enable a child to listen to the tape without distracting other children in the center.

And still more:

1. After children listen to the tape, ask children to draw what they would like to be with crayons. When they have finished, have them dictate what they would like to be while you write what they say.

2. Share the pictures and dictations with parents or bind the pictures into a book to be placed in the library.

Our Flannel Board Picture

Objective: To tell about a picture constructed from felt shapes

Materials needed: A small flannel board, felt or flannel shapes such as circle, square, rectangle, triangle

What to do:

1. Have children work in pairs designing a picture with shapes. Young children may make a design that is pretty to them. Older children may create objects or a scene.

2. As the children work, encourage them to talk about what they are making and how they are making it.

And still more:

1. Use the flannel board to follow up small or large group story telling or reading.

2. Place pictures or puppet characters in the center and encourage children to tell their versions of the story using the characters. This activity can be important in a multicultural emphasis with stories from many cultures. (*Note:* a simple flannel board can be created by pasting flannel or felt inside a box lid. Flannel board shapes and characters can be stored inside the box.)

Shapes

Watch My Shape

Objective: To talk about one's own creative design or picture with shapes.

Material needed: Basic shapes cut from colored construction paper; sheets of 9 by 12 inch newsprint or manila paper; glue or paste; clean styrofoam trays

What to do:

1. Have precut construction paper shapes in trays for easy selection by the children.

2. Encourage children to select shapes and make a picture or design on the paper. (The design or picture should be the child's idea, not predetermined by adults.)

3. Have each child name or tell about the picture according to his or her language ability. Use statements or questions such as, "What name would you like to give your picture? Do you have anything else you would like to say about your picture?" Print exactly what the child states.

And still more:

1. Use only one shape but in different colors for children to use in creating their designs or pictures.

2. Either before or after the activity, read *Shapes, Shapes, Shapes* by Tana Hoban, which contains photographs of shapes in the environment. Pause after asking questions so children have an opportunity to name and find shapes.

3. Accept and expand upon the answers children give encouraging further dialogue.

4. Encourage parents to find and talk about shapes in the environment with their child.

References

Burnett, C., G. Mendoze, & S. Secunda (1975). *What I want to be when I grow up.* NY: Simon & Schuster.

Cohen, M. (1983). *See you tomorrow, Charles*. NY: Greenwillow Books.

Edwards, L.C. (2002). *The creative arts: A process approach for teachers and children*. Columbus, OH: Merrill/Prentice Hall.

Hoban, T. (1986). *Shapes, shapes, shapes*. NY: Greenwillow Books.

Jensen, E. (1998). *Teaching with the brain in mind*. Alexandria, VA: Association for Supervision and Curriculum Development.

Jewell, M. & M. Zintz. (1986). *Learning to read naturally*. Dubuque, IA: Kendall/Hunt.

Machado, J.M. (1995). *Early childhood experiences in language arts: Emerging literacy* (5th ed.). Albany, NY: Delmar.

Mayer, M. & M. Mayer (1975). *One frog too many*. NY: Dial.

Morrow, L.M. (1997). *Literacy development in the early years* (3rd ed.). Boston: Allyn & Bacon.

Neuman, S.B., C. Copple & S. Bredekamp. (1999). *Learning to read and write: Developmentally appropriate practices for young children*. Washington, DC: National Association for the Education of Young Children.

Peterson, J.W. (1977). *I have a sister: My sister is deaf*. NY: Harper & Row.

Read, K. (1993). *Early childhood programs: Human relationships in learning* (9th ed.). NY: Holt, Rinehart, & Winston.

Rivkin, M.S. (1995). *The great outdoors: Restoring children's right to play outside*. Washington, DC: National Association for the Education of Young Children.

Sendak, M. (1963). *Where the wild things are*. NY: Harper & Row.

Slobodkina, E. (1947). *Caps for sale*. NY: W.R. Scott.

Seuss, Doctor. (1960). *One fish, two fish, red fish, blue fish*. NY: Random House.

White House Conference on Early Childhood Development and Learning (1997). *Brain development in young children: New frontiers for research, policy and practice*. Chicago, IL: University of Chicago.

Checklist for Evaluating the Library Center

Rate the items below on a scale of 1 to 4 with "needing improvement" as 1 and "outstanding" as 4.

_____1. Children frequently choose the library center.

_____2. Children have many opportunities to speak and to listen.

_____3. The center contains soft furnishings to provide a relaxing, warm atmosphere.

_____4. The center has shelves or a book stand where books are displayed within easy reach of children.

_____5. Stories depict a variety of cultures and ethnic groups in positive ways.

_____6. Stories depict a variety of ages in positive ways.

_____7. Stories convey prosocial themes and perspectives.

_____8. Books have large, colorful pictures and are easy for children to handle.

_____9. The library center has quality books that appeal to children.

_____10. The library center has table space or other appropriate spaces where children can work with language arts and literacy materials.

_____11. The library center is equipped with engaging pictures, puppets, flannel board story sets, cassette tapes or other recordings, a listening post, and other materials for building language and literacy skills.

_____12. Adults are available to interact with and assist children's use of the library center and to share books and reading experiences.

About the Author

Mary Ann Waldon, Ed.D. is a retired professor of Early Childhood Education at Texas Southern University where she served for 25 years. In addition to teaching, she directed the summer early childhood laboratory for children 3- through 5-years-old. She has also taught kindergarten and elementary school in Nebraska and has been in the education profession for 39 years. She currently serves as an early childhood consultant and a mentor for programs seeking national accreditation. She is past president of the Houston Association for the Education of Young Children and the Texas Association for the Education of Young Children.

Chapter 15

Cooking in the classroom? What better way to reinforce children's cognitive, motor, cultural, social, math, and language skills? Cooking activities help children learn cooperation and collaborative teamwork, develop self-discipline and independence, and gain a basic understanding of nutrition and kitchen science. Food preparation activities offer teachers opportunities to reinforce nutrition, health and safety concepts. Language and  *math skills develop as children investigate size, shape, texture, weight, temperature, quantity, and flavor. The overall value of cooking experiences earns this center a place in every early childhood classroom.*

Cooking

Louis Parks

Social and Cultural Impact of Cooking

In their experiences with food in the early childhood classroom, children will learn that growing and preparing foods is a cooperative effort. Through food related activities children may pose many questions and reveal some of their misperceptions about food. The adult needs to be responsive to children's questions about food sources and production and plan projects that clarify these curiosities. For example, children might compare bread, rice, or bean products and learn the geographic source of these foods and how they are prepared in families of various cultures. Simple discussions and picture flow charts of how foods get from the farm or other place of origin to the meal table is a sequence that children find interesting. Such a project assists children in learning about food production and distribution. Consider growing food to use in cooking activities. Herbs, for example, can be grown in small containers, or vegetables planted in a small garden plot. Hike through a pecan grove in the fall and collect nuts for examination and snack. Grow sprouts for sandwiches and salads.

Young children are keenly aware of the social nature of preparing and eating food. The social interaction that spontaneously evolves during food preparation activities provides a nice opportunity to dialogue with children about the foods of various cultures. When choosing foods and planning cooking activities, adults should be mindful of cultural diversity, food stereotypes, and dietary restrictions. The cooking center can be used to enhance understanding of similarities and differences among people while recognizing our universal need for food. A cooking activity alone will not promote cultural awareness and understanding. But in the context of a culturally responsive classroom environment, learning about foods offers another fundamental dimension to our knowledge of each other.

Food study and preparation activities provide an excellent opportunity to get parents involved. Invite parents and other significant adults to share recipes that can be adapted to a classroom cooking plan. An additional hand on cooking days will make the activity easier and the children will enjoy having a special guest share their culinary creations. Send home copies of rebus directions and encourage parents to let their children prepare food for the family. Parents are impressed with the independence and confidence children show when they can follow directions and make a tasty dessert "all by themselves."

Nutrition

A cooking center provides a natural and appropriate setting for discussions about nutrition. Help children understand what food is and how our bodies use it. Explain, in developmentally appropriate ways, that wholesome food provides the nutrients necessary for growth and good health. The way food is prepared affects its nutrient value, appearance, and taste. Teachers can teach the basics of good nutrition and encourage healthy food habits through careful menu planning, food preparation, and attractive presentation at regular meals and in the cooking center.

A variety of nutritious food choices offered to children help them to balance their intake of nutritious foods while introducing them to new food experiences. One should never insist that a child eat foods which may be aversive to them or for which they simply have no appetite. Plan cooking activities that use nutritious foods such as whole grains, fresh fruit and vegetables, and milk products. Avoid processed foods, excess salt and other seasonings, sugar, and sugar-rich foods such as marshmallows and chocolate.

What about the use of food for purposes other than nutrition? Using pudding as finger paint, potatoes for art printing, or cornmeal in the sand and water table confuses young children. If yogurt is a medium for smearing on the art table one day, why would we expect a child to eat it with a spoon the next? Consistency is a key to good teaching and effective learning. Help children understand that food is nutrition for their bodies and a resource that should not be played with or wasted. Demonstrate respect for food by encouraging children to serve themselves only as much as they will eat. Illustrate food economy by casually remarking that yesterday's leftover peas are in today's chicken casserole. Be receptive to children's suggestions about favored and disliked foods and plan accordingly.

A less tangible aspect of nutrition and cooking are the feelings and attitudes associated with food. We often use food to ease stress, help celebrate a special event, or provide a reward. These uses of food often reinforce poor nutrition habits and contribute to obesity. Changes in lifestyles and the quest for convenience, combined with the lack of basic nutritional information make packaged, processed products, eating out, fast foods, and junk snacks a way of life for many. Take advantage of the positive influence nutritious cooking activities can provide.

Skill Development

Language is enhanced through cooking activities. Children learn and practice new vocabulary, e.g., *sift, stir, grind, grate,* and *spread,* or *pinch, drop,* and *dash.* The connection between written symbols and spoken language is reinforced through rebus charts and labels on food containers. Motor skills are developed and refined when kneading bread, pouring milk, breaking an egg, and slicing a banana. Perceptual skills are strengthened through practice in sequencing, following directions, predicting change, and observing and comparing differences.

Children acquire math concepts and numeracy relationships through cooking activities. Recipes illustrated on rebus charts help children learn to sequence. Measuring tools invite comparisons and offer hands-on evidence of many math concepts such as one half is smaller than a whole. Counting and correspondences build basic numeracy skills. Making graphs and charts to show comparisons and preferences is a meaningful way to help children visualize numbers and concepts such as *more, less,* and *equal.*

Cooking Plans

In planning cooking and tasting activities for children, it is essential to know about individual food allergies and avoid foods that cause allergic reactions in children. Adults must obtain this information from parents in advance of planning these activities.

Plan One: Group Cooking

The most frequently used cooking plan is one in which the teacher demonstrates and performs the cooking tasks. This is the easiest plan to implement, but since hands-on learning is the most meaningful for young children, activities that include children in the process provide more opportunity for learning. Children should participate in the activity not just watch it. Group cooking does not require a special cooking center. Whether the activities take place in an established classroom center, or as a special project, food preparation, tasting and sharing has value in promoting cooperative attitudes and group effort.

Almost every class makes Stone Soup after reading the book. Making applesauce is a favored fall cooking activity for even the youngest cooks. Plan these cooking activities to allow all children to practice such skills as washing, chopping, measuring, and mixing ingredients. Avoid having children wait for a turn. Excessive waiting often causes children to misbehave and lose interest. Rather, the tasks can be divided so that three or four children can work on cooking while other children in the group are engaged in other learning centers. Because group cooking experiences tend to be the least hygienic, take special precautions with hand washing before each activity begins.

Plan Two: Food Preparation Trays

Food preparation trays offer a child the opportunity to work with food products and cooking techniques in a manner that is self-directed and self-paced. Trays offer a novice the time to practice such skills as sifting, using level measures, pouring, and spreading. All necessary supplies are arranged on portable trays.

In tray cooking children choose a cooking tray as they might choose a particular manipulative from a shelf. A child carries the tray to a work surface, follows the directions for the cooking activity, and returns the tray to the storage shelf for another child to use. It is best to make two food preparation trays available to avoid squabbles about sharing. The tools and materials should be changed often to encourage exploration and discovery. Again, it is important to remind children that food is not a toy but a valuable resource that must be respected. Since food preparation trays are always available to the children, take special precautions to ensure that supplies and work surfaces are sterile, utensils are easily handled and safe to use, and food products are fresh and kept free of contamination. Examples of successful tray cooking activities are shelling nuts, shaking cream into butter, sifting flour into a cup, shelling green peas or black-eyed peas, and grinding corn into cornmeal.

Plan Three: Individual Servings

Cooking centers designed for the preparation of individual servings are well suited to children of all ages and have the advantage of being the most hygienic. Preparing individual servings offers each child the opportunity for maximum independence and self-direction by using rebus charts that sequence the steps or directions for a particular recipe.

Select a recipe and break it down into simple steps. Three-year-olds can usually manage four to five steps. Older, more experienced children can be challenged by more steps. Illustrate each step on charts made from large sheets of heavy paper. For younger children, the illustrations need to be the same size as the measuring equipment that will be used. This allows children to compare the chart pictures with the actual equipment. Laminate the charts and store each recipe in a separate folder. Label the folder with the recipe name, the number of steps, and the necessary ingredients and equipment.

To use, arrange the charts in left-to-right order on the work surface. Place appropriate utensils and supplies next to each card. Equip each child with a labeled container and demonstrate each step of the recipe. Talk about the recipe with the children and encourage independence, investigation, and discovery. Children are usually eager and proud to eat their own creations even if inaccurately prepared.

Plan Four: Independent Cooking Center

In this plan, the cooking center is as integral to the early childhood environment as unit blocks and the art center. Once the center is introduced and the children have some food preparation experience, selected independent food preparation tasks offer children maximum autonomy and requires less teacher supervision.

Arrange the center in a quiet area of the room with labeled equipment displayed and accessible. Arrange a file box of no-heat recipes (peanut butter and jelly sandwiches or green salad, for example) and place clearly labeled non-perishable ingredients on a nearby shelf. Experiment with self-serve breakfast or snack in this center. Limit the number of cooks to two or three at a time. Use an ice chest for ingredients that must be kept cold. Perishable ingredients must be removed from the learning center at the end of the cooking period and stored safely for the next day. Set an attractive place for

eating the prepared food. After the cooking activity, assist children in learning to clean up and restore the center for another activity.

Space Requirements

Space requirements for the cooking center will vary according to frequency of use, children's ages and experience, and the cooking plan. A quiet corner or wall area will allow children to cook without being distracted by other activities. A firm and sturdy work surface is essential and should be an appropriate height for the children. Chairs are not necessary and are best removed from the area. Accessibility to running water makes preparation and clean-up easier.

Many cooking activities can be performed without electric appliances. The best equipped cooking centers will need only a crock pot for soups and stews and an electric fry pan with securely fitting lid for simmering and heating. With the lid in place, the skillet works as an oven for baking. Pour batters for breads and cupcakes into wax-coated paper cups. The bottom of the cup may darken with the skillet heat but the wax coating keeps food from burning. To bake cookies, warm tortillas, or make skillet pizzas, for example, line the bottom of the pan with aluminum foil, cover, and bake. Make certain that any appliance used is clean and in good repair.

Heated appliances should be strategically placed on a secure and sturdy surface with the electrical cord in a protected position to prevent pulling or tripping. Never run long cords across the floor. The placement of the appliance should be away from the main traffic patterns and a "hot zone" marked off with red plastic tape. Only the adult should manage the use of the heated appliance, and should closely supervise the cooking activity.

Basic Supplies

- wooden spoons
- plastic or metal mixing bowls
- plastic knives with serrated edges
- small plastic pitcher
- measuring spoons
- measuring cups, both liquid and dry
- egg beater
- vegetable peeler
- plastic grater
- cutting boards
- aluminum foil

- pot holders
- electric frying pan with secure lid
- crock pot with secure lid
- storage container for equipment

Other supplies may be needed depending on the recipe. Teachers should check each recipe in advance so that needed supplies and equipment can be made ready for children's use.

Sanitation and Safety

It is essential to practice basic sanitation and safety procedures when incorporating cooking activities into classroom activities. Follow the safety and health precautions below, making modifications according to your own experience and the capabilities of children in the group. Consistently follow health and safety routines with children, and be prepared to frequently remind children of healthy and safe practices. Repetition and clear expectations foster self-discipline and contribute to the success of each activity.

Safety Precautions

- Adults must provide vigilant supervision.

- Have hair and clothing pulled back and out of the way. Talk with the children about why chefs and commercial cooks wear hairnets, hats, and aprons.

- Encourage children to wear special cooking aprons, not the smocks they use for art or water-play activities.

- Mark off a "hot zone" around electric appliances with red plastic tape.

- Demonstrate and teach respect for cooking utensils and supplies. Plastic serrated knives work well for most cutting and spreading tasks. Help children learn to push a vegetable peeler away from their bodies and toward the work surface. Consider safety over efficiency when choosing tools for the cooking center. A wire whip, blender, electric skillet, plastic grater, and toaster oven are safer than their counterparts eggbeater, mixer, hot plate, metal grater, and kitchen range.

- Use care in selecting foods. With toddlers, avoid grapes, nuts, raw vegetables, coin cut hot dogs, popcorn, and other slippery or difficult to chew and swallow foods. When preparing food with older children, demonstrate and insist on small bites and careful chewing with a closed mouth. Children should not walk about (or run and play) while chewing and eating.

Health Precautions

- Post a hand washing reminder. A hand washing rebus chart posted above the sink teaches children to do an effective job of getting their hands clean. Have children wash their hands thoroughly before and after handling food.

- Color code preparation and serving utensils with plastic tape. Teach children that the spoons with red tape, for example, are used for mixing and never tasting.

- Teach children to turn their bodies to sneeze or cough. Insist that hands are rewashed after touching the eyes, blowing the nose, or coughing or sneezing into the hand.

- Rewash and sanitize all cooking and eating utensils following the activity.

- Be aware of food allergies and restrictions. Choose recipes that all of the children in the group can prepare and eat.

Planning for Children with Special Needs

In *Anti-Bias Curriculum: Tools for Empowering Young Children*, the authors assert that "People with disabilities are not handicapped by their conditions but by prejudice, lack of accessibility, and discrimination" (Derman-Sparks, 1987). The limitations of prejudice and discrimination are personal and complex. But in every classroom cooking center, however, every child can be an able participant through equal access. Teachers can affix cooking trays to wheelchairs and provide a work surface that is suitable to use with a body board or wheel chair. Purchase adaptive utensils or adapt your own to facilitate grasping and handling. Develop a file of recipes with strongly scented ingredients. Use rebus charts to allow children to work independently and at a comfortable pace. Allow children sufficient time to complete a task and enjoy its product.

Activities

Grow Bean Sprouts

(Group cooking. Prepare with groups of four children, 3 years and older)

Objective: To observe and participate in the production of food

Materials needed: 1 tablespoon of alfalfa or mung

seeds, a large, clear plastic jar with lid, cheese cloth to cover the jar's mouth, a rubber band, running water, a bowl, a tablespoon

What to do:

1. Introduce the activity by telling the children that they will grow food that they can eat. Discuss food farming, production, distribution, and marketing.

2. Wash hands.

3. Place one tablespoon of seeds in two cups of water in the jar. Cover the jar with cheese cloth and hold the cloth in place with the rubber band. Let the seeds soak overnight.

4. The next morning, fill the jar with water to rinse the seeds. Drain thoroughly through the cheesecloth.

5. Place the jar in a cool and dark place.

6. Repeat the rinsing process daily for an additional three days. Engage children in observation and discussion of the seed growth.

7. On the fourth day, rinse and drain the seeds, and place the jar in a sunny place. The seeds will produce chlorophyll that changes the seeds from pale to bright green.

8. On the fifth day, rinse the seeds and drain. Pour into a bowl and encourage the children to taste them.

9. Discuss how the seeds grow and make tiny plants called sprouts. Compare bean sprouts with other plants that must grow for a long time before they are ready to eat (e.g., squash, green beans, broccoli, and potatoes). Compare the taste of the sprouts with other greens such as parsley and spinach.

Extension: Combine the sprouts with another cooking activity. Sprouts are tasty on cheese sandwiches, stir-fried with rice, in a green salad, and on top of bean and cheese nachos.

Dry Grapes

(Group cooking. Prepare with groups of four to six children, 4 years and older)

Objective: To observe changes in food after sun exposure

Materials needed: Bunch of Thompson seedless grapes, cookie sheet, wire rack, purchased raisins, fresh green grapes

What to do:

1. Introduce the activity by telling children that they will compare the appearance and taste of dried grapes, raisins, and fresh grapes. Explain to the children that raisins are commercially dried grapes.

2. Wash hands.

3. Invite the children to remove the grapes from the stems.

4. Arrange the grapes with space between them on a wire rack resting on a cookie sheet.

5. Dry the grapes in hot, dry sun for several days. Observe and record the changes.

6. Place the dried grapes, raisins, and fresh grapes in bowls. Observe and record the differences in appearance.

7. Taste the dried grapes. Compare the taste to the raisins and the fresh grapes.

Raisins are a good source of iron but are also sweet and will stick to the teeth. Serve raisins with celery or apple slices; these are natural tooth cleaners. Follow all meals with thorough tooth brushing.

Peanut Butter Fondue

(Individual servings. Prepare with groups of six children, 4 years and older)

Objective: To prepare a healthy snack while practicing cutting and stirring skills.

Materials needed: rebus charts, ½ cup peanut butter, ½ cup yogurt, 3 bananas peeled and cut in half, 3 pears, sliced, electric skillet with lid, 2 measuring spoons, 6 paper cups labeled with children's names, 6 spoons, ingredients in labeled containers

What to do:

1. Prepare the rebus charts.

2. Label each cup with a child's name.

3. Have children wash their hands

4. Prepare the fruit in advance or have the children prepare it as a separate activity.

5. Set up the skillet but do not preheat.

6. Create five work stations by placing each chart on the work surface next to the necessary tools and ingredients.

7. Introduce the activity by telling the children that

Peanut Butter Fondue

1. Wash hands.

2. Add tablespoon of peanut butter.

3. Add tablespoon yogurt.

4. Stir.

5. Place in skillet.

they will make a snack for themselves. Review health and safety rules and instruct the children to avoid touching the hot skillet.

8. Demonstrate the sequence of the recipe using the charts and reading them from left to right. Spoon peanut butter into cup; add yogurt then stir and place the cup in the skillet.

9. Tell the children that you are turning on the skillet to warm the fondue. Again, caution them to keep away from the skillet area by staying on the outside of the red tape. Heat the fondue at 250 degrees for about 15 minutes. Allow to cool a bit, then serve the fondue for snack with banana halves and apple slices.

Seed, Fruit, Leaf, Pod, and Root Salad

(Individual servings. Prepare with groups of six children, 4 years and older)

Objective: To make a salad that includes all plant parts.

Materials needed: rebus charts, 1/3 cup sunflower seeds, 6 cherry tomatoes, 6 green beans, 6 lettuce leaves, 6 radishes, ½ cup salad dressing, 6 paper bowls labeled with children's names, 6 forks, 6 plastic serrated knives, 2 cutting boards, measuring spoon, ingredients in labeled containers

What to do:

1. Prepare a rebus chart.

2. Label each bowl with a child's name.

3. Have children wash their hands.

4. Wash the vegetables, slice the radishes, and remove the stem tips from the green beans.

5. Create eight work stations by placing each chart on the work surface next to the necessary utensils and ingredients.

6. Introduce the activity by talking about and showing the parts of a plant. Examine the plants together pointing out that different parts of plants are used for food, e.g., we eat cabbage leaves but not the root and we eat carrot roots but not the leaves.

7. Reading the charts from left to right, demonstrate the sequence of the recipe. Tear lettuce into bowl, cut green beans and put in bowl, cut tomato in half and add to the bowl, add radishes, then measure salad dressing into bowl, toss gently, and sprinkle

sunflower seeds on top. Refrigerate the salads and serve with lunch.

Pineapple Cheese Spread

(Individual servings. Prepare with groups of six children, 3 years and older)

Objective: To prepare a healthy snack while practicing measuring and grating skills.

Materials needed: rebus charts, 6 paper cups labeled with children's names, 8 ounces mild cheddar cheese cut in 6 cubes, ½ cup crushed pineapple, measuring spoon, plastic cheese grater, cutting board, whole wheat crackers, 6 plastic knives for spreading

What to do:

1. Prepare the rebus charts.

2. Label each cup with a child's name.

3. Have children wash their hands.

4. Create three work stations by placing each chart on the work surface next to the necessary utensils and ingredients.

5. Introduce the activity by talking about how foods are prepared for visual appeal or ease of eating. For example, a slice of cheese on a cracker with drippy pineapple on top would be messy to eat and would look unappealing. In contrast, grated cheese mixed with crushed pineapple makes an appetizing and easy to use spread.

6. Reading the charts from left to right, demonstrate the activity: wash hands, grate cheese on cutting board and place in cup, spoon pineapple into cup, and stir.

Refrigerate the children's cups unless served immediately.

Egg Salad Sandwiches

(Independent cooking. Two children, 5 years and older)

Objective: To independently make egg salad and spread it onto bread.

Materials needed: rebus charts, hard boiled eggs in ice chest, mayonnaise in ice chest, mustard, dill pickles, whole wheat bread, cutting boards, bowls, spoons, plastic serrated knives, garbage bag, serving plates

What to do:

1. Prepare the rebus charts.

2. In advance of the class activity, boil the eggs. Place

Pineapple Cheese Spread

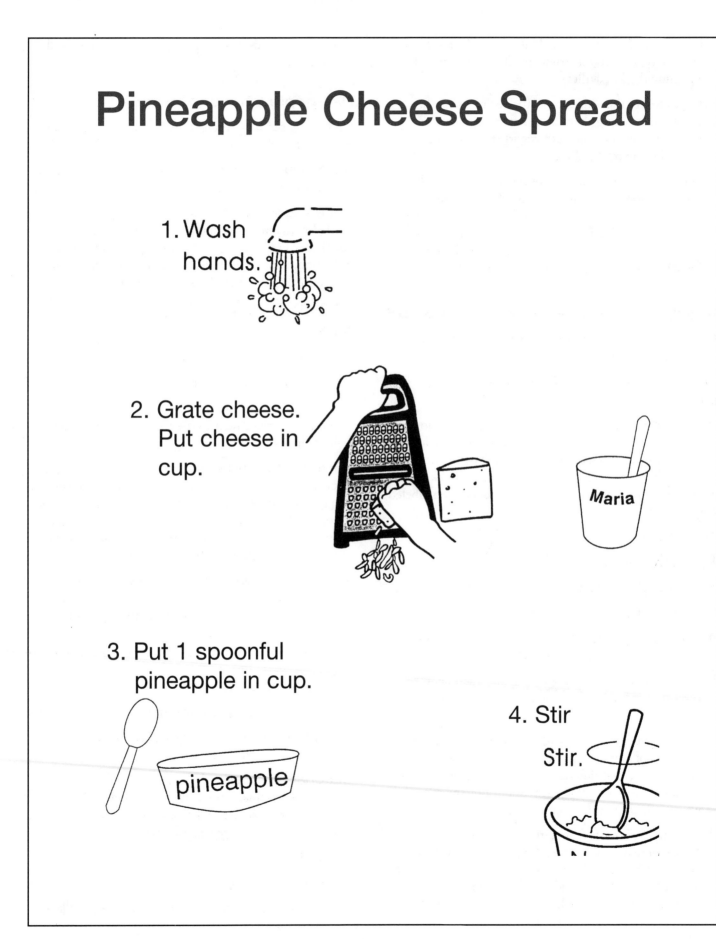

1. Wash hands.

2. Grate cheese. Put cheese in cup.

Maria

3. Put 1 spoonful pineapple in cup.

pineapple

4. Stir Stir.

eggs and mayonnaise in ice chest. Place other ingredients and equipment on nearby shelf.

3. Have children wash their hands.

4. Reading the charts from left to right, demonstrate the sequence of the recipe: peel and chop the eggs, put egg shells in garbage container; chop pickles and add to the chopped eggs; stir in mayonnaise and mustard; spread egg salad on bread; return perishables to ice chest, clean work surface, and enjoy eating the sandwich.

Variation: Encourage children to experiment with adding one or more herbs to the salad. Parsley, dill weed, tarragon, and fennel are good choices

Spring Rolls

(Independent cooking. Two children, 5 years and older)

Objective: To independently make spring rolls

Materials needed: rebus charts, cutting boards, bowls, spoons, plastic serrated knives, purchased wonton wrappers, fresh spinach, cabbage, carrot sticks, precooked rice, soy sauce, garbage bag, serving plates

What to do:

1. Prepare the rebus charts (Chapter 15, Figure 5).

2. Place wonton wrappers, spinach, carrots, cabbage, and rice in ice chest. Put other ingredients and equipment on shelf.

3. Have children wash their hands.

4. Share the rebus directions with the group.

5. Talk with the children about the ingredients. Encourage children to think about and suggest other ingredients that could be added to the recipe in the future.

6. Reading the charts from left to right, demonstrate the sequence of the recipe: grate carrots, shred cabbage, tear spinach in small pieces, mix vegetables in bowl, add rice to bowl, add soy sauce, mix together, spread on wonton wrapper, wrap roll envelope style, return perishables to ice chest, clean work surface, and enjoy eating the spring rolls.

Variation: Bean sprouts grown by the children and thoroughly washed and chopped might be add to this recipe.

Evaluation of the Cooking Center

Rate the items below on a scale of 1 to 4 with "needing improvement" as 1 and "outstanding" as 4.

_____1. Thorough hand washing is a first step in every cooking activity.

_____2. The center is a safe place for children to learn.

_____3. The cooking center encourages independence and builds self-help skills.

_____4. Children learn and use proper sanitation and food storage procedures.

_____5. All children have equal access to the center.

_____6. All recipes contain wholesome, nutritious foods from the bottom of the food pyramid.

_____7. Recipes reflect ethnic and cultural diversity.

_____8. The center encourages the involvement of all of the senses.

_____9. Activities are introduced in a way that encourages discussion, prediction, and comparison.

_____10. The activities of the center are shared with parents.

References

Johnson, B. (1978). *Cup Cooking: Individual Child-Portion Picture Recipes.* Lake Alfred, FL: Early Educators Press.

Veitch, B. & T. Harms (1981). *Cook and Learn: Pictoral Single Portion Recipes, A Child's Cook Book.* Menlo Park, CA: Addison-Wesley Publishing.

About the Author

Louise Parks is editor of *Texas Child Care Quarterly*. She has worked in early childhood education for the past 20 years as a preschool teacher, program director, and college instructor. She has served in multiple capacities in the Texas Association for the Education of Young Children and in its Austin chapter. For the past two years she has trained Self-Arranged Child Care providers for the Capital Area Workforce Development Board.

Egg Salad Sandwiches

1. Wash hands.

2. Peel egg and chop. Put in bowl.

3. Chop pickle. Add to bowl.

4. Add mayonnaise and mustard.

5. Spread on bread.

6. Return perishables to ice chest.

7. Clean work area.

Chapter 16

Manipulatives

Joan Wyde

Jessica takes a square board with nails in it and a container of colored rubber bands from a low shelf and sits on a corner of the rug. Her small hands stretch a band to fit over two nails. Selecting the other bands, she starts a pattern with the same colors going in the same direction. With her tongue sticking out, she concentrates, not looking up for a full five minutes. When she finishes the pattern, she looks up with a radiant and satisfied smile. Then she shoves the board and the container back on the shelf and skips to the housekeeping area. Bill, who has been waiting for her to finish, takes the board and container, removes the bands from the board and starts his own design.

Manipulatives Across the Curriculum

In their concentrated work, Jessica and Bill show that the process they are involved in is more important than the product they make. That process involves skillful control and coordinations of eyes and hands. During manipulative play the child handles objects and toys comprised of a number of small parts that must fit together in some meaningful or creative way. Gaining manipulative control is important for all areas of a child's development because children need manipulative skills in nearly everything they learn to do. Manipulatives are fundamental in an early childhood environment.

Teachers in early childhood programs have long been aware of the need to provide toys and activities that help children develop their fine motor skills. Manipulatives need not be provided for the manipulative center alone. Many other learning centers incorporate the same kind of materials. Manipulative materials and activities are integral to the block center, art center, science, music, and dramatic play centers where they support and enhance essential learning. Manipulative activities also occur in outdoor play.

The Manipulative Center

Although manipulative toys and activities are found in all areas of the early learning classroom and playground where they support and enhance specific types of learning, a separate area can be devoted for manipulative toys and activities. Here materials can be selected to facilitate the development of specific types of fine motor coordinations.

The manipulative center, also referred to as the table games center, the toy center, or the fine-motor center, is a quiet place where children work independently or in small groups. The materials in this center allow children to practice emerging fine motor skills in many different ways gaining visual acuity, dexterity, and fine motor strength. Manipulatives also engage cognitive processes as children discover relationships and solve problems. As children choose games to play, they interact with other children in a non-teacher-directed experience. It is always emotionally satisfying to a child to complete a puzzling or creative task, game or activity just for the fun or satisfaction of doing it. No judgments, no mistakes, no comparisons are made. Children gain inner control as they make choices and complete such manipulative activities.

According to Dodge (1988), many teachers consider the table toy area the most versatile in the classroom. A wide variety of table toys facilitate children's development in a number of areas. In their cognitive, social, emotional, and physical development, children can reach numerous learning goals through the use of these toys. In selecting goals appropriate for children's needs, teachers should consider the ones below.

Goals for cognitive development:

- To enhance creativity and problem-solving ability
- To develop concepts of color, size, shape, and function

- To sort, classify, and sequence objects in logical ways
- To learn number and quantity concepts, and
- To develop matching, pairing, and contrasting skills
- To develop awareness of symbols and other early literacy concepts and skills

Goals for social and emotional development:

- To gain experience in working with others in a small group
- To learn to work cooperatively with others
- To make choices and develop self-discipline
- To stay with a task to completion
- To learn to take intellectual and creative risks, and
- To develop self esteem and a sense of competence

Goals for physical development:

- To develop and refine fine-motor coordinations
- To enhance eye-hand coordination
- To refine visual and auditory discrimination

Materials Matched to Developmental Levels

In selecting manipulatives for the early childhood classroom the teacher should seek materials that match the developmental levels of individuals in the group. With age and individual appropriateness in mind, a variety of manipulatives should be provided that encourage children to make choices, explore, experiment, and create from a variety of materials. This process builds cognitive skills, such as sorting, classifying, observing, and learning about cause and effect. Manipulatives can also be selected for their social interaction benefits as when children share the manipulative to construct or to play games together.

Since there is always a range of abilities and experiences among children in each group, there should also be a range of activities provided in the manipulatives center (Bredekamp & Copple, 1997). A range of levels of complexity among the materials and activities allows children to work at their level. They will be able to challenge themselves with the next hardest task when they feel ready and comfortable with it.

Three-year-old children enjoy blocks of many types and sizes; objects to sort, classify and organize; materials to explore, take apart and put together, (e.g., one-inch beads and string); and puzzles consisting of eight to twelve pieces. Sewing cards are usually too difficult. Dressing frames should be limited to buttoning and zipping. Number concepts to five are being mastered.

By the time children are 4- and 5-years-old, they have gained a great deal of knowledge and experience with materials, toys and activities, and they can choose and carry out a task to completion. They are moving into a period in which they engage in more cooperative play and love to play simple games such as lotto, concentration or board games. They continue to use many types of building materials to construct, tear down, and reconstruct and to manipulate objects to learn about relationships among them. The more difficult 18-piece puzzles, as well as half-inch beads, lacing and buckling dressing frames are good. Number concepts up to 10 are being mastered now.

Activities are best planned with the young child's typically short attention span in mind. The same materials can sometimes be used to plan different levels of activities. For example, Jody might need to work on simply stringing beads, while Manuel is ready to repeat a complicated pattern sequence of different colors and shapes of beads.

Equipment and Materials

The manipulative center is a quiet center located in a low traffic area. It must have storage shelves accessible to children, a table and chairs and access to floor space. Materials must be appealing and attractively displayed on the shelves. The manipulative sets should be complete and in good repair since their condition influences the way children use and care for them. Items can be placed in clear, sturdy tote boxes and cut down plastic milk jugs or other clean recycled plastic containers. Containers should be labeled or coded with symbols, words, pictures or colors to help children know which pieces go together and where they fit on the shelves. Pictures and symbols can be cut from catalogs, box tops, or magazines and attached with clear contact paper or tape. Collections of items can be placed on a tray with baskets for sorting.

Organized shelves allow children to put toys away and gain a sense of order. The toys should be neatly displayed at the child's eye level. It is important for children to have as much control as possible over their environment. Good organization provides an opportunity for success in doing something for themselves and for others. There should be enough toys on the shelves for each child in the group to have one if he or she chooses to play with a manipulative toy. Having 12 to 15 choices available on the shelf, while the other items are stored and then rotated weekly will keep the children's interest high.

There are five types of manipulatives.

1) Toys that advance coordination abilities – dressing frames, sewing cards, strings and beads, inset puzzles, pick up sticks;

2) Construction toys of various types – interlocking plastic blocks; various interlocking items such as stars, geometric shapes and gears; and small wooden table blocks;

3) Put-together and take-apart items many of which are self correcting or have only one way to put them together – puzzles, nesting boxes, sorting boxes; (Some Montessori items such as cylinder blocks, the pink tower and color tablets fall into this category.)

4) Items that can be sorted, classified, paired, or seriated – colored cubes, attribute blocks, counting bears, nuts and bolts, plastic lids, a collection of keys or buttons, and other collections; and

5) Simple games that encourage children to work together – lotto, checkers, card and board games. (Older preschoolers are more successful with games because they are beginning to understand that games have rules, and they can remember and follow game procedures.).

Although manipulatives can be separated into these five categories, many items fit into more than one category, such as pegboards and pegs which can be used for both coordination and put together toys.

The manipulative center is designed to facilitate, reinforce, or extend learning as a child explores and experiments independently with the materials and activities. Manipulatives are meant to be handled. Materials are likely to get dirty, crumpled, lost or chewed upon. Hence, items selected for the manipulative center should be sturdy, durable, washable, and safe. Dangerous materials such as fragile items (glass, brittle plastics) or items that look edible such as plastic jellybeans, or small parts that can be swallowed or pose a choking hazard should not be used.

Materials for the manipulative center can be found in many places and are often free or inexpensive. These sources include hardware stores, grocery stores, fabric stores, lumberyards and natural settings. Many and varied types of manipulatives designed to meet many developmental goals and to address various curriculum areas are available commercially through school supply catalogs.

Use and Care of Materials

Children should be introduced to safe handling of the materials and know the rules governing their use and care. It helps children to understand the rules of the center when the teacher introduces and demonstrates how to use and care for items in the manipulative center. This can take place at circle time or with small groups of children as they move through the various centers, and should occur when new materials are added to the center.

A sensitive and supportive teacher who is ready to assist as needed guides children's use of the manipulative center. According to Piaget (1952), children construct concepts and knowledge through their exploration and play with objects. Vygotsky (1987) points out that learning is facilitated through collaborations between teacher and child. The teacher should try to strike a balance between the amount of instruction given to children and the amount of independence that can reasonably be expected to allow children to explore and discover for themselves.

Teachers should introduce new manipulative materials slowly and deliberately, and allow enough time for children to understand and adjust to the activity. When planning activities for the manipulative center, children should be involved whenever possible. For example, if a trip to the zoo is planned, the teacher might place a map layout of the zoo in the center and have the children plan which animal models are needed. Such planning helps children see that they can be active doers and make things happen for themselves.

Each activity must be available to children to use independently. How materials are displayed is important in inviting their use by children; how materials are put away is important to the sanity of teachers. Nothing is worse than having to sort and pick up thousands of little pieces at the end of a tiring day.

Safety Considerations

Adults must be constantly aware of conditions that affect the safety of all children. Younger children tend to put objects in their mouths. Small manipulative pieces are especially prone to mouthing. When setting up a manipulative center for children it is wise to check the dimensions of all of the objects by using a "choking tube" that can be obtained at many teacher's supply stores. If a choking tube is not handy, a plastic canister that 35mm film comes in can serve as a measuring device. If the toy or toy part can fit all the way inside either the tube or canister, it poses a choking hazard for children. Keep in mind that the younger the child, the larger the manipulatives must be.

Multicultural and Nonsexist Perspectives

Differences in child-rearing practices, parent's expectations, and children's role models affect the social develop-

ment and play interests of children. These prior experiences and expectations are often reflected in children's choices of play activities and the manner in which they respond to others. The manipulative center can provide positive images of all cultures represented in the class through puzzles, books, types of collections used for sorting, and visual displays. Puzzles for example, can include portrayals of people of different ethnicities; small plastic models of people and the clothes they wear can do the same.

Similarly, gender bias can be avoided when materials portray girls and boys, men and women in many contexts and roles. Again puzzles, games, stories, and illustrations can convey nonsexist perspectives. As children work along and beside other children, they gain knowledge and experience in interacting with people who may be different from themselves. By planning manipulatives that will interest all children and support learning goals in conjunction with the other areas of the curriculum, both boys and girls of many cultures will be attracted to the manipulative center.

Planning for Children with Special Needs

Administrators and teachers in early childhood programs must acquaint themselves with both the laws and the unique needs of children with disabilities. Planning for children with special needs involves working with parents to learn about individual needs, capabilities, and interests. Setting developmental and educational goals for children with special needs is a collaborative effort between parents and teachers. Other health care professionals may be involved in this planning as enlisted by the child's parents.

In planning the manipulative center with children with special needs, it is important to consider the physical spaces that the children will use and attempt to navigate. Entrances, exits, seating, pathways, table and shelf heights, and so on may need to be adjusted to accommodate the child. Some manipulatives may need to be placed in containers with handles, or trays with a lip to prevent run-away parts. Items on shelves will need to be reachable, for example, a child on crutches may not be able to reach the lower shelves to access and return materials. Children with special needs may need more assistance in handling manipulative materials. Partnering these children with a helpful playmate may provide all the assistance needed and support social interactions as well. Teachers can observe the fine motor abilities of children and select materials and activities with which a child can succeed, or adapt the materials in ways that make them more manageable and enjoyable.

Curriculum Planning

Some strategies that will help in curriculum planning include:

1) Accurately observing and recording present behavior. This may be achieved through checklists of expected behaviors, anecdotal records, standardized assessments, or even a simple count of the number of times a behavior occurs. *Note:* These records are used for setting developmental and educational goals for children and are shared with the parents only, unless otherwise directed by the parents to share with other professionals who have a legitimate reason to be informed.

2) Design a pleasant, stress-free and satisfying learning environment. Be aware that children need to learn to relax, so alternate periods of quiet and active play help children to be aware of their feelings, bodies, and muscles.

3) Offer materials and activities that encourage free and active exploration and that children may choose of their own accord.

4) Provide enough time for children to explore and practice.

5) Vary the tasks (increasing the complexity in small increments) to add interest and challenge.

6) Provide positive feedback and authentic praise for effort and success, and assist only when necessary.

7) Allow for errors, multiple attempts, and repetition.

Activities

Drawing Tray
(4- to 5-year-olds)

Objective: To increase the manipulative strength of children's hands, to practice making shapes and lines, and to track from left to right.

Materials needed: A 12- by 18-inch cookie sheet with a raised edge, about four sticks of plasticene oil-based modeling clay, various blunt drawing implements such as blunt pencils, popsicle sticks and defunct ball point pens, a small tray or cup to hold the implements.

What to Do:

1. Teacher preparation: The adult prepares the clay by warming it on the cookie sheet in a slow oven and spreading it to about 3/8 inch depth.

2. Encourage children to draw, write, poke, push or pull the implements to make marks in the clay.

3. When the clay gets too choppy, help smooth it out or put it back in a warm oven. It is also helpful to warm the tray (only slightly) before a child uses it.

And still more:

If at first the clay is too difficult for the children to use, provide trays of sand, salt or cornmeal for the children to draw in with their fingers.

Matching Bead Game
(5-years-old and older)

Objective: To sequence, take turns, and use descriptive language.

Materials needed: Two boxes or baskets with the same assortment of stringing beads and two laces; two trays lined with corrugated cardboard to keep the beads from rolling and to serve as a work surface.

What to Do:

1. Have the children work in pairs and sit back to back with the box of beads in their laps.

2. One child picks up a bead and describes it to the other child, "a small, round, red bead," for example, and strings it on to his or her lace.

3. The other child then picks up the same bead and strings it on his or her lace. After stringing five or six beads, the children compare strings to see if they are the same.

And still more:

1. Have the children take turns calling out bead descriptions.
2. Try longer strings or a more complicated bead collection.

Matching Photos
(3-years-old and older)

Objective: To match pictures and printed names, recognize self and others, name self and others.

Materials needed: Disposable color camera or a camera with color film, cardboard, glue or non-toxic photo mounting spray, marker, laminating equipment, storage box.

What to do:

Teacher preparation: Take a photograph of each child and order a double set of prints. Cut the cardboard into pieces that are the same size as the prints. Mount the photographs on the cardboard pieces, print each child's name at the bottom and laminate each card.

1. Encourage children to use the sets in different ways – recognizing themselves and friends, matching sets, or sorting.

2. Teach the children how to play concentration with the photo sets.

3. Use photographs in cubbies to help children find their belongings.

4. Make name cards to be matched to the photographs.

And still more:

Make another set of photos for a get-acquainted bulletin board.

Ask for photographs of parents or the child as a baby and make a matching game board with string extending between matched photos.

Make a class collage.

Sizes
(4-years-old and older)

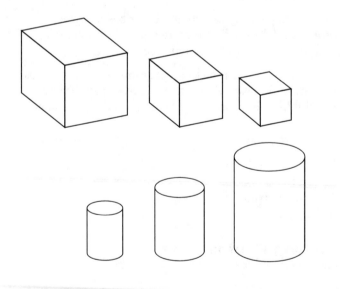

Objective: To recognize and order sizes

Materials needed: Sets of small, medium, and large items that are alike, for example, balls, boxes, toy cars, basket for storage.

What to Do:

1. Have the children sort the items by size, for example, all the small balls, boxes or cars together, followed by grouping the medium size items and then the larger ones.

2. Have the children arrange the items in rows from small to large.

And still more:

1. Have the children describe or classify objects in the room as small, medium, or large.

2. Have three children arrange themselves by height; add more children and then more. Talk about ordinal positions, first second and third.

References

Bredekamp, S. (Ed.). *Developmentally appropriate practice in early childhood programs* (Rev.ed) Washington, DC: NAEYC 1997

Dodge, D. T. (1988). *The creative curriculum for early childhood.* Washington, DC: Creative Associates International Inc.

Piaget, J. (1952). *The origins of intelligence in children.* NY: International University Press.

Vygotsky, L.S. ((1987). *Mind in society: The development of higher psychological processes.* Cambridge, MA: Harvard University Press.

Checklist for Evaluating the Manipulative Center

Rate the following items on a scale of 1 to 4 with 1 as "needing improvement" and 4 as "outstanding". Ratings that fall at 1, 2, or 3 need to be improved.

_____1. Materials are attractively displayed.

_____2. Materials and activities are stored so that children can handle them independently.

_____3. Materials are complete with no missing pieces.

_____4. There is a wide enough range of activities to challenge children. Puzzles with different numbers of pieces, games and activities with different levels of difficulty.

_____5. Shelves are clean and attractive.

_____6. Materials and activities are changed often enough to prevent boredom.

_____7. Materials and activities are safe.

_____8. Materials are included from all five types of manipulative toys – coordination, construction, problem solving, collections and games.

_____9. There is enough space for children to work comfortably on the floor or at child size tables.

_____10. Spaces and materials are provided or adapted for children with special needs.

_____11. Materials represent diverse cultures and are free of bias or stereotypes.

About the Author

Joan Wyde, Ph.D. is the Department Chair in Child Development and Education at the Houston Community College System. Her background includes studies in Studio Art, English as A Second Language, Curriculum Development, Family Counseling, Early Childhood and Educational Psychology. She has served on the board of the Houston Area Association for the Education of Young Children, various boards, task forces and community organizations and is a frequent presenter at conferences and workshops. She is also the author of journal articles and the co-author of the textbook: *Early Childhood Growth and Development: Connecting Theory and Practice*.

Geometric Inset Shapes

Chapter 17

Woodworking

Gordon D. Bacon

Whack, Whack. John, 4 years old, hammers a nail into a scrap of wood at the workbench. He enjoys making a little noise after sitting quietly through circle time. He glances through his goggles at Juanita, 5 years old, while she glues together two small pieces of wood. She has just finished sawing the wood she plans to use to make a baby bed for her doll."Want to use the hammer?" he asks."No, I want it to look pretty," she replies. Holding the two pieces of wood tightly, she runs off to show the teacher what she has done.John adjusts his goggles, grasps the hammer, and goes back to whacking nails into the board.

Woodworking encourages children to learn more about themselves and the world around them. Through woodworking, children can broaden and refine their cognitive, physical, emotional, and social skills. Woodworking encourages in children the development of creative expression and pride in accomplishment. It aids in both small and large muscle development as well.

The woodworking center is sometimes referred to as the carpentry or construction center. No matter what it is called, developmental theory and research support the value of woodworking. Through the years, child development scholars have stressed the importance of first hand, concrete experiences to enhance children's development. This widely accepted belief about how young children best learn is for the most part, attributed to Jean Piaget, a Swiss psychologist whose theories of cognitive development continue to guide early education practice. There are a number such benefits to woodworking. Woodworking gives children the opportunity to:

- develop small and large muscle coordination;

- improve hand-eye coordination through the manipulation of tools;

- stimulate thinking and problem solving;

- release emotional and physical stress;

- build concepts of size, form, equality and other proportional relationships;

- create and develop good work habits; and

- learn social skills through sharing and working together.

One could argue that many other early childhood activities provide these same or similar opportunities. However, woodworking offers several unique possibilities. First, children can investigate and experiment with a variety of tools. As in cooking, for example, early mastery of certain tools provides the basis for other skills. Second, basic construction activities allow children to plan and execute ideas which produce a tangible product for them to evaluate and improve. Third, the children can develop specific motor and cognitive skills related to building such as measuring, hammering nails, sanding wood, sawing wood, drilling holes, and gluing. Fourth, the center provides the teacher with an opportunity to reinforce safety guidelines.

Despite its many benefits, the woodworking center is available only on a temporary or part-time basis for children's use in many early childhood programs. The limited number of children who can participate at any one time, the need for constant supervision, the time required to complete a project, the cost of tools and materials, the potential for injury, and limited teacher knowledge of woodworking are all obstacles that can be overcome. By offering woodworking in a planned and caring environment, teachers and children reap its engaging and rich benefits. Among other benefits, both adults and children learn that in this world of plastics it feels and smells good to work with wood.

Getting Started with Woodworking

Before setting up a woodworking center, a teacher should learn about tools and wood. Knowledge about woodworking will give a teacher the confidence to introduce the activity to children. A good place to start is the reference list at the end of this chapter. After reading about woodworking one should get some hands-on practice. Ask a high school shop teacher or a parent skilled in woodworking to explain different types of wood and show you how to use the tools. Plan an on-site workshop for staff in working with wood.

Woodworking is a noisy activity that requires a clearly defined space. A work space of 3 feet by 4½ feet allows enough elbow room for two children to work at the same time while preventing crowding and accidents. Avoid placing the workbench near quiet centers, and for safety reasons, locate the center away from the flow of traffic. Help children working in the center learn to focus on their activity. Distractions are dangerous when children are working with tools.

Consider setting up the woodworking area in an empty room, in a hallway, outdoors or in an area away from the flow of traffic yet easily viewed and supervised by adults. Placing the woodworking center in a corner helps because distractions can come from only two directions. However, the woodworking center should not be so isolated that children feel cut off from everyone else or do not have reasonable access to other learning activities. Constructed items can often be incorporated into other centers; for example, the "wall plaque" of nature twigs might be hung in the science center.

The area needs special storage for tools and other materials. For a permanent center, some teachers use a pegboard frame that has been painted with a dark outline or shadow for each tool. This helps children match shapes so they can easily return tools to their proper hooks. The hooks should lock in place so they will not fall out. For a temporary woodworking center, a tool box is helpful for tool storage. Since children searching for a tool may cut themselves or damage tools, the teacher should place only selected (non-cutting or blunt) tools such as hammers and files in it and carefully supervise access. Children should not be able to use tools until after the adult has given a careful orientation to the nature and function of each tool.

For safety and maintenance, tools should be stored in a secure place at the end of each day and during the weekends and holidays. This is particularly necessary when the facility spaces are shared with another group that may not be familiar with proper tool use and safety rules.

Equipment and Materials

Although specific projects may entail the use of specialized tools, a woodworking center requires certain basic equipment:

Workbench A workbench must be sturdy and solid so that it will not move when children hammer or saw. The proper height for a workbench is a little shorter than half a child's height or approximately a child's waist height, typically around 24 inches. An alternative to purchasing a child size workbench, is to shorten the legs of a sturdy kitchen table to an appropriate height. A solid wood door placed on wooden packing boxes might also be used. One should make certain that all units of this workbench are secure and properly reinforced for stability and safety.

Hammers The woodworking center should have at least two hammers. The best type is a steel-shank, curved claw hammer. Ten ounce hammers are best for preschoolers and 13-ounce hammers are better for kindergarten and primary school children. Teach children to hold the hammer near the end for maximum power and leverage. Children tend to hold a hammer near the head when it is too heavy. This causes nails to bend and their arms to tire. A hammer that is too light causes children to use too strong a stroke. A toy hammer is never acceptable because it does not work correctly.

Saw A quality steel backsaw, which has a ridge top edge or back and 10 to 14 teeth per inch, is best for children to use. The steel back keeps the saw from bending, a great frustration to any saw user. A dull saw is more dangerous than a sharp one because it requires more force to use, and children can hurt themselves in the struggle to make the saw work.

Nails A variety of nails creates interest. Start beginners with nails that have large-size heads, such as roofing or common nails. Use them with sheets of styrofoam or cardboard to practice hammering techniques. As children get more experienced, nails with smaller heads such as finishing nails can be introduced. Four-penny (4d) and six penny (6d) nails as well as 1-inch and 1-inch nails are good to have on hand. Store nails in clear plastic (not glass) peanut butter jars. Glue a different size nail to each jar lid for a sorting exercise. Buying nails by the pound is less expensive then by the box.

Vise A vise mounted on the workbench holds wood securely and allows children to use both hands in sawing, hammering, and sanding. Consider having a vise on each end of the workbench. C-clamps, which are less expensive, can be used in place of a vise. C-clamps enable a child to hold firmly large pieces of wood.

Eggbeater-type Hand Drill and Bits The drill should be introduced only after the children have had ample experience in the woodworking center. Children should have fairly well coordinated motor skills (usually 5-years-old and older) to succeed with this task and to safely use these tools. Show the children how to tap a small nail hole that will help center the bit for drilling. Buy several different standard bits that are available in sizes from (1/16-inch to 1/4-inch). Bits smaller than 1/8-inch break easily and frustrate children and their teachers. Have one drill and two or three bits available.

Wood Wood scraps of various sizes and shapes stimulate a child's imagination. Visit a lumberyard and ask a salesperson to show you standard wood types, sizes, and prices. Inquire about scraps that the lumberyard might be willing to donate. In selecting wood, remember that with children, white pine, poplar, cedar, and spruce are best to use. Construction grade yellow pine is not appropriate in the woodworking center. It is hard, knotty, and splinters easily making it difficult for even experienced woodworkers to manage. Since lumber can be expensive, obtaining wood scraps from a local professional cabinetmaker or someone who does woodworking as a hobby is a good option. These scraps will be varied and more interesting than those from a construction site and hard woods can be used for gluing.

An old tree limb (bark removed) is another satisfactory woodworking material. Children can use it to practice hammering, sawing, and sanding. Help children understand that all lumber begins as tree wood. Call children's attention to the grain and the annual rings that indicate the tree's age. Sometimes a limb suggests a form for sculpture; some hard work with a saw and sandpaper can produce a work of art. For inexpensive wood substitutes, use fiberboard, acoustical tile, styrofoam, plasterboard, and bundles of cardboard taped together.

Sandpaper Sandpaper comes in a variety of grades. Garnet or aloxite paper is more economical than flint paper. A good woodworking center keeps at least three grades of sandpaper on hand: coarse, medium, and fine. Sandpaper wrapped around and tacked to the back of a clean chalkboard eraser is easier for children to use than a flat sheet. The new sanding sponge blocks work well and unlike regular sandpaper, can withstand water.

Glue Yellow wood glue works best and is waterproof when dry. Wood glue is easy to clean up with water but hard to paint when dry.

Safety Goggles Require children to wear safety goggles when sawing or nailing. Most other woodworking activities can be performed without goggles. Flying sawdust, nails, and wood chips can injure an eye. Goggles should be comfortable for the child wearing them and should not restrict breathing. Help children learn to adjust the elastic strap so the goggles are neither too tight nor too loose. Check for properly worn goggles before children begin their woodworking activities. Plastic visors that can be easily raised or lowered are popular with children

In addition to the larger equipment, the woodworking center should have materials such as:

- carpenter's apron
- a carpenter's pencil
- dust pan with brush magnet for picking up nails
- pliers
- spoon dowels of different size structures
- glue
- clamps such as rubber band, masking tape, and clothespins
- mallet or soft rubber-headed hammer
- ruler and yardstick in metric and standard scale
- tongue depressors

As children become more experienced, the following items might be added:

- crosscut saw
- coping saw
- nuts and bolts of different sizes
- phillips and flat head screws and screwdrivers, (stubbles work best)

Interesting props and accessories help to make woodworking more realistic and meaningful.

Examples of appropriate props and accessories include:

- native woods and tree bark
- mounted pictures showing forests, lumber jacks logging, sawmills, logs in transport, cabinet makers, wood working tools, and construction projects in progress
- books, audio cassettes tapes, and finger plays on wood related topics
- hardware items such as hooks, knobs, wooden wheels and casters.

Thrift stores and garage sales are good sources for these items. Be judicious in the use of props, as too many can be distracting. Remember that the primary function of the woodworking center is to provide opportunities for children to learn new skills and to have fun.

Engage the interest and resources of parents of children enrolled in the early childhood program. Parents can provide used tools and materials that are still workable and in good repair. If they have carpentry skills, invite them to demonstrate and assist children in the use of specific tools.

Activities

Tool Concentration Game

Objective: To introduce children to tools

Materials needed: Two sets of pictures cut from magazines or catalogs of common tools such as hammer saw, pliers screwdriver, vise, 3- by 5-inch index cards, glue, scissors, and markers

What to do:

1. Cut two pictures of each tool. Glue each picture to an index card, making a matched pair.

2. Print the name of each tool above the picture. Although reading ability is not necessary to participate in this activity, labeling helps children develop print awareness and word associations.

3. Instruct the children on how to play Concentration: First, turn all the cards face down. Then each child turns up two cards and attempts to find a match. In finding a pair, the child names the pictured tool and takes another turn. When all pairs are matched, shuffle the cards and start over.

Wood Gluing
(2 years and older)

Objective: To become familiar with wood and its properties: texture, weight, smell, and uses.

Materials needed: Small pieces of wood, wood glue, butcher paper, brushes and water-based paint.

What to do:

1. Cover the table with butcher paper. Place an assortment of wood pieces on the paper.

2. Encourage children to stack, arrange, and make designs with the wood pieces.

3. Discuss how the wood feels and smells. Encourage children to compare the wood texture to their clothing, hair, plastic, and other objects around them.

4. Show the children how glue will make the wood pieces stick together. Encourage them to build structures.

5. After the glue has dried, the children may paint the structures.

Wood Clamping and Sawing

Objective: To introduce children to the vise, C-clamp, and backsaw.

Materials needed: Goggles, workbench vise, C-clamp pieces of soft pine l-inch by 4-inch, backsaw, pencil, square

What to do:

1. Have children put on their goggles. Make certain the goggles are worn comfortably and securely in place.

2. Show children how to clamp a piece of wood to the workbench using a vise or C-clamp.

3. Allow the children to practice securing their wood with these tools.

4. Working with one or two children at a time, demonstrate how to mark a line on a board and then cut it in half with the backsaw.

5. Encourage children to practice using the backsaw.

Hammering

Objective: To gain skill in hammering

Materials needed: Goggles, claw hammer weighing 11 to 13 ounces, golf tees, 3-inches thick styrofoam

sheet, roofing nails, cardboard sheets stacked and taped together to a 3-inch thickness, common nails, soft pine (1-inch by 4-inch strip)

What to do:

1. Place the golf tees and styrofoam in the woodworking center, and encourage children to hammer the tees into the styrofoam.

2. When children lose interest or are sufficiently skilled in hammering the golf tees, add the roofing nails and cardboard to the woodworking center.

3. Gradually encourage children to hammer common nails into pine.

Drilling

Objective: To use a hand drill and bit.

Materials needed: Goggles, hand drill, ⅛-inch bit, soft pine (1-inch by 4-inch strip)

What to do:

1. Demonstrate how to use the hand drill, including how to open and close the chuck to insert the bit. Allow children to practice.

2. Show children how to hold the drill, and encourage them to drill a hole.

Name Plaque
(4 years and older)

Objective: To recognize that the wood in carpentry products comes from trees

Materials needed: One 6" board (cut to accommodate the letters of the child's name, usually 8 to 10 inches long) twigs ranging from 1 to 4 inches long, backsaw, clamp or vise, ruler, glue, hand drill with 3/8- inch bit, cord.

What to do:

1. Gather twigs in a wooded area. Discuss how trees grow from thin saplings to gigantic trees with spreading branches. Examine the bark and core of large fallen branches. Explain how trees are milled into boards.

2. Working with one or two children, let each child decide what name to put on his or her plaque.

3. Have each child write her or his name on paper, or the adult can provide a written model for the child to use as a guide.

4. Have the children place the twigs on the board to form

the letters of the name. Once the letters are placed, use the ruler and pencil to draw a cutting line across the end of the board to obtain the correct length.

5. Clamp the board to the table and saw it to the desired length.

6. Drill a hole in the two corners of the board. The holes will be used for hanging the plaque.

7. Place the twigs on the board again to form the letters of the name. Carefully remove one twig at a time and apply a few drops of glue. Replace the twig in its proper position.

8. Allow the glue to dry one to two hours.

9. Loop the cord through the drilled holes and knot the ends.

Woodworking Safety Considerations

Woodworking requires close supervision. To protect the children's safety, engage children in a dialogue about the need for safety when working with tools and wood. Examine each tool and discuss its possible hazards. Then together set clear and logical limits and rules for the woodworking center. Limit the number of woodworkers to no more than two at a time, perhaps one person only, depending on the size and configuration of the woodworking table and center. Supervise constantly and be prepared to remind children frequently of the safety rules. Children are usually careful when they understand the reasons for caution and safe use of materials and equipment, but with distractions and enthusiasm may from time to time forget the rules.

The following are some suggested safety rules. You may wish to modify them as needed so that every child in the group understands the rule and why it is necessary.

- Use each tool only for its intended purpose. For example, hammers are for hammering nails, saws are only for cutting wood, and so on.

- Use tools only in the woodworking area and only when an adult is present to help. Children should understand that tools are not toys and can be dangerous if not properly used and stored in safe place.

- No more than two children should occupy the woodworking center at a time.

- Use a vise or C-clamp, not another person, to hold tools or equipment in place.

- Keep the workbench free from clutter. Return tools, nails, and lumber to the proper storage area when they are no longer in use.

- Be certain there are no nail heads or points protruding from lumber.

- Saw, hammer, or drill only on construction wood, never into the work bench.

- Keep nails and any other woodworking objects away from mouth and eyes.

Adults must continuously and conscientiously check tools (and the woodworking center) for damage, and remove hazardous or damaged items. Teach children to watch for and report any needed repairs or hazards. Be firm and consistent in enforcing the rules that you and your group have established. Be prepared to remind children frequently of the rules. Children should know in advance the consequences (such as losing a turn at the workbench) that result from their misuse of tools or materials. Finally, observe children as they work, noticing those who find woodworking difficult or frustrating so that you can offer help and encouragement when needed or suggest an alternative activity.

Anti-Bias Consideration

Woodworking interests both boys and girls. Teachers should encourage both girls and boys to participate in woodworking and provide the support, assistance, and modeling needed to make woodworking a successful and enjoyable experience. Books, visual props, and supporting materials can be used to illustrate that men and women, boys and girls enjoy working with wood.

Planning for Children with Special Needs

Encourage children who have special needs to accomplish as many large and small motor activities as they can. Modify the workbench and the space around it to allow easy access for children who use assistive or adaptive equipment such as wheelchairs, walkers or other apparatus. Provide a large surface area as needed to facilitate the child's handling of wood. Place tools within easy reach for children. Encourage independence while observing all children as they use the tools and equipment, and provide assistance when they want or need it.

Checklist for Evaluating the Woodworking Center

Use the following checklist to determine the quality of your woodworking center. Rate the items below on a scale of 1 to 4 with "needing improvement" as 1 and "outstanding" as 4.

_____1. Tools are good quality and in good repair.

_____2. An adult supervises the center at all times.

_____3. The center has clear rules that the children follow.

_____4. The workbench stays clear of tools when the materials are not in use.

_____5. Tools are stored out of reach when the center is closed.

_____6. Only two children use the center at one time.

_____7. Storage is organized to encourage independence and proper care of tools.

_____8. Children use the center at least weekly either indoors or outdoors.

_____9. The center offers a variety of materials that are rotated to maintain interest.

_____10. The teacher recognizes and responds readily to signs of fatigue and frustration.

_____11. The schedule allows adequate time to finish woodworking projects.

_____12. Woodworking is a center choice for both boys and girls.

_____13. The children are provided age-appropriate woodworking activities to promote success.

_____14. Teachers are familiar with the proper use of tools and model skills for the children.

References

Adams, P. K., & M. K. Taylor (1990). A developmental approach to woodworking. *Dimensions 18* (3), 16-19.

Ard, L. (Spring, 1990). Building skills with wood and hammers. *Texas Child Care*. Austin, TX: Texas Department of Human Services.

Dawson, S. R. (1984). *"I can build it myself:" A home and school course in hand tools for young children*. San Diego, CA: Children's Woodshop Publications.

Hubbard, L. K. (1999). Woodworking with young children: You can do it! *Young Children 54* (6), 32-34.

Hubbard, R. S. (1998). Creating a class where children can think. *Young Children 53*(5), 26-31.

Leithead, M. (1996). Happy hammering: A hammering activity with built-in success. *Young Children 51*(3), 12.

Skeen, P., A. Garner; & S. Cartwright (1984). *Woodworking for young children*. Washington, DC: National Association for the Education of Young Children.

About the Author

Gordon D. Bacon is chairperson of the Early Childhood Professions Department at Central Texas College in Killeen, Texas. He has spent seventeen years as the director of the Child Development Center and as an early childhood instructor at Central Texas College. Previous to that, he served as Department of Defense project officer for establishing family child care homes on military installations and coordinated various child development and family advocacy programs for the United States Army. He holds a master's degree from the University of Montana.

Chapter 18

In the shade of the arbor in the playground, 3-year-olds Stephanie and Brian are hard at work digging in a center designed for sand and water projects. Carefully they scoop the sand and shape an oblong mound.

When the caregiver walks over to watch the children, they explain: "We're making a place for a big alligator and a little alligator to lay when they come out of the water."

The caregiver gets a yardstick and helps the children measure the mound. "Let's dig a lake tomorrow," Stephanie says.

Sand and Water Play

Nancy H. Beaver

Because children have had sandboxes at home and schools for many years and children naturally gravitate to playing in water and dirt, it's easy to underestimate the value of sand, soil, and water as media for learning. It is also easy to dismiss this kind of play as too much trouble for the mess it creates. However, sand and water play offer tremendous developmental opportunities for children that outweigh any disadvantages for adults.

Value of the Sand and Water Center

Therapeutic. Who doesn't love to climb into a hot bath after a hard day at work, or wiggle toes in the sand at the beach? Water and sand are soothing to children as well as adults. Time alone at the sand and water table can help calm a child who is out of control.

Physical development. Children strengthen and coordinate large muscles in pouring, carrying, and lifting activities. Children strengthen and coordinate small muscles in pouring, measuring, scrubbing, grasping, and squeezing activities. They develop eye-hand coordination when reaching for objects under water, shaking sand through a sifter, pouring, ladling, digging, and using eye droppers. The pincer grasp, which is so important for cutting and writing, is developed as children grasp a scoop to pour sand, dig with a hand shovel, and squeeze a baster or eye dropper.

Cognitive development. Sand and water play combine the use of all the senses such as seeing wet sand drip from their hands, feeling the grainy texture of sand, smelling the earthy scent of mud, and hearing water splash as they pour. They learn scientific concepts such as the properties of water and sand, volume, weight, con-

sistency, cause and effect, durability, and mutability which is how a substance changes form. They gain experience in predicting, problem solving, measuring, comparing, observing, experimenting, and evaluating. The teacher can guide discovery by asking questions such as: "Which holds more?" "I wonder what would happen if...?" "Why did it do that? "Will that happen again?" Sand and water are also excellent props for creative play and can stimulate the child's imagination as described in the scene at the beginning of this chapter.

Language development. Children discuss their actions informally or evaluate an activity with the teacher. As children play with sand and water, they are learning words to describe concepts like full or empty, deep or shallow, wet or dry, and sink or float.

Social development. Sand and water play encourages cooperation, social interaction, and self-discipline as children work together and share materials. Children explore adult social roles as they wash baby dolls and build construction sites.

Space Requirements

Sand and water play can take place indoors or outdoors, The best place for this play indoors is near the art area where water is near and the floors are not carpeted so they can be mopped or swept easily. If the sand and water play area is carpeted, the floor can be protected with a thick sheet of vinyl from a local hardware store or an old plastic shower curtain or tablecloth. The vinyl sheet can be taped to the floor with 2-inch duct tape to prevent children from tripping. Some teachers put towels or newspaper down to absorb sand or water spills.

When older children engage in projects such as making a yard around a doll house, creating the place where dinosaurs lived, or paving an area around a filling station made of blocks, slightly dampened soil can be brought in and spooned where needed on cookie sheets or cardboard trays lined with foil or plastic. These can be located on a relatively small table in the science center or on top of the soil and water table when not in use.

Outdoors the sandbox and water table are best placed in a shady area that can be easily supervised. When placed near dramatic play structures, play in both areas can be integrated. Placing the sandbox away from the building entrance will reduce the amount of sand tracked indoors.

When deciding where to have a center with natural soil as the medium, one should think about shade, the possibility of having to clear the area, and drainage. There may also be a need to add sand or compost to loosen packed, hard, or sticky soil. The area need not be a traditional box shape; it can be any shape or size and have borders made of different materials such as old tires or landscape lumber.

Equipment and Materials

Basic materials are soil, sand, and water, which can be used independently or in combinations. Sand is loose, granular particles of disintegrated rock, finer than gravel and coarser than dust, usually found along seacoasts. Soil is dirt, commonly suitable for gardening. It differs greatly from place to place because it is composed of different proportions of humus, fine particles of silt and clay, coarser particles (including sand), and coarse materials such as pebbles.

The basic equipment includes a variety of containers to hold sand and water, e.g., dishpans, under-the-bed storage tubs, washtubs, and large plastic tote trays as well as commercial sand and water play tables. Anything that is wide (but at least 6 inches deep) and doesn't leak will serve the purpose. Individual dishpans put side by side work well for toddlers who have trouble sharing materials and space.

Materials are ordinary, inexpensive ones found in the kitchen or closet. Materials for measuring and pouring include cups, measuring cups, measuring spoons, ladles, spoons, spouts, small pitchers, scoops, butter tubs, small plastic rakes and shovels, and plastic bottles of various sizes and shapes.

Materials that can promote experimentation include cookie cutters, sand and kitchen molds, bulb-type basters, sponges, sieves, plastic tubing, colanders, funnels, whisks, eggbeaters, paintbrushes, PVC pipes and guttering, colored ice cubes, pumps (from window cleaners or ketchup) and spray bottles to dampen sand.

Dramatic play can be provided by having dolls to bathe, clothes to wash, clotheslines with pinch-type clothespins, dishes to wash and dry, toys to be cleaned, boats to sail, trucks to build roads for, pots to "cook" in, and construction toys to excavate building sites.

Materials can be mixed with sand or water to increase the sensory impact and renew interest. Some good medium mixtures include Dawn© dishwashing liquid, which contains glycerin, or baby shampoo and water; food coloring and water; glitter and sand; and aquarium gravel and sand.

While sand, dirt and water are the basic mediums for this sensory play, other materials can be used in sand and water table to provide a variety of experiences. Some choices of dry materials include: birdseed, cardboard tubes, confetti, cotton balls, dry leaves, feathers, grass seed, landscape mulch or bark chips, potting soil, ping pong balls, plastic eggs, shredded paper, straw, packing squiggles, and wrapping paper. Avoid using food products, especially in edible form such as cooked spaghetti.

Wet materials such as shaving cream, cornstarch and water, and "clean mud" which is made of torn paper, Ivory© soap and water should be treated like water, which means that the water table should be emptied every day and sanitized.

Health and Safety Precautions

Children's clothing should be protected when playing with water. The vinyl smocks used for painting are also good for water play. Smocks must be of different sizes to fit various ages of children and long enough to cover a child's stomach and thighs. Roll up children's long sleeves for both sand and water play. Because, warm water and damp sand offer a perfect medium for bacteria growth, children must wash their hands before and after sand and water play. Sand boxes and tables should be covered when not in use.

Children most likely to spill should have their feet protected. Teachers can place a washtub on the floor, surround it with towels, and have children kneel to use this sand and water play arrangement, so feet stay dry and free of sand. Children should have a second set of clothes in case they get too wet or sandy, or have an accident of any kind. Spills on the floor should be swept or mopped as soon as possible to prevent slipping.

Rules and limits for sand and water play must be clearly established with the children when the activity is first introduced. Children older than 3 years can help come up with good rules. Examples include:

- Wear a smock while playing at the water table.

- Help clean up after play.

- Keep the sand or water in the play table or in containers used there.
- Try not to get wet or to get anyone else wet.

Limit the number of children who can play in the area at one time. The exact number will depend on the space and arrangement of the area and the children's ages. A good way to limit the number of children is to have only three or four smocks at the sand and water play table. When no more smocks are available, children must choose another activity.

Cleanup is part of the process. Empty water containers at the end of the day and sanitize them. Fill with fresh water the next morning. Children enjoy helping empty and fill water tubs if they have pitchers and buckets for this purpose. Children can also help by wiping tables, mopping water spills, and sweeping away sand. Allow plenty of time for clean up. It is an important extension of the sand or water play itself.

Planning for Children with Special Needs

The sand and water center is a favorite activity area for children with special needs and requires little adaptation. Plan activities and materials in the same manner as one would for younger children, using large utensils that are easy to grasp, matching the complexity of activities to the child's capability levels and protecting clothes. The foam cylinders from curlers can be slip over the handles of utensils to make them easier to grasp. Some commercial sand and water play stands are designed so that children in wheelchairs can use them efficiently. To make an accessible sand and water table, build a stand of four posts with a frame to hold the plastic or metal tub at a height where a wheelchair's arms can slip under the bottom of the tub. Use a small to medium size tub that can be lifted out of the frame to empty or install a drain in the tub. Make a cover, if sand will remain in the tub more than one day.

Activities

Washing Dolls of Diverse Cultures
(2- and 3-year-olds)

Objectives: To develop an awareness of likenesses and differences in skin color, develop eye-hand coordination and small muscle control.

Materials Needed: Washable multicultural dolls, tubs or water table, baby shampoo or Ivory© soap bars, sponges or wash cloths, towels, a mirror, and smocks.

What to do:

1. Have the children wash the dolls.

2. As they are washing them, point out the different skin colors of the dolls. Have the children look at your skin and their skin and discuss how we all have our special skin color and we are all different. Use the mirror to look at hair and eyes to extend the activity.

Water Transfer
(3-year-olds)

Objectives: To develop small muscles, practice using the pincer muscles (a good precutting exercise), enhance problem-solving skills, and enhance self-help skills

Materials needed: Sponge, meat baster, or eye dropper; 2 shallow bowls or tubs or a two-sectioned container (similar to a pet food dish); food coloring; water

What to do:

1. Place bowls side by side. Fill one bowl with water. Instruct the children to dip the sponge into the water. Squeeze the water out of the sponge into the empty bowl. Compare the water in the two bowls.

2. Fill one bowl with water, adding a bit of food coloring to make it more visible. Challenge children to transfer the water from one tub to the other using the meat baster.

3. Fill each tub about one-third full and put a different color of food coloring in each. Encourage the children to transfer the water from one to the other, discovering the new secondary color that appears.

Construction Sites
(4-year-olds)

Objectives: To strengthen eye-hand coordination, develop small and large muscles, and learn about building and construction.

Materials needed: Sandbox or sand table, toy trucks, bulldozers and other heavy construction equipment; shovels, scoops, and blunt-ended trowels, small boxes or other rectangular molds for making bricks; sprinkler cans or spray bottles of water for moistening sand, props such as construction hats, carpenter's apron or belt, lunch box, small wheel barrow, metal tape measure, pieces of cardboard to brace excavation work, sticks or dowels, string or surveyor's tape which is available at any hardware store and comes in bright colors, books with pictures of construction activity, the book, *Mike Mulligan and His Steam Shovel*, by Virginia Lee Burton, an engineer's or architect's blueprint, large pieces of paper (for making blueprints), blue crayons or markers (other colors can be used if a child chooses), carpenter's pencil, craft sticks, pieces of smooth wood, juice cans, and other items to add to sand buildings

Note: This activity can be done with fewer materials, but the greater the variety of props and equipment, the more complex the play will usually be.

What to do:

1. Read books to the children about building and construction work. Discuss what construction workers do.

2. If possible, take a field trip to a construction site.

3. Discuss with children an engineer's or architect's blueprint. Discuss with children what they want to build and have them draw blueprints. Discuss various jobs involved in constructing buildings or roads, and ask children which roles they would like to play (roles may change as play progresses). Discuss safety rules and engage children in developing the rules.

4. Help the children map out the construction site using a metal tape measure and marking it with dowels and string or surveyor's tape. Encourage the children to start digging and building. Act as a resource to discuss possible solutions to construction problems and conflicts the children cannot resolve without support. It is important that the children guide the direction and flow of this activity.

5. Make this activity a long-term project by covering the sandbox daily to protect the children's work.

Siphoning
(5-year-olds)

Objectives: To gain experience in problem solving and cooperating with others. The key concept is that gravity and suction makes a siphon work. New words include *siphon*, *gravity*, and *water pressure*.

Materials needed: Small hose or plastic tubing (clear if possible) for each child, 2 to 3 small buckets or containers, food coloring

What to do:

1. Show the children how to use a siphon. This can be introduced as a different way to fill or empty the water play table.

2. Instruct the children to experiment with water pressure by raising and lowering the buckets they are filling, and by placing the hose near the bottom and top of the water from which they are siphoning.

3. Add food coloring to the water to allow the children to better observe the flow of the water through the tube.

Measuring Sand and Water
(3- years-old and up)

Objectives: To identify different measures, develop a beginning understanding of volume and addition, develop small muscles and eye-hand coordination, and obtain experience in problem-solving

Materials needed: Tall thin container and low wide container that hold the same amounts; clear plastic measuring cups, measuring spoons of various sizes, water colored with food coloring (or sand)

What to do:

1. Typically two- and three-year-olds simply pour the water or sand from one container to another. They are developing concepts of empty and full and that water and sand take the shape of the container.

2. Four- and five-year-old children can use sand or colored water and measuring utensils to fill containers. Ask questions such as: "How many spoons will it take to fill one cup?" "How many cups will it take to fill this pitcher?" "Which holds more?" This interaction is informally carried out as children are using measuring cups and spoons with the sand and water play table.

Note: When using the equal volume containers of different shapes, children may not be able to recognize at first that the amount remains the same when sand or water is transferred from one to the other. When they do, they have learned conservation of volume, a cognitive skill characteristic of children in what Jean Piaget, a Swiss psychologist, defines as the concrete operations stage of cognitive development. During the concrete stage of cognitive development children begin to enlist more sophisticated, less egocentric and less perception-bound ways of thinking (Piaget, 1963).

Mud Pies and Other Cooking
(3-years-old and up)

Objectives: To learn about different measures, develop a beginning understanding of volume and addition, develop small muscles and eye-hand coordination, learn to use tools, and explore adult tasks.

Materials needed: Kitchen props such as pots, pans, spoons, spatulas, egg poachers, cookie cutters, rolling pins, measuring cups and spoons, sand, water in milk cartons and pitchers, pebbles, acorns, leaves or other small natural items to use as recipe ingredients, spice shakers filled with sand, index cards and pencils for recipes

What to do:

1. Place this activity adjacent to the sandbox or sand table. Encourage the children to play.

2. As children play, they develop concepts of measurement.

Color Mixing
(4-years-old and up)

Objectives: To identify the primary colors (red, yellow and blue) and secondary colors (green, orange and purple) and to develop eye-hand coordination, pincer grasp, and small muscle control.

Materials needed: Three clear plastic cups; egg cartons, muffin tins or several cups, water in a small pitcher or large measuring cup, red, yellow, and blue food coloring, 3 eye droppers, bucket and sponge for cleanup

What to do:

1. In the clear plastic cups, mix water and food coloring to make strong deep primary colors.

2. Have the children pour water from the pitcher to fill egg carton cups half full of water.

3. Have the children use eye droppers to mix different colors and create new colors and tints.

Holey Bottles
(4-year-olds and up)

Objectives: To discover the concepts of surface tension and air pressure, to develop eye-hand coordination, pincer grasp and small muscle control.

Materials needed: 20 ounce clear plastic soda bottles with caps, an ice pick (for the adult to use), water in a small pitcher or large measuring cup, water table or a tub or bowl of water, food coloring, bucket and sponge for cleanup

What to do:

1. Before use, the adult should prepare the soda bottles by making a small hole in the bottom with a hot ice pick.

2. Have the children pour water from the pitcher to fill the bottles half full of water and screw the top on tightly. This works best if the bottle is held in the tub of water while it is filled.

3. Lift the bottle out of the water and watch. The bottle should not leak if the top is on tightly. Unscrew the top slightly and watch the water flow. Close the top again and see the water flow stop. Ask, "What Happened?" or "Why did it stop?" Now squeeze the bottle. What happens? Why?

Color Surprise
(2-years-old and up)

Objectives: To identify the primary colors (red, yellow and blue) and secondary colors (green, orange and purple) and to develop eye-hand coordination and small muscle control.

Materials needed: Two liter clear plastic soda bottles with tops, duct tape or electrical tape; ice pick (for adult use only), water table, red, yellow, and blue food coloring, bucket and sponge for cleanup

What to do:

1. Before use, the adult should prepare the soda bottles by cutting them about 1/3 down from the top to make funnels out of the tops and containers from the bottoms. Use the tape to cover the rough edges where the bottles were cut. Then the adult makes a small hole in the bottle tops with a hot ice pick.

2. Before water play, put two or three drops of food coloring in each bottle top.

3. Instruct the children to use the bottom containers to fill the funnel tops and watch as the color drips out of the tops. As children use different tops, the colors will mix in the water table.

Drops on a Penny
(5-year-olds and up)

Objectives: To discover the concept of surface tension, to develop eye-hand coordination, pincer grasp and small muscle control.

Materials needed: Shallow bowls or trays, pennies, eye droppers, cups

What to do:

1. Fill cups with water and put eye droppers in the cups. Place the pennies in the trays or bowls.

2. Have the children use the eyedropper to drop water drop by drop onto a penny, counting the drops as they go. See how many drops the penny will hold. Inquire, "Why does the penny hold so many drops?"

Note: This is a great challenge for school-agers! The best record I know of is 62 drops! It takes care and patience.

Mud Sculptures/Adobe Bricks
(3-year-olds and up)

Objectives: To develop small muscle control, to develop the pincer grasp, and to promote creativity and problem solving.

Materials: Potting soils, flour, water, a bowl, a measuring cup and spoons. Small boxes or shoe boxes, straw, and sticks can be added if making adobe bricks.

What to Do:

1. Have the children mix 4 parts soil and 1 part flour in the bowl. Children will enjoy mixing with their hands.

2. Slowly add water and stir until the mixture is the consistency of play dough.

3. The dough can be molded into any shape the child desires.

4. The dough will dry, so sculptures can be saved.

5. To make adobe bricks, add straw and more water to the mixture.

6. Mold brick shapes in the boxes and turn out on to a hard surface such as the sidewalk to dry. Bricks can be stacked while wet to build an open topped structure such as a fort. If a roof is desired, place sticks across the top of the structure to support the roof bricks. Wait until the next day to add the roof bricks. Roof bricks should be thinner than wall bricks to reduce the weight needing to be supported.

Checklist for Evaluating the Sand and Water Environment

Rate the items below on a scale of 1 to 4 with "needing improvement" as 1 and "outstanding" as 4.

_____ 1. The sand and water play center is located near the art center (or other easily cleaned area) indoors and in a shady area near a water source outdoors.

_____ 2. The sand and water play center is available to the children three or more times a week.

_____ 3. When playing with water, children wash hands and wear protective smocks and shoe coverings to stay dry; an extra set of clothing is available.

_____ 4. The sand and water play center is used frequently by all children.

_____ 5. Props and materials are adequate in quantity, variety, and condition.

_____ 6. Props and materials are rotated to maintain interest.

_____ 7. Children are involved in keeping the center clean and well maintained.

_____ 8. Children help set limits, and limits are enforced to allow children to play in the center safely and with little conflict.

_____ 9. Accommodations and adaptations are made to support the inclusion of children with disabilities.

References

Piaget, J. (1963). *The psychology of intelligence*. Patterson, NJ: Littlefield, Adams.

About the Author

Nancy Beaver, M.Ed. is a Teaching Administrator in the Child Development Department of Eastfield College. She holds a Masters of Education degree in Early Childhood Education from the University of North Texas. She is a past president of Dallas AEYC and a past vice president of Texas AEYC. She has raised over $1,000,000 in grants for Early Childhood Programs.

Chapter 19

Mathematics for 4- and 5-Year-Olds

Laverne Warner

Bailey struggles to match a red bead in a prestructured bead sequence her teacher has placed in the math center. "Mrs. R.," she calls, "I need help with this bead!" Mrs. Rodriquez, who is watching Anita sequence a group of straws from shortest to longest, looks in her direction and suggests, "Be patient, Bailey, you've put all the other beads on the string. You can do this one, too."

Raul approaches the teacher and says, "I can count to 10; you want to hear me?" Mrs. Rodriquez nods and says, "Of course, Raul, count these for me." She gives him some number chips, which he begins to count. In the meantime, she gives another sequence of beads to Bailey to match, smiling to let her know that she has formed the previous bead sequence correctly.

Some adults believe children are supposed to learn how to count when they are young, especially if they are enrolled in a preschool. On a regular basis, preschool teachers report to parents about the cognitive learning children are doing in their classrooms, and always include information about understanding numbers and counting objects. Teachers should observe children in meaningful activities such as measuring, sorting, and counting objects for a specific purpose or reason, not because memorization or rote counting is required (Bredekamp & Copple, 1997).

The National Council of Teachers of Mathematics (NCTM) reports that by the time children enter kindergarten, they have many practical, though informal, math skills, which range from understanding concepts about position and length, simple addition and subtraction (with concrete objects), making simple estimates, and correctly counting to 10 (and some can count beyond). *Principles and Standards for School Mathematics* (NCTM, 2000) defines *Standards for Pre-K –2* on their web site at http://nctm.org. These standards are in five categories: (1) number and operations; (2) algebra (patterns and functions); (3) geometry; (4) measurement; and (5) data analysis and probability.

However, it is impossible for children to have the same perceptions of math at age 5 than older children and adults have. Children are just beginning the abstracting process to acquire information about mathematics from the activities in which they participate. By using concrete objects, children learn the quantitative qualities of objects - their sizes, shapes, and numbers (Copley, Ed., 1999).

Knowledge of number is abstract, and children acquire mathematical information through experiences. Math understanding is differentiated from physical knowledge, (e.g., trees move when the wind blows), and information about relationships that are not observable but exist in the minds of those who understand the relationships. For example, to comprehend that there are two wagons on the playground, the listener must comprehend the relationship between the two wagons, which is not inherent in the objects but rather in the learner's understanding of *twoness* (or that the numeral two represents two objects) (Wortham, 2002).

Generally, educators agree that early childhood mathematics programs should assist in the development of mathematical knowledge by addressing specific areas of learning in concrete ways (Seefeldt & Barbour, 1998). These areas include:

Classification - putting objects in sets or groups according to a specific characteristic (color, shape, size, or other attributes);

Comparing - looking at two objects and describing their likenesses and differences;

Ordering (or seriating) - placing objects in sequence (from largest to smallest or from thinnest to widest, for example);

Measuring - using informal techniques to compare objects and discovering that objects can be expressed as a multiple of units;

Counting (cardinal and ordinal) - being able to count a group of objects sequentially (one, two, three, four) and being able to tell which is first, second, third, last (ordinal counting);

Numbers - being able to recognize numeral names and the many ways that children and adults use numbers;

Operations - learning that numbers can be manipulated (that is, they can be changed by putting them together or taking them apart to form new groups);

Spatial relationships - understanding the relationships of objects in space (on top of, behind, over, under);

Time - acquiring basic information about time (morning, afternoon, night, yesterday, today, tomorrow);

Sets - understanding that objects grouped together have certain characteristics;

Patterns - understanding simple to complex relationships among objects in order to form an established pattern;

Graphing - organizing mathematical information into a visual display in order to communicate the information to an audience.

Other scholars add **geometry** (experiencing flat and solid geometric shapes) as important learning in the preschool (Copley, 2000). The major goal of this knowledge is that children can use it to solve problems (Seefeldt & Barbour, 1998). In recent years, experts emphasize children's abilities to **represent** and **communicate** the knowledge they have about mathematics (Copley, Ed., 1999).

When preschool teachers begin developing a math center, they need to consider the knowledge their children have about counting and number. Four-year-olds, for example, need an abundance of objects to count, seriate, classify, compare, measure, and talk about. But 5-year-olds, especially if they have had many experiences with number, can be doing simple problem-solving activities.

Materials

Initially, the center should have some of the following items:

- Objects for classifying such as dollhouse furniture, large beads of different shapes and colors, various collections, e.g., small vehicles, small plastic animals, large buttons, and leaves, seeds and other raw materials.

- Materials for making comparisons, e.g., objects that are large and small, heavy and light, long and short and have dark and light hues of the same color;

- Materials for measuring such as strings or yarn, measuring cups, scales, a trundle wheel, homemade rulers;

- Many materials for counting such as tongue depressors, counting chips, an abacus, jar lids, nuts, stones or other other natural items;

- Materials for seeing part/whole relationships, e.g., unit blocks, foam or wooden geometric shapes;

- Materials for patterning such as varied beads to string and a variety of commercially available items.

Patterning materials that are commercially produced include:

- Cuisenaire rods© - centimeter-square rods in lengths from one to 10 centimeters in various colors);

- Pattern blocks — wooden blocks that come in six colors and shapes and are uniform in thickness;

- Parquetry blocks - wooden blocks of assorted colors and shapes with uniform thickness and pattern cards which children match;

- Multibase blocks - wooden or plastic cubes showing base relationships;

- Attribute blocks - wooden or plastic blocks that vary in color, shape, thickness, size;

- Geoboards - plastic or wooden boards with nails or pegs in an array, typically 5 inches by 5 inches; and

- Geoblocks - pieces of unfinished hardwood cut into a wide variety of shapes and sizes.

Usually commercially manufactured materials are expensive. However, many can be created by the preschool teacher and if raw materials are used, parents and children can be encouraged to bring specific objects to be used in the mathematics center. A number of preschool teachers report that garage sales yield excellent mathematics materials, because some child has outgrown their use and the parent is selling the materials to dispose of them. Later, when children require more difficult challenges, center materials can be teacher-made in order to meet the individual needs of the children.

Space and Location

Since the math center requires children's active involvement, it will probably become noisy when a number of children are in it. Placing it in a moderately quiet area of the room is appropriate and limiting the number of children who work in it becomes critical at specific times. However, the teacher should be prepared to expand the center if it becomes particularly interesting or attractive to children. This center should allow the teacher to carry out occasional directed activities, preferably if they are conducted with a small group of children at a time.

A rug or carpet in the area will reduce the noise level in the center when materials fall or are dropped. A solid color carpet is preferable to a patterned one for ease in finding a missing block (or other item). Possibly, the math center could become an extension of the manipulative center and as such, should be placed near it.

Teaching math skills to children needs to be relevant to their lives. Integrating mathematics skills into daily discussions will help children understand the reasons for knowing math. Math activities can be used with thematic topics that are often a part of the school year curriculum.

All children should be encouraged to use this center. Preschool teachers need to develop a number of ways for children to use math knowledge in the classroom and demonstrate that both girls and boys use math in everyday activities. In so doing, they avoid the stereotype that math is for boys.

The teacher's role in the math center is critical. She must be observant to perceive when children need more challenges and when to ask appropriate questions that will help children think in a different way about number and number concepts. Because of the individualized nature of this center, working with children with special needs is not difficult. Allowing the child to play in the math center who needs more experiences with objects in order to form mathematical knowledge is appropriate. Or the teacher may suggest that the child move into the manipulative center to experience materials at a sensory level as a prerequisite to the acquisition of math knowledge.

Record Keeping

Record keeping becomes quite important in the math center in order to show the skills children are acquiring. Teachers will need copies of checklists (shown at the end of this chapter) for each child and plenty of time to record classroom observations.

Skill Activities

Matching Numerals
(4-year-olds and older)

Objective: To help develop understanding of the numerals from one to five

Materials needed: Three or four purchased sets of house numerals of varying styles; counting chips or other objects that can be counted; handmade (and laminated) cards with written numeral symbols on them (use the print guide for numerals shown at the end of this chapter).

What to Do:

1. Place the house numerals in the math center for children to match. Encourage them to match the different styles—for example, the gothic style three with the block style three.

2. After children have gained experience with step 1, begin with real objects, placing three counters on the table for children to count. Show children the numerals to match what has been counted.

3. After children can do step 2 successfully, ask them to name the numerals written on cards.

And still more:

Make the activity more complex by adding numerals beyond five (through nine). As you work with the numerals with children, help them form the concept that smaller groups are part of larger sets of numbers (one bead is part of a set of three, for example, or three beads are part of a set of five). Helping children see this relationships will form foundation knowledge that will be important for later understanding of addition and subtraction when they see a problem such as $5 - 3 =$ ___.

What Comes Next Sequence Cards
(5-year-olds and older)

Objective: To help develop the concept of sequential patterning and do simple problem solving

Materials needed: Beads or attribute bocks that can be arranged in a pattern for children to match; laminated teacher-made pattern cards and handmade shape pieces (also laminated) that match the size of the shapes on the pattern cards (the cards must progress in difficulty level from simple to more complex, which can be accomplished by using color, size, and a variety of shapes. (See suggestions below).

What to do:

1. Place the patterned sequence cards in the math center and allow the children to use them individually as puzzles. Observe carefully in case a child needs instructions about the use of the cards.

2. Add washable markers so children can draw the appropriate "what comes next" shape onto the cards (which they will be able to do if the cards have been laminated). The cards can also be used with small groups of children.

Note: Make sure children have had many experiences with real objects before beginning the abstract patterning required in this activity.

And still more:

1. Continue to add more difficult cards for learners who need greater challenge.

2. Allow children to make their own sequence cards or use objects in the math center to form patterns for other children to tell what comes next (or match).

Graphing Made Easy
(5-year-olds and older)

Objective: To understand simple graphs and their uses and set a foundation for later learning about graphing.

Materials needed: An old sheet (a solid color is preferable), which has a line either painted or stitched length wise down the middle (use hemming tape); a number of classroom materials to use for graphing purposes. Attributes and preferences of the children can also provide graphing materials, e.g., color of clothing, number of pockets, how many prefer what kind of pizza, and so on.

What to do:

1. Explain to children that adults like to make charts that describe the way we live and behave. Show them the sheet and say that we are going to make a living graph.

2. Spread the sheet on the floor and ask all the children who have on blue clothes to stand on one side of the sheet. Ask the children who have on green to stand on the other side.

3. Count the children on each side and record the results on the chalkboard or on a chart.

4. Ask children to translate the information they are graphing by drawing pictures onto large pieces of paper that have a line drawn down the middle.

5. Repeat the activity but use other differences in clothing such as the number of children who wore sweaters that day compared to those who wore jackets and coats and the number who have sneakers with laces compared to those that hold together with Velcro©.

6. Try graphing other facts such as how children get to school (car or bus) or which type of pet they have or would like to have (cat, dog or fish). Note that it is difficult for children to count others if they are standing together as a group. If the numbers of children who ride a bus to school are large, try a paper plate face to represent individuals and then count them.

7. Eventually show children how to make marks to represent people and demonstrate how to use the tally mark when numbers go beyond four.

And still more:

1. Ask children to make simple surveys to determine who prefers watching which television show.

2. Divide a sheet into thirds or fourths and expand the number of options (not only blue and green clothing but also red and yellow, for example).

Theme Activities

Over in the Meadow Rhyme

Objective: To visualize differences in objects (animals, in this instance) and compare objects; to do simple sorting

Materials needed: *Over in the Meadow, A Counting-Out Rhyme* (Wadsworth, 1985); teacher-prepared animal shapes (the book has simple animal shapes that can be traced and cut out for this activity). This is easily prepared as a flannel board story.

What to do:

1. At circle time, show children the collection of animal shapes represented in the book, and ask children to

identify each. Ask individual children to count each animal.

2. Read the book to small groups of children, letting them count each animal on individual pages as the book is read.

3. Place the animal pictures in the math center. Give children opportunities to compare the animals. Ask: "Which ones live underground?" "Which ones live in the water?" "Which ones could become pets?" "Which are your favorites?"

4. Ask children to organize the animal shapes to demonstrate the progressive order from one animal to ten animals.

And still more:

On an individual basis, show children how to make paper plate turtles. Count the number of turtles as they are made. If these are made out of varied colors and sizes of paper plates, suggest that children sort them by color or size.

Measuring from Corner to Corner
(5-year-olds and older)

Objective: To understand the fundamental concepts of measurement

Materials needed: A variety of measurement tools (these should not be formal instruments but such items as string, rope, teacher-made "footprints" made of posterboard and laminated, measuring cups, or plastic cups, pint, quart, and gallon containers); water or sand; objects to measure.

What to do:

1. Add measurement tools to the math center one at a time over time.

2. During circle time or with small groups in the math center, demonstrate how each tool will be used.

3. Allow children to use the instruments informally to measure the tables or chairs in the center or to pour water and sand into the plastic containers. The "footprints" can be used to measure the height of individual children, a bulletin board, classroom murals, how far the table top is from the floor (string or tape could be used here, too), or the size of the math center (this could be premarked with masking tape in preparation for the activity).

Print Guide for Numerals

1234567890

4. After several weeks, instruct the children to measure the classroom floor using the teacher-made "footprints." If it takes 16 "footprints" to measure one wall, record the results on a permanent chart for display in the math center.

And still more:

Use the measurement tools outdoors in sand play or water play. If the playground is not too large, use the "footprints" to measure its size. Record the results. Compare the playground area to the size of the classroom.

References

Bredekamp, S. & C. Copple (Eds.). (1997). *Developmentally appropriate practice in early childhood programs* (Rev.ed.). Washington, DC: National Association for the Education of Young Children.

Copley, J. (Ed.). (1999). *Mathematics in the early years*. Reston, VA: National Council of Teachers of Mathematics.

Copley, J. (2000). *The young child and mathematics*. Washington, DC: National Association for the Education of Young Children.

Seefeldt, C. & N. Barbour (1998). *Early childhood education: An introduction* (4th ed.). Upper Saddle River, NJ: Merrill/Prentice Hall.

Wadsworth, O. (1985). *Over in the meadow, a counting-out rhyme*. NY: Puffin Books.

Wortham, S. (2002). *Early childhood curriculum: Developmental bases for learning and teaching*. Upper Saddle River, NJ: Merrill/Prentice Hall.

About the Author

Laverne Warner is Coordinator and Professor of Early Childhood Education at Sam Houston State University. She is a Past President of the Texas Association for the Education of Young Children (TAEYC, 1995-1997) and a charter member of the Sam Houston Association for the Education of Young Children, to which she currently serves as advisor. She has written numerous articles for state, regional and national journals and is co-author of a textbook about early childhood education in public school settings (Allyn and Bacon, 2004). She is a regular presenter at conferences for TAEYC, the Southern Early Childhood Association (SECA) and the National Association for the Education of Young Children (NAEYC).

Checklist for 4-Year-Olds

Child's Name _____

Teacher's Name _____

Directions: Record information four times a year to show growth in mathematical knowledge. (Suggested months are September, December, February, and May). Write yes, no, checkmark, or the child's answer.

Concept	Date	Date	Date	Date
Sorting Objects				
• big/little				
• heavy/light				
• long/short				
Matching Objects (one-to-one correspondence)				
• more than				
• less than				
• equal				
• as many as				
Classification (based on likenesses/differences)				
Ordinal Counting (record how far child counts each time using objects)				
Simple Patterns				
• shows what comes next				
• verbalizes what comes next				
Seriates				
• three objects by size				
• five objects by size				
• ten objects by size				

Concept	Date	Date	Date	Date
Draws Shapes				
• square				
• circle				
• triangle				
Basic Activities (demonstrating knowledge of the following concepts)				
• the same as				
• different than				
• alike				
• one to one				
• under				
• over				
• above				
• below				
• in front of				
• far away from				
Matching Sets (demonstrate knowledge of the following concepts)				
• what is a set				
• form a set				
• show equal sets				
• show set with more/less				

Note: Checklists will take several days to complete. Teachers may discover that having the checklist handy when observing in the math center will facilitate the type of assessment that needs to be done.

Checklist for 5-Year-Olds

Child's Name _____

Teacher's Name _____

Directions: Record information four times a year to show growth in mathematical knowledge. (Suggested dates are September, December, February, and May). Write yes, no, checkmarks, or child's answer.

Concept	Date	Date	Date	Date

Rote Counting
- 1–10
- 1–20

Recognizes Numerals
- 1–10
- 1–20
- 1–30

Orders Numerals
- 1–10

Names Coins
- penny
- nickel
- dime

Matches Sets
- same
- different
- more than/less than

Matches Objects
(one-to-one correspondence)

Sorts Objects
- sorts using colors
- sorts using shapes
- sorts using size
- sorts like characteristics

Uses Vocabulary For:
- long/short
- heavy/light
- big/little
- up/down
- behind/in front of

Concept	Date	Date	Date	Date

- beside/next to
- first
- second
- middle
- last
- half
- whole
- plus sign
- minus sign
- equal sign

Time Units
(understands the following concepts)
- morning
- afternoon
- today
- tomorrow
- yesterday
- tonight

Graphs
- forms simple graphs
- verbalizes information on graphs

Patterning
- matches simple designs
- matches complex designs

Ordering
(with objects)
- by length (long to short)
- by colors (light to dark)
- by size (little to big)

Addition/Subtraction
(using objects)
- solves easy story problems (sums less than five)
- solves more difficult story problems (sums more than five)

Note: Checklists will take several days to complete. Teachers may discover that having the checklist handy when observing in the math center will facilitate the type of assessment that needs to be done.

Chapter 20

Writing for 4- and 5-Year-Olds

Laverne Warner

Four-year-old Jesse patiently cuts out a large circle, which he has traced onto yellow construction paper. He plans to use it as a headlight on a car he and his friends are building in the art center.

Kesha makes script-like marks on a piece of stationery and says excitedly, "I'm writing a letter to mommy." Abby imitates her friends' activity, but it's obvious to most observers that neither child is actually writing anything that resembles print.

Bryce, sitting nearby, watches carefully to determine whether he could possibly join his peers in the writing center.

Most adults, parents and teachers alike, recognize young children's interest in learning to write. Preschoolers watch adults write checks, prepare grocery lists, fill out forms, as well as write letters, and they observe older siblings doing school work after hours at home. Print abounds in the environment, and children show their awareness when they recognize familiar signs such as Wal-Mart and MacDonald's and ask about specific letters (EXIT), or when they scribble or ask for help in writing their names. Most parents react with dismay when they see children scribbling in inappropriate locations, but these scribbles are the first indication that children are trying to make sense of the symbols in their environment (Jalongo, 2000).

The classroom writing center provides an opportunity to experiment with print and attempt to make sense of it all. Writing becomes relevant to children in a safe atmosphere, and they play with forming letters without fear of mistakes. When children use their personal scripts, they can write any word or any letter the way they want it to look. The time for conventional print will come soon enough (Seefeldt & Galper, 2001).

Writing in a protected environment provides the opportunity to acquire basic skills in a meaningful way without having to memorize letters that probably do not relate to the child's understanding of language. Initially, children's playing with letters and words is more appropriate for young children than direct instruction. Children should be doing pretend writing or experimenting with magnetic letters on a magnetic board long before adults present formal teaching about what letters and words do (Bredekamp & Copple, 1997). Eventually, learning about sentence construction is another step in the process.

Art plays an important role in prewriting experiences. When children are finger painting, drawing with a crayon, painting at an easel, or making a paper plate puppet, two things are happening that relate to their later ability to write: (1) they are expressing themselves (formulating a thought that is projected onto paper or other art material) and (2) they are strengthening muscles in their hands that will allow them to better hold a writing tool.

Preschool teachers need to provide numerous and varied art experiences daily for children so they will be ready for writing when writing becomes essential to their school success. Providing instruction about holding art instruments increases children's ability to hold a pencil more easily at a later time.

Parents need to understand the relationship between art experiences and writing. If teachers collect art samples at specific times during the year (September, November, February, and April) to share with parents when conferences are scheduled, they can talk about the cognitive growth evidence in children's art. Information sent home in newsletters or shared during open house hours should emphasize that children who feel comfortable in expressing themselves well through an art activity will feel no differently when it's time to begin conventional writing in first grade.

Preschoolers may need a stimulus to move them away from the scribbling and drawing they are doing in art.

Setting up a writing center in classrooms when children are 4- or 5-years-old will prompt them to begin their own personal forms of writing and lead to an understanding that print conveys meaning. The emphasis on relevant, personal involvement in writing experiences is clear from research literature about early writing (Texas Association for the Education of Young Children, 1997).

Space and Equipment

The writing center does not require much classroom space. A table approximately 4 by 6 feet and four to six chairs are enough to get started. Paper and pencils are interesting in themselves, but later the center must become more challenging and stimulating to children. This center is the type that is used more as the year progresses, not less so. It is probably better to place the center next to the library or book center (which naturally emphasizes print concepts) or near the manipulatives center (which promotes fine-motor skills development). If a computer is available in the classroom, it should be placed next to the writing center as its use can complement the writing process.

A bulletin board behind the writing center provides a perfect place to display children's writing and notes the teacher might leave for individual children. As children progress in skill or as their interest in the center begins to lag, other materials and equipment may be added. Some suggestions are:

- Writing paper of all types - unlined tablets and notebook paper; stationery; computer paper; construction paper;

- Writing tools - markers of all colors; regular size pencils with dull points; chalk and chalkboard; crayons; brushes and water-color sets;

- Commercially prepared stencils (all sizes and shapes) for promoting children's tracing skills;

- Stamps and stamp pads for the beginning experimentation with putting "thoughts" on paper;

- Child-size scissors for both left- and right-handed children;

- Textures for crayon and pencil rubbings—sandpaper, nubbed fabric (such as corduroy), lace, leaves, tiles, a brick, corrugated paper (anything rough);

- Alphabet letter box filled with various sizes and type of letters cut from newspaper or magazines for children to glue and experiment with;

- An alphabet chart showing capital and lower-case letters;

- A chart showing the names of the children in the classroom to promote children's writing notes to their peers; and

- Scrap paper collected in a box labeled "Scraps: (children can be taught to collect scraps from other projects to put into this box).

Literacy Activities

The writing center is a great place for a message board. The teacher can write messages to children such as: "Caitlin, thanks for dressing the dolls. Miss June" "Maria, please feed the fish today. Mrs. Chi" Children will enjoy writing or drawing messages to the teacher or to their classmates.

Other literacy activities promoted by the writing center are making class books or children's personal books, developing rebus charts and stories, and writing experience stories. Collecting books that children write and bind themselves is an ideal communication technique to share with parents as evidence of children's learning in the preschool.

Experience stories are excellent records of classroom experiences, which children dictate to their teachers as they write the children's words on a chart. Or they may be developed individually as children dictate sentences to an aide or a parent volunteer who places them in the child's personal journal or on a sheet of paper. Often experiences evolve from group discussions about a special topic, as an extension of a class field trip or as a consequence of other classroom interactions children have enjoyed together, such as a visit to the classroom by a police officer or a local dentist. (Machado, 1999).

Rebus writing is a combination of pictures and words that assist children in following directions for a specific center activity (such as recipe in the cooking center or feeding the class rabbit). An example of a rebus chart is shown here:

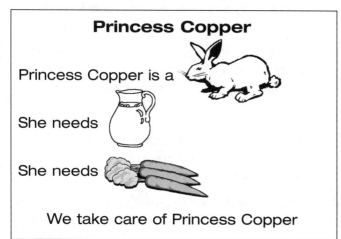

Princess Copper

Princess Copper is a

She needs

She needs

We take care of Princess Copper

Of all the centers in a preschool classroom, the writing center is the most easily adapted to individual needs. Basically, writing is a personal experience during the preschool years, and the writing center will accommodate several levels of performance and interest. Children with special needs will require more time to participate in the center, and their instructional needs will vary based on the specific problems they deal with every day. Working with children with special needs should be an extension of what is happening with other children.

The writing center should be a permanent fixture in the classroom; but if space is limited, only a portion of the materials need to be placed into the center at a time and then rotated to increase interest in the center. Other specific items will become part of the center as individual activities are planned and presented to children (Herr & Libby, 1994).

Evaluation in the writing center will take two basic forms: (1) observing children while they are writing and attempting to write, and recording that observation (see the sample checklist shown at the end of this chapter); and (2) collecting samples of children's writing on a regular basis. If teachers are observing appropriately and recording what they observe, they can step in and give specific instruction as the need arises. Some children will need information about holding a pencil or marker, while older children may request instruction about forming specific letters.

The checklist and the collection of writing samples serve two purposes: they help children see their own growth in writing, and they serve as an excellent starter for parent conferences. Parents are delighted to see the growth children have made in writing.

Young children can learn to assess their own writing and suggest ideas for improving their skills (Seefeldt & Galper, 2001). Teachers can ask youngsters questions to develop the self-assessment process, such as:

"What do you like best about your writing?"

"Which letter is the most fun to write?"

"Which letter matches best the alphabet chart?"

"How do you feel when you write?"

"Look at this writing you did in September? How do you feel about it? Is there anything you might want to change to make it better?"

Skill Activities

Recognizing that Print has Meaning
(4-year-olds and older)

Objective: To develop awareness in children that print in the environment has meaning

Materials needed: Print samples commonly found in the home and in the environment (print from cereal boxes, detergents, candy bars, canned goods, product logos cut from magazines, and many more); involve parents by asking them to help children collect familiar print samples to bring to preschool

What to do:

1. During circle time, spend five or ten minutes discussing various product logos children have brought in (concentrate on one type, perhaps logos from canned products, as an example, or logos of local familiar restaurants or business establishments). The objective is not to recognize the message of the logo, but rather, that the logo has a specific purpose.

2. Place the logos on the floor including a different one from another food category and ask children to find the one that does not belong. Ask children why the selection they made is different.

And still more:

1. Place the logos in the writing center and find an opportunity to informally assess the child's knowledge of the print.

2. Develop specific print awareness scrapbooks with each showing one category of product logos (one showing food items, another one representing clothing stores or another displaying photographs of local gas stations).

3. Encourage children to add to these scrapbooks throughout the year. Eventually, add pages that have the logos written in manuscript. If sheet protectors are placed over the logos and manuscript examples, children will be able to use markers to copy the print.

4. Place various signs in the classroom such as a rebus for washing hands, brushing teeth, or toileting procedures.

5. Add commercially prepared traffic signs in the block center or on the playground to encourage dramatic play.

Print in the environment

Adding Print to Classroom Centers
(4-year-olds and older)

Objective: To give children an understanding that print is used in a variety of ways in everyday life

Materials needed: Print material that represents how people use writing and reading during everyday living (recipe books, blueprints, calendars, books, etc.)

What to do:

1. During circle time, ask children what items they observe in their homes have writing on them. Add suggestions of your own as the discussion progresses.

2. During the next few days, use children's suggestions to collect and add materials to classroom centers to

enhance children's understanding that print is used in everyday life by all people.

Here are some suggestions:

- Dramatic Play or Home Center - Books, calendars, recipe books, dictionaries, magazines, daily newspapers, date books, address books, TV guides, telephone books and note pads; pencils or markers to taking messages; message boards

- Library Center - Develop check out procedures so children can take a favorite book home for several days; paper and pencils

- Science Center - Books about animals and plants; logs for keeping records about plant growth or scheduled feeding times for animals; charts describing scientific phenomena; paper or journals and pencils for data collection

- Art Center - Books showing famous art illustrations; directions for a specific art activity; signs showing where children's art is to be dried or displayed; pencils for putting their names on their art

- Grocery Store Center - Specials flyers from area grocery stores; pads for writing grocery lists; signs showing sections of the grocery store (dairy, produce, canned goods, bakery, etc.); paper and pencils for writing grocery lists

- Block Center - Teacher-prepared diagrams showing children how to build a selected block structure; signs indicating where blocks are to be stored; large pieces of paper and markers for children to develop their own designs for others to use

And still more:

1. Place signs around the room to assist children in remembering routines or locating supplies and materials they enjoy.

2. Call attention to signs in the building (EXIT, Gymnasium, Cafeteria, Nurse's Office, Library, Custodian).

3. Ask parents to point out print in the community while they are in their cars with their children. Children could prepare their own print scrapbooks at home with parental assistance.

Class Prepared Thank-You Note
(4-year-olds and older)

Objective: To give children an understanding that people who write have reasons for doing so

Materials needed: Two large pieces of white posterboard (18 by 24 inches or larger) prepared ahead of time and fastened together on the left with three or four pieces of yarn; felt-tipped markers or pencils

What to do:

1. After a field trip in the community, talk to children at circle time about writing a thank you note to the specific individual visited.

2. Guide them to understand that this is one reason why people write.

3. Try these questions:

   - What did we do on our field trip?

   - What was the most fun?

   - Who helped us have fun?

   When people help us, what should we do?

   - Have you or your parents ever received a written thank you letter?

   - What would you like to write in our thank you letter?

4. Allow children to brainstorm other reasons why adults and older children write.

5. As a group, compose a dictated story to the person visited and record what the children have said. Place the card in the writing center (or in a prominent spot in the classroom) so children can take turns signing their names. Encourage children to use their own personal scripts for writing their names, but adults can help children who insist that they want assistance. Suggest to children that drawing a picture is one way to write.

And still more:

1. Deliver the card to the appropriate person, and have your camera ready so that someone can take a picture of you giving the card to the recipient. Best practice would be to take children when the thank you note is delivered, but this plan might not be practical. Once the photograph has been processed, it makes a wonderful addition to the scrapbook of

the year's activities. Or it can be placed on the writing center bulletin board with a caption describing what's happening in the photograph.

2. Add purchased thank you notes to the writing center.

Theme Activities

Shapes Chalk Writing
(4-year-olds and older)

Objective: To draw simple shapes

Materials needed: Colored chalk, paper sacks or scrap pieces of paper, bulletin board space

What to do:

1. Provide children an opportunity to draw simple shapes on paper sacks.

2. Display their drawings on a bulletin board titled "Chalk Shapes" or "Chalk Magic." At another time, children could be encouraged to cut out shapes to drop into the sacks on the bulletin board.

And still more:

1. When the weather is warm outdoors, have children draw with chalk on a concrete sidewalk (or on an appropriate playground wall). Moisten the area with a water hose before the chalk is applied, and the drawing will remain for a longer time.

2. Observe each child to assess their ability to draw a square, circle, or triangle, but also encourage children to draw other figures as well.

Thematic Content Logs or Journals
(5-year-olds or older)

Objective: To assist children in recognizing the conventions of writing such as spaces between words, word order, and marks on pages other than alphabet letters, and to help children record their thoughts in a sequence over time to read and enjoy later.

Materials needed: Fifty pages of unlined paper stapled together in booklet form with a construction paper cover, a pencil for each child

What to do:

1. As thematic studies are introduced to children, ask them to keep a log (or journal) describing the information they are learning about the topic.

2. Encourage children to draw pictures and use invented spelling to tell their knowledge about the topic. In a unit about farm animals, children could draw pictures about the cat, dog, cow, horse, pig, duck, goose, turkey and other animals studied and attempt to write something about each animal. The emphasis should be on communicating through writing and not how letters are formed.

3. Suggest that this journal is a private one that only the teacher and child will read.

4. Give children information about writing casually, as they request it.

And still more:

1. Brainstorm topics with children relating to an event happening in the school or community to determine children's interests. Plan other thematic studies based on children's suggestions.

2. Encourage children to write or draw anytime they want. Also, use writing in logs as a transitional activity while waiting for lunch or for other children to finish center activities.

3. The teacher should keep a journal, too, and write at the same time as the children.

4. Allow children to take their content logs home to their parents to read. Prepare another journal and encourage children to continue the activity throughout the year. This is an excellent instructional tool for showing parents children's growth in writing.

Word Walls
(5-year-olds or older)

Objective: To secure children's understanding that words have meanings and conventional spellings

Materials needed: Chalkboard or bulletin board space to record words children suggest for their Word Wall (Some teachers use large pieces of butcher paper taped to a wall in the classroom.)

What to do:

1. As the school year emerges, call on children to tell specific words they need for their stories and descriptions of daily events. Write their suggestions on the word wall for consultation when they write in the writing center or during a preset writing time (some teachers invite children to write in their logs

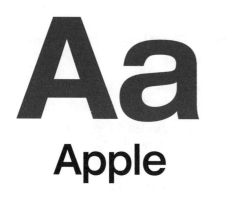

Aa
Apple

Bb
Ball

Cc
Cat

as they arrive each morning). Children could contribute the following words for a thematic study of the pond, as an example: *pond, water, water lilies, frogs, tadpoles, scum, trees, moss, polliwogs.*

2. Leave the words on the word wall for several days (or weeks) until children no longer need this assistance in their individual writing.

3. As new themes evolve, add new words to the class word wall.

And still more:

1. Introduce the alphabetic principle to children by reading an alphabet book to them during circle time (*T is for Texas* by Anne Bustard or *Chicka Chicka Boom Boom* by Bill Martin, Jr. and John Archambault are favorites).

2. Place a posterboard or large pieces of butcher paper in the classroom to demonstrate to children how the alphabet is organized.

3. Continue to introduce the alphabetic principle to children by placing flash cards showing each alphabet letter (capital and lower-case samples) at children's eye level. As words are requested, write them on flash cards to place *under* the appropriate alphabet letter (the word *basket* would be placed under *Bb*, for example).

4. Use the same flash cards described above to place children's names under the first letter of their name (*Cara* under *Cc*; *Harold* under *Hh*; and so on).

References

Bredekamp, S. & C. Copple (Eds.). (1997). *Developmentally appropriate practice in early childhood programs* (Rev.ed.). Washington, DC: National Association for the Education of Young Children.

Bustard, A. (1989). *T is for Texas.* Stillwater, MN: Voyageur Press, Inc.

Herr, J. & Y. Libby (1994). *Early childhood writing centers.* Fort Worth, TX: Harcourt Brace College Publishers.

Jalongo, M. (2000). *Early childhood language arts* (2nd ed.). Boston, MA: Allyn &Bacon.

Machado, J. (1999). *Early childhood experiences in language arts* (6th ed.). Albany, NY: Delmar Publishers.

Martin, B. & J. Archambault (1989). *Chicka, Chicka, Boom Boom.* NY: Simon and Schuster Books for Young Readers.

Seefeldt, C. & A. Galper. (2001). *Active experiences for active children: Literacy emerges.* Upper Saddle River, NJ: Merrill/Prentice Hall.

Texas Association for the Education of Young Children (1997). *Early childhood literacy development: A position statement.* Austin, TX: Author.

Checklist for Evaluating Children's Writing

Use the following checklist to evaluate children's participation in the writing center. Assess each item by circling the answer option that best describes a child's observed writing behavior.

Child's Name_____

Child chooses the writing center at least once a week.
Yes   No

Child requests information about writing on a routine basis.   **Yes   No**

Child holds pencil correctly.
Yes   No

Child forms letters and/or words.
Yes   No   Sometimes

Child's writing attempts can be described as:

uses own printscript

attempts conventional print

Child includes all letters of own name when attempting to write it.   **Yes   No**

Child understands and uses spaces between words.
Yes   No   Sometimes

Child reads his or her own writing at a later time.
Yes   No   Sometimes

Child shares his or her writing with others.
Yes   No   Sometimes

Child begins to evaluate his/her own writing.
Yes   No   Sometimes

Checklist for Evaluating the Writing Center

Rate the items below on a scale of 1 to 4 with "needing improvement" as 1 and "outstanding" as 4.

_____1. Adequate space is provided for writing activities.

_____2. The center contains basic equipment, tables, chairs, shelves, and writing materials.

_____3. The center offers writing activities for several levels of development (from inexperienced to very experienced).

_____4. Children choose the writing center on a regular basis.

_____5. The teacher routinely monitors the writing center to remove unsafe materials.

_____6. The teacher observes and instructs children who have specific individual needs in writing.

_____7. The teacher provides a good writing model.

About the Author

Laverne Warner is Coordinator and Professor of Early Childhood Education at Sam Houston State University. She is a Past President of the Texas Association for the Education of Young Children (TAEYC, 1995-1997) and a charter member of the Sam Houston Association for the Education of Young Children, to which she currently serves as advisor. She has written numerous articles for state, regional and national journals and is co-author of a textbook about early childhood education in public school settings (Allyn and Bacon, 2004). She is a regular presenter at conferences for TAEYC, the Southern Early Childhood Association (SECA) and the National Association for the Education of Young Children (NAEYC).

Chapter 21

Creating Spaces for Technologies

Deborah Diffily

Just a few short years ago, cutting-edge technology in early childhood classrooms consisted of a VCR, relatively slow computers, and diskettes that held computer games. Today, companies roll out new technology on almost a weekly basis. More and more adult lives are filled with Palm Pilots, digital cameras, scanners, DSL connection to the

Internet, MP3 players, CD players, and CD burners. The remarkable technologies being developed to assist children with special needs hold promise for helping children become more independent and functional. The World Wide Web is being brought into classrooms with increasing frequency connecting teachers and children to sites around the world. The question becomes which of these technologies can be or should be used in classrooms for young children and how can educators become discerning and informed consumers.

Some early childhood experts believe that technology can be used in developmentally appropriate ways with young children, ages four to eight. These educators view technology as a way to expand curriculum topics and themes beyond the child's immediate environment and to offer opportunities for children to develop listening skills, follow directions, hone hand-eye coordination, expand vocabulary and literacy, practice and solve mathematical problems, and enhance creative writing and artistic efforts (Luntz, (1999).

Other experts are diametrically opposed to young children using computers and other technological devices. In a position statement endorsed by dozens of education experts and pediatricians, the Alliance for Children asserts, "Computers pose serious health hazards to children. The risks include repetitive stress injuries, eyestrain, obesity, social isolation, and for some, long-term damage to physical, emotional, or intellectual development" (http://www.allianceforchildhood.net/projects/computers/computers/_articles_call_for_action.htm, p.1).

Technology and Developmentally Appropriate Practices

Despite the disagreement about whether young children should use technology, there is general consensus that technological devices are not appropriate for children three and under. Speaking specifically about computers, Claire Lerner, a child-development specialist for Zero to Three contends, "Children don't need computer activities in any shape or form to thrive or master the basic skills of early childhood" (Reek, 2000/2001, p. 126). Susan Hauglund (1999, p. 26) echoes this opinion by writing, "Computers simply do not match their learning style. Children younger than 3 learn through their bodies, their eyes, ears, mouths, hands, and legs." Therefore, space for new technology is not a consideration for classrooms of the youngest children.

By entry into prekindergarten programs, children are typically ready to explore selected computer programs. This is true when children control the learning experience and the computer provides concrete experiences (Papert, 1998).

In kindergarten, children are ready for expanded uses of computers (Haugland, 2000). They benefit from a wider range of software programs, consult CD-ROMs for particular information, use word processing to compose letters, and view adult-selected web sites to gather information through photographs and digital streaming.

From first to third grade, children grow in their abilities to use technology as a tool for both research and producing products that share what they have learned with others. Primary-age children readily learn to scan their work or photograph it using a digital camera. They can order their work, label it, and create presentations. They can use DSL connections to the Internet to locate specific web sites. However, adults should supervise any exploration of the Internet by young children. One good place to start the search for the sites that are right for young child is the American Library Association's 50+ Great Web Sites for Parents & Kids (www.ala.org/parentspage/greatsites/50.html). But adults should always be aware of potential links to other sites that are not appropriate for young children.

Space Requirements

Creating spaces for technology depends on how the technology will be used. With 4- and 5-year-olds, children will typically use only computers with prepackaged software. Most experts and practitioners believe that, at this stage, children learn best when they work with a partner at a computer. The verbal interaction between children enhances the computer experience. Given this limited use by pairs, computers in classrooms for 4- and 5-year-old children should be arranged so that two chairs are placed in front of them. Also given the rambunctious nature of children this age, computers should be placed as far away from the messier learning centers as possible. Spilled sand, water, or paint can ruin equipment.

As children begin using computers more for research and creating products and as they incorporate other technologies into their work, other factors about space must be considered. As with younger children, it is important to place technological equipment away from anything that could damage it. This may become more complicated because more computers should be made available to kindergarten and primary-aged children. Haugland (2000) strongly recommends that the ratio of computers to children should be one to five. Creating space for four or five computers in a single classroom may not be easy.

First of all, five computers take up a significant portion of the classroom. Because of the issue of electrical outlets, computers are usually positioned against a wall. So, most likely, computers would fill one entire wall of a classroom. Second, the cost of the computers is just the beginning of technological-related expenses. Peripherals are needed, such as printers, zip drives, scanners, and digital cameras, and furniture to house the equipment.

A variety of types of workstations can be purchased to hold computers and other equipment at a range of prices. An individual workstation needs to be no less than 24" wide, 30" deep and should have shelf space for software and other supplies.

Workstations can be purchased or designed to accommodate two or more computers. In planning and designing spaces and equipment for computers, consideration must be given to the need for flat surfaces large enough to house any extra peripherals or storage for discs or CD-ROMs. Additional furniture may need to be purchased for this equipment and other add-ons as they become available and are deemed appropriate for use with young children.

In addition to the hardware and software space needs, reference materials and writing supplies are placed near the technology center. Many software programs require that children use reference materials such as atlases and almanacs. Occasionally, children need graph paper to complete activities suggested in the software program, and quite often, children need scratch paper so they can jot notes about their work.

Selecting Appropriate Software and Web Sites for Young Children

It has been said that today's children are "the first generation of the Digital Age" (Center for Media Education, 1996, p.2). Indeed, new technologies are entering into our daily lives and tasks at astounding speed. Many adults are having to learn new ways to carry out old tasks. The teacher of young children does not escape this bombardment. Hence, it is critical that those who teach young children be informed about technology's possibilities while remaining focused on the human needs of the growing child.

This means making sound judgments about if, when, and how to use technology with children, and how to make wise selections of software and other resources. The following are criteria for selecting appropriate software for children's use (Puckett & Black, 2000).

- Children should be able to boot up the software program independently or with minimal help.

- The directions for use should be easily explained and understandable to children.

- The vocabulary of the program should be appropriate to the child's developmental level.

- The program should provide feedback to let children know when their responses are correct or incorrect.

- The program keyboard functions should be simple and manageable.

- The program graphics should be simple, appealing, content appropriate. It should not be distracting.

- The program's audio component should be clear, accurate, supportive, and not distracting.

- The program encourages choice, decision-making, problem solving, creative thinking, and prosocial perspectives.

- The program fosters social and intellectual interaction with others.

- The program complements and supports the current curricular themes and class activities, and/or can be extended through concrete, hands-on materials and social interaction activities that are provided in other learning centers.

- The content is congruent with developmentally appropriate practices and the goals of the early childhood program.

As with software, educators who choose to access the Internet need to become discerning consumers. There is widespread concern over the content and quality of materials made available to children through cyberspace. Today, there are millions of web sites of every conceivable genre beckoning the attention of educators, children, and families. Educators and parents must make decisions about those sites that serve the best interests of children and the goals of early education. Selection of web sites should be based on several criteria (Roempler, 1999):

1. Is the web site easy to navigate and use?

- What types of web browsers (e.g., Netscape Navigator© or Microsoft Internet Explorer©) are required to connect to the web site? Are these browsers installed in your equipment?

- How long does it take for the site to appear on the screen? Sites that take a long time are loading large files that may include more material than is needed. Children (and adults) lose patience and interest if the wait becomes too long.

- Is the site available when it is needed? Some very popular sites become very busy and cannot be accessed during a particular instructional period.

- Is the web site's home page clean and uncluttered, and does it provide a simple table of contents?

- Is it easy to follow a path (or links) to information one is seeking?
- Does the web site include irrelevant advertising?

2. Who or what entity is the author of the web site?

- Does the address provide clues as to the source of the information on it? Generally, this information is partially found in the URL (web address) extension which is the part of the address that comes after the "dot," (e.g., ".com," usually represents commercial businesses; ".gov," represents a government agency, ".edu," represents an education agency or institution, and ".org," represents some business, faith-based, social, civic, philanthropic, educational or other type of organization). A tilde (~) usually means that the web page is created and maintained by an individual rather than a business, organization, or school.
- Does the web site provide information about how to get in touch with the author(s)? It is important to determine the affiliation or credentials behind the material offered on a web site. Reliable web sites make this information available along with how users might get in touch with the author(s) by phone or postal address.

3. Is the content valid?

- Is the information accurate? Accuracy of information is important if it is to be used for education purposes. Simply being on the screen or being presented in a colorful, clever, or appealing format, does not assure that the material is accurate and true.
- Is the information bias-free? The material (as with all other classroom materials) must be free of bias and stereotypes, and should not promote only one point of view.
- Is the information current? How recently has the information been updated? The web site should provide this information.

4. Does the web site engage young learners?

- Is the material age-appropriate?
- Is the material relevant to the curriculum goals and meaningful to students?
- Does the web site format get children actively involved in a learning process?
- Can the knowledge or skills learned on the web site be transferred to other activities in the classroom?
- What types of interactive features does the web site offer?

Planning for Children's Use of Technologies

While new technologies offer hope and promise for enriching curriculums and expanding children's knowledge and skills, it is important to keep in mind the precautions mentioned in the beginning of this chapter. Children need real play with real people. They need the social and linguistic interactions that come from playing and talking with others. They need to manipulate, pretend, explore, experiment, construct, and create using real objects. They need to explore their surroundings and take real field trips to places in their communities. They need to share and test their own ideas as they play, dialogue, inquire, and reflect. They need to express and receive affection. They need the human voice to provide instruction, assistance, feedback, and authentic praise. No matter how sophisticated, technology cannot meet these needs.

Throughout childhood the purposes for using technology changes. Younger children use computers, for example to play games or to practice selected skills. As children get older, their use of computer technology to access information and carry out homework tasks increases. As children gain independence in the use of computers and access to web sites through the Internet, adults must take precautions to protect children from inappropriate content and contacts.

While there are a number of electronic devices and software programs designed to block reception of inappropriate material, the American Academy of Pediatrics urges parents and teachers to help children become discerning users suggesting that "media literacy" affords protections when adults are not present to over-see and guide their choices (AAP, 1999). The following suggestions are made to increase children's media literacy (Buriss, 1997):

1. Set clear rules for computer use, Internet access, on-line contact sources, communications, and behavior.

2. We teach children not to talk to or share personal information (name, address, phone number, family names, school or center name, and so on) with people they do not know, and this includes talking with strangers on-line.

3. Adults need to know and be able to talk with the person on the other end of the Internet communication (e-mail, chat-room, or other communicating device).

4. Advise children to tell an adult when they receive messages that are frightening, or inappropriate.

5. Help children identify best sources of web site addresses and other electronic resources.

6. Help children learn to evaluate the material provided by software and Internet sources on the basis of some of the criteria listed above.

7. Monitor children's use of technology; limit children's screen time; and clearly define how computers and other technologies are to be used. (Arrange computers in the classroom so that the monitors face outward in clear view of adults, so that both monitoring and assisting is facilitated).

Technology in early childhood classrooms requires a significant investment of money and the dedication of a large portion of the classroom space and knowledgeable teachers capable of selecting, instructing, and guiding its appropriate use. It is important that early childhood educators determine if the investment in dollars and space is commensurate with the time and use that can or perhaps, should be given to the equipment. If screen time or other technological pursuits detract from the principal goals of early childhood education rather than augment them, then the investment may be excessive. Further, if the equipment and its use are beyond the technical skills of the teachers and adults who work with children, the full potential of the technologies cannot be realized.

References

Alliance for Children (2000). Children and computers: A call to action [Online]. Available: http://www.allianceforchildhood.net/projects/computers/computers_ articles_call_for_action.htm

American Academy of Pediatrics (August, 1999). Media education. *Pediatrics, 104,* 341-43.

Center for Media Education (November, 1996). *Connecting children to the future.* Washington, DC: Author.

Buriss, L.L. (Winter, 1997). Safety in the Cybervillage: Some Internet guidelines for teachers. *Association for Childhood Education International Focus on Elementary (Ages 7-10), 10*(2), 1-6.

Haugland, S.W. (2000). *Computers and young children.* ERIC Document Reproduction No. 438926.

Haugland, S.W. (1999). What role should technology play in young children's learning? *Young Children, 54*(6), 26-31.

Luntz, I. (Winter, 1999). Using computers in the kindergarten. *Association for Childhood Education International Focus on Pre-K and K (Ages 4-6), 12*(2), 4-6.

Papert, S. (1998, September 1). Technology in schools: To support the system or render it obsolete [Online]. Available: http://www.mff.org/edtech/article.taf?_function=detail&Content_uid1=106

Puckett, M.B. & Black, J.K. (2000). *Authentic assessment of the young child: Celebrating development and learning* (2nd ed.). Columbus, OH: Prentice Hall.

Roempler, K.S. (1999). Using the Internet in the classroom: Becoming a critical consumer of the Web. *Eisenhower National Clearinghouse Focus, 6*(3) 11-13.

Reek, A. (2000/2001). Raising kids in a wired world. *Parenting, 14*(10), 126.

Checklist for Evaluating Spaces for Technology

Rate the items below on a scale of 1 to 4 with 1 representing "needs improvement" and 4 representing "outstanding."

_____1. Computers are positioned far away from materials – sand, water, paint – that could damage them.

_____ 2. More than one chair is available at each computer station so that children can work in pairs.

_____ 3. Computers are connected to electrical outlets with surge protectors.

_____ 4. Printers, scanners, and digital cameras are easily accessible by children working in the computer area.

_____5. Criteria for developmental appropriateness and alignment with curriculum goals are applied in the selection and use of computer software and web sites.

_____ 6. Children are helped to become media literate through guidance and instruction on how to evaluate software and web sites.

_____ 7. Adults both monitor and limit screen time for children.

About the Author

Deborah Diffily is an assistant professor of Early Childhood Education at Southern Methodist University, in Dallas. Her primary areas of interest are supporting emergent and scientific development, teaching young children through projects, and working with families.

Section IV

Environments for School-Age Children

Chapter 22

It is Friday of the first week of the new school year. It has been a challenging week for everyone in Ms. Beck's class of 6-year-old children. The beginning of the school year always is. Fortunately for most of the 18 children in this class, Ms. Beck is the same teacher they had last year in kindergarten. The children know her teaching style, are acquainted with her ways of interacting with them, and have enjoyed a positive and supportive relationship with her over the preceding months. They are happy to be back in their familiar classroom, and are eager to show Ms. Beck "how smart" they now are. While much about the classroom looks the same as it did during kindergarten, there is a sense of change, newness, anticipation. For some children there is a twinge of anxiety. For some, a whole new experience awaits them.

Organizing Classrooms for 6- and 7-Year Old Children

Margaret B. Puckett

Ms. Beck has the advantage of knowing her former pupils' capabilities, interests, unique personalities, their family expectations, and where each child "left off" at the end of the previous school year. During kindergarten, she kept copious assessment records through portfolios, school tests results, family conferences, and health and special school diagnostics as needed. She has had a week to get reacquainted after the summer break. But she must also know more about several newcomers who did not attend her kindergarten last year. Her informal assessments (observations, anecdotal notes, and selected check-lists), during this first week have given her much to think about as she begins to match what she knows about the children with the predetermined expectations and standards set by local and state authorities for primary grade education. Though she has already put in place her preliminary first-of-school preparations, there is much planning she now must do.

Classroom Preparations

Wisely, Ms. Beck has kept the basic features of her kindergarten classroom in place. There are learning centers, a large group meeting area, a small half-circle shaped table for small group direct instruction, and there is a bank of 4 computers arranged to be used as an added learning center. Then, of course, there is Ms. Beck's familiar "granny chair" (the children named it last year), a small cushioned rocker that she sits in when they hold class meetings and share stories, that is, if she doesn't join them on the floor.

Yes, the room does differ from last year's however, there are taller tables and chairs, the room's color schemes have changed and there are a number of different artifacts and visuals on the walls bulletin boards, and shelves. A new blue tweed carpet remnant spreads over the dual purpose block center/large group meeting area, and fresh plants are spotted about the room. There is a new dark blue canvas slipcover on the old love seat with no legs. An there are assorted colorful floor pillows fluffed and inviting. There are one or two waist high stands that will be used to accommodate Jeremy who wears leg braces and depends on a walker to get around. The higher work surface will allow him to stand rather than sit when that is more comfortable for him.

Curiously, there are some very plain wooden indoor window boxes on the seal of each window, but there is nothing in them. There is a sizable aquarium waiting to be assembled, and what was once a large walk-in closet opening into the adjacent hallway, has now been opened into the classroom and new cubbies installed there along one wall. The other wall of the closet now has shelves for storage of school supplies, books, and materials yet to be rotated.

Because there are school supplies that children bring during the first week or two at the beginning to the year, Ms. Beck, anticipating the clutter and confusion, assessed the new storage shelves and considered the following:

- Which materials need to be on the lower or eye-level shelves to facilitate child access?

- How can materials be made accessible to Jeremy?

- Which materials need to be nearest the door for frequent access?

- Which materials need to be stored out-of-reach and accessed by adults only?

- Which materials will be used during these first weeks and thus, need to be handy?

- Which materials can be stored on higher shelves for later use?

- In what sequence might the need for certain materials arise?

Once these decisions are made, Ms. Beck is prepared to involve the children in the storage plan. During class meeting time on the second day of school, the children were invited into the new cubbie room to look it over and get acquainted with the space. Ms. Beck suggested that each student could create a label to identify their own cubbies. During center time, they could choose to: draw a small picture and write their name on it to be taped to the back of their cubbie; they could use Kid Pix© at the computer and create a picture or a name plate to use; they could select a special sticker to put on a name card created from a section of sentence strip; or they could write their name on a sentence strip and bring a photograph from home to glue to their name strip. By the end of the day, she expected each student to have labeled a cubbie for themselves.

The following day, in the class meeting Ms. Beck led a discussion of the types of supplies that had been brought by students and purchased by the school or district for the first grade glass and how they would be used. After a show and tell examination of the types of materials that had been and would be brought, the discussion led to how they should be organized in the new storage area. She again invited the children to peruse the storage space. Returning to the blue rug she engaged the children in a discussion about how the materials might be stored in the new space to make them easy to find. She shared her own ideas and prompted that it would take work and cooperation to get the storage space arranged so that everyone could use the materials efficiently.

The class was divided into committees. One committee would stack the manilla paper in its agreed upon location, a lower shelf near the closet door for quick and easy access. Another committee would sort the colored papers into color stacks and place them next to the manilla paper. Another would sort and stack the writing tablets and notebooks. Other committees would sort and store crayons, pencils, erasers, glue, math counters, and other small items in labeled bins. Still another would sort the school supplied beginning reading books and other textbook materials. A place would be selected for

the aquarium supplies, extra library books, science equipment, and Ms. Beck would label and arrange the prop boxes on higher shelves. This process consumed the better part of two mornings, but as we shall see, was well worth it. As supplies continued to arrive in the next several days, children knew where to store them and could do so independently.

Ms. Beck always takes the first several weeks to, as she says "build our nest," with the children. She provides the "infrastructure," having predetermined the placement of centers to minimize interferences, maximize natural lighting, allow for appropriate storage, allow for both horizontal and vertical display areas, and provide efficient pathways to restrooms, water and clean-up supplies, drinking fountains, and doorways. She has made certain that centers with equipment that need electricity are placed near an outlet that is protected and from which cords can be secured to avoid accidents. She has located a small space near the hallway door for a family communications center. She has considered placement of centers and furnishings to facilitate quick and easy exit in the event of an emergency, and will practice with the children in the next few days how fire or weather emergencies are handled.

For the first week, she has placed a minimal number of items in the centers to allow her an opportunity to introduce or reintroduce them and talk about the use, care, and placement of materials in their respective centers. She engages the children in discussing what other materials they think they will need in the centers. For example, the math center may need more paper, pencils, rulers, additional counters, and perhaps some numeral strips taped to the table. A committee is formed to carry out the task of adding the needed items during center time. The library center needs some more books, but what topics will we be discussing? And what are some of your favorite remembered titles? Three students are assigned the task of selecting four books each from storage to add to the library center. We will be learning about and talking about the aquarium, what can we add to the science center to help us learn more about fish and how to care for them and how to keep their aquarium clean and healthy for them? Two students are assigned the task of locating books about fish, a tray to hold a week's supply of food and other aquarium supplies, a magnifying glass to look more closely at the fish, and so on. Each of the existing centers — art, writing, library, math, blocks, science, puppets, and sociodramatic — are addressed in this fashion.

As the weeks progress and the curriculum evolves, the centers will take on different personalities with altered purposes, added materials, and perhaps, physical reconfiguration. Additional centers may be added, such as a center for paired reading, a current events center, a listening station, a book publishing center, and a geography circle. Theme centers may also be added during the year as extended or long-term projects are included in the curriculum. Such themes as "All about our school;" "How animals help people;" "Where our food comes from;" "Authors whose books we have read;" and so on, may require a designated space for children to focus on the associated research and activities.

So what has Ms. Beck done so far to organize space for 1st grade children? She has:

- reacquainted herself with individual children, their capabilities, needs, and interests;

- begun to informally assess new pupils in the class to ascertain their capabilities, needs, and interests;

- maintained continuity from kindergarten to first grade by keeping many of the features of the kindergarten setting while embellishing it to engage and meet the needs of older children;

- prepared the environment by first establishing an infrastructure that provides the necessary room arrangement and health and safety precautions;

- planned for the storage of materials;

- planned for children's independent access to the materials;

- reviewed the use of learning centers with the children;

- introduced 1st grade materials to the students;

- engaged the children in a storage plan;

- engaged the children in provisioning the centers with necessary and wanted supplies; and

- anticipated future center themes and curricular extensions.

Notice that arranging and organizing space and materials involves both pre- and on-going planning. This is not an isolated teacher task; nor is it about furnishings and teaching materials only. What the teacher can know about her students in advance is essential to planning a functional primary grade classroom, one that can meet the needs of a student with a physical/motor disability, and a classroom that is culturally authentic and responsive to the needs and expectations of families of diverse cultures. Moreover, the students themselves can and should be an integral part of the process. Effective learning centers cannot be prepared without considering the capabilities, interests, and needs of the users. Learning centers are used more fully and productively when the

users (students) have a say in what they think they need to carry out school tasks.

Selection and Use of Materials is Based on:

- Specific learning objectives

- Knowledge of specific individual or group needs and interests

- Usability and appeal to children

- A range of levels of difficulty

- Flexibility and multiple uses

- Cultural authenticity

As well, when the children are engaged in the process of storing and organizing materials at the very beginning of the school year, they begin to mentally process and internalize the notion that the classroom and its contents are theirs to use in appropriate ways. They learn how to access and neatly store their materials. They become reacquainted with the learning centers and classroom procedures and rules. Importantly, their awareness of what is to come during this 1st or 2nd grade experience is quickened and their curiosity and interest is aroused.

Invitational Display and Accessibility

Every center is surrounded by low open shelves, peg boards, wall ledges, and other features to hold the necessary materials in ways that make them handy for children to retrieve and replace. There are bulletin boards, wall display space, wall pockets, and improvised systems for promoting focused attention to the learning objectives and tasks that are intended for the center. The manner in which materials are stored and displayed in each learning center either invites constructive and focused participation or discourages and negates it.

Creative teachers use innovative ways to make centers inviting. The types of instructional materials that will be used dictate the types of containers, organization, and display that is needed. Because 1st and 2nd grade children are using and honing their language, speaking, writing, spelling, reading, and mathematic skills and do so in each center, instructional materials to support these skills need to be provided in each center. Further, the content or subject matter, the theme, or projects taking place in each center require specific types of theme related materials, artifacts, supportive literature, and visual and auditory supports.

These display materials can be color coordinated to designate their center home and items used in the center marked with a color dot sticker, so that when borrowed for other uses they can be readily returned. Grouping display containers that belong to "families" in individual centers creates a sense of order and place. For example, a center can be organized using mostly baskets of different shapes and sizes, another can use plastic containers more appropriate for activities with water, paint, or food, another might use wooden containers, and yet another, cardboard/corrugated containers, such as decorated boxes, corrugated files boxes, commercial corrugated units, and so on. Following is a partial list of the types of containers and display strategies that can be used to store, display, communicate instructions, and convey content. The use and strategic arrangement of these items creates centers that are not only functional but aesthetically appealing as well.

Small objects such as counters, pegs, beads, small manipulatives:

- baskets (natural fiber or painted, small and large, deep or shallow, with or without handles as needed)
- small clear plastic buckets with handles
- shallow square or rectangular boxes covered in color coordinated Contact© paper
- trays artistically painted with picture or print labels to convey their contents
- small plastic stacking bins

Writing implements, crayons, craft sticks:

- color coordinated Contact© paper covered juice and coffee cans
- plastic cups, cylinders, small pitchers
- heavy pottery cups, tumblers, small vases, or bowls
- commercial wooden or wire marker and crayon holders

Writing and art papers

- office supply in/out trays
- shallow tray-shaped baskets
- labeled and attractively decorated rectangular boxes
- larger plastic stacking bins
- clip boards
- trays of different shapes (square, rectangle, round, hexagon, oval)

- vertical magazine file boxes
- wooden folding plate drying rack
- wire collating stands
- wall-mounted pockets (single or multiple units)
- attractively decorated corrugated barrels for wide rolls of paper and larger items

Manipulative sets

- small canvas bags with carrying handles and drawings or painted labels on them (either a picture of the objects or printed word label or both can convey the contents of the bag.). The handle allows the bags to be hung on a peg board.
- baskets
- plastic open bins and stacking bins
- see-through plastic shoe boxes

When assorted but related supplies must be assembled:

- lazy susan tray with small plastic cups or containers
- divided plastic carry-all such as is used with housekeeping supplies
- open top carpenter's box
- pigeon-hole shelf
- wall hung shoe bag with clear plastic pockets for individual floppy disks
- commercial CD, DVD, and floppy disk shelves and/or file boxes
- hanging file stand or box (found at office supply and container stores)
- divided trays as used for thread or jewelry

To convey instructions or information

- clear plastic stand-alone 5" x 7,"8"x 10," or 10"x 12" photo frames can hold rebus instructions, assignments, snack recipes, news articles, or other informational pictures or print.
- clear plastic stand-alone cook-book holders can position and hold an open book or small chart
- stenographers tablet stand
- clip board hung on a hook at the center's entry
- small table easel
- photo easels
- small white or chalk boards with stands and chalk or markers

To designate individual work spaces

- laminated paper placemats (purchased or teacher-made)
- large trays with shallow lip
- commercial finger paint trays
- 12" x 14" sections of Masonite© board or laminate material
- color coordinated carpet samples
- small 3"x 4" grass mats

This list is certainly not exhaustive, nor does it address all of the types of items that need containers for display and efficient use. Hopefully, reading through the list sparks creativity and generates new, functional and attractive ideas. The purpose in selecting and arranging attractive and functional display materials is to create inviting learning spaces and to make school tasks manageable for 6- and 7-year-old children. Orderly display of materials facilitates the care and maintenance of school supplies and the orderly conduct of learners.

Sights and Sounds in the Environment

Every primary grade classroom should have well chosen and strategically placed visual and auditory supports for learning. Without being overstimulating, distracting, superfluous, or disneyesque,[1] visual displays can at once add to the pleasing aesthetics of the learner's environment and support learning in significant ways. In like manner, there can be auditory supports for children's learning through well-chosen recorded background music, voice, or sounds. Teachers who observe their children carefully to ascertain the types of environmental supports that encourage productive, focused work, soon learn to select or avoid the types of sounds, sights, textures, and other qualities that facilitate or distract their pupils' on-task behaviors.

The visual supports to learning include eye-level instructional materials. The alphabet at ceiling height is not as useful as a small alphabet chart with both lower and upper case letters at the writing table, or a laminated alphabet page that each child owns and can store in their individual work folders. Likewise, numeral strips with introduced mathematic symbols (+, -, <, >, =,) taped to the math table work space is handier than large numerals displayed across the top of the chalk board at the front of the classroom. Rebus charts in small display frames at the learner's work site are easier to follow than

focusing far away to a large easel chart, then back to the work space to carry out its directions. On the other hand, a collection of environmental print, or a display of spelling words that have been mastered can occupy the vertical wall space near the writing center. A montage of photographs depicting many types of aquarium fish can fill the bulletin board near the science center. A large map of the school's surrounding neighborhood can be posted in the block area to encourage road building and directional orientations. A display of important signs that are found in and around the school or center (*Exit, Nurse's Office, Principal, Boys' and Girls' Restrooms, Auditorium, Library, and Do Not Cross, Stop, Fasten Seat-Belt,* and so on) can be posted in the class meeting area for discussion and review of important locations and school procedures. A big book open and ready to read displayed on a ledge or stand in the meeting area or reading center enlists interest. A list of two or three goals for the day can be neatly printed on the chalk board at the front of the room to review and set the tone for the day, and to revisit at class meeting time at the end of the day. In short, visuals should be chosen and placed for their relevance to what children are expected to do and for their ability to enrich and clarify the learning environment.

Auditory supports are chosen with these same caveats. Some children are calmed and focused by softly played soothing background music. Different forms of music can provide a pleasing backdrop for creative expression: written, painted, movement, or dance. Selected classical works introduce children to classical musicians and orchestral instruments, and are pleasing to hear in the background and may be helpful during rest time. Familiar songs with which to hum along or sing while working on a project in the block center lightens the heart and increases the enjoyment of work. Transitions that are sung, chanted, clapped out, or sounded on a musical instrument rather than spoken enlist cooperation and reduce the number of times students must "stop and listen" to the teacher's verbal instructions. Recordings need not only be musical. Recorded poetry, chants, pleasing environmental sounds also can be used. In the listening station, professional voices are not the only ones that are auditorily pleasing and interesting to children. Enlist parents to read and record favorite stories and poems. Create a recorded montage of parents' or family members' voices each reading a passage from a book, a nursery rhyme, or a verse of poetry. As children listen, they are intent on hearing the most familiar voice! A family member for each child should be included in the montage. In like

---

[1]*Disneyesque* is a term often used by Dr. Lillian Katz of the University of Illinois at Urbana, a well known scholar in early childhood education.

manner, a montage of the students reading from a familiar book, or their own writings can create similar interest and auditory discrimination.

What Time Is It?
(*Tune: Muffin Man*)

"O do you know what time it is?

It's story time you see."
(*or clean-up, lunch, snack, etc.*)

Won't You Come and Sit Right Here
(*Tune: Mary Had a Little Lamb*)

Won't you come and sit right here, sit right here,
sit right her.

Won't you come and sit right here, for our story.

Schedules

Ms. Beck begins each day with a class meeting. Members of the class share news while others are arriving and putting their book bags and wraps in their cubbies. To help the children settle in and begin to focus, Ms. Beck recites a number of finger-plays with them, sings a song or two, or plays a brief game of *I Spy*. Usually she selects finger-plays, songs, or games related to the current curriculum concepts or themes. When all are assembled, the children recite the Pledge of Allegiance followed by one of several patriotic songs that they now know. Announcements are made, and an overview of the day's activities and learning center procedures is given. Ms. Beck reviews with the children the activities and lessons of the previous day and assigns completion tasks. On the chalk board she has written today's assignments which she explains to the children:

Complete cubbie name labels.

Read a book in the library center.

    Write the book title in your reading log

Meet with Ms. Beck at the lesson table.

Copy new words from the words board.

Prepare a math journal:

    Your name on page 1

    Write numerals from 1 to 20 on page 2

Prepare snack using the rebus recipe

The instructions will remain on the chalk board throughout the day. Children are instructed to complete unfinished tasks from the previous day, and then begin today's assignments. They may begin with their choice of task and find the most appropriate place to carry it out. A book can be read on the love seat; the math journals are filed in the math center, but one may carry their journal to a rug area if they would prefer to work on the floor; the new words board is on a wall in the writing center, cubbie labels are being completed in the art and computer centers, and snack preparations and rebus recipe are set up in the science center. Students can prepare a snack as they feel hungry for it, so long as there is a space in the center for them. The students know that each center has spaces for a certain number of students who can work there at any one time. It is usually designated by the number of seating or individual work places. Other centers have a numeral suspended from the ceiling (e.g., the blocks center has a large laminated cut-out of a block with the numeral 2 on it).

When the students have completed their tasks they may select other related activities in the centers. However, they must make every effort to complete the assigned tasks before lunch time. Ms. Beck is very conscientious about helping students use their time wisely and productively. All items in all centers are strategically selected to impart some aspect of the curriculum requirements.

During this period, Ms. Beck will summon 4 to 6 children at a time to the lesson table to introduce the basal reader or other beginning literacy material which has been adopted by the school for first grade. She will ascertain each child's ability to read the 1st level books and thereafter, determine what types of readers and other literacy supports are needed for individual children.

After a substantial time period to complete assignments and work in centers, the children are given the "5-minute-signal" that conveys that there are five minutes left to complete what they are doing and put away their materials. They will now assemble on the blue rug to review and discuss what they have accomplished, while hands are washed and lunch bags and lunch tickets are retrieved from cubbies. After lunch, they return to the classroom for a story time, a quite rest time for about 15 minutes. After rest time, Ms. Beck plays the recorder for a brief sing-along as children gather their wraps and outdoor play items for a 25-minute outdoor play period.

After recess, the children return to their centers to complete tasks begun during the morning. Ms. Beck circulates among the centers providing encouragement, assistance, feed-back, taking dictations, and clarifying instructions. Individuals who have completed their tasks may be given a more advanced or an extension assignment to carry out. During this process, Ms. Beck continues to observe and record her assessments of individual accomplishments and challenges — an on-going process that has become almost second-nature to her. From this information she is able to anticipate curriculum advances and generate ideas for augmenting the state, district, or school required skills and content (National Research Council, 2001; Puckett & Black, 2000).

Across the hall from Ms. Beck's classroom is Mrs. Ruiz's 2nd grade. Mrs. Ruiz 2nd grade classroom is similar in infrastructure to the 1st grade class with the addition of small desks arranged in groupings of two, three, or four about the room. These groupings are situated near or within selected learning centers. She too, has created a number of learning centers, (science, art, geography, current events, blocks/meeting area, puppetry, communications center), and while she would like to have the whole room configured with tables instead of desks, she has found a way to make the desks work for her students in this context. She too has utilized every nook and cranny to create a parent interest corner, a reading loft, a listening station, and a computer bank.

Recognizing that there is always a range in developmental rates and academic achievements among children of the same age and grade, Ms. Beck and Mrs. Ruiz collaborate to find ways to integrate their activities and extend experiences for their children. During center work times in the afternoons, they may provide opportunities for paired reading between 1st and 2nd grade partners, or they may have students sharing their creative writings with one another in the class writing center. They may participate in a shared long-term project with mixed-grade committees assigned specific tasks for the project. As needed, they share learning center materials to extend the ranges of complexity: a 1st grade student may need items more complex and challenging, and a 2nd grade student might benefit from reinforcement from learning center materials that are more basic. Sometimes, just for the pleasure of it, they have class sing-alongs to share and learn together new songs and rhythms; or the children may work together on a mural for the hallway display for the school's open house.

The day culminates with a class meeting to go over accomplishments and anticipate the activities and assignments for tomorrow. Children who wish to do so can share their drawings, writings, or other projects with the class. Home notes and assignment sheets are distributed for children to place in their homework pocket folder, and children retrieve their book bags from cubbies in preparation for dismissal.

How does Ms. Beck allocate the time during the school day to obtain maximum instruction without being rigid or inflexible? Rather than listing activities in small time increments throughout the day, Ms. Beck plans within large and small blocks of time. Notice that group meetings or large group instructional activities occupy the smaller blocks of time. Her schedule looks something like this:

8:30 - 9:00	Arrival, class meeting, announcements, daily plans and assignments. Introduction and instruction in use of new materials. Time permitting: introduce a finger play, song, poem, or share a story. Usually on Monday, children are given a time to share their news with others through guided group conversation. Sometimes (only as essential) the morning meeting is used to discuss a class behavior issue and restate rules and limits (Developmental Studies Center, 1996).
9:00 - 11:00	Concurrent assignment work in learning centers and direct instruction at the lesson table. Time permitting, teacher-student conferences to set individual learning goals and plan portfolio contents. (These conferences occur on an on-going basis throughout each week to ten days, until each child has had a conference.)
10:50 - 11:05	Complete tasks, assemble on the blue rug to prepare for lunch (wash hands, obtain lunch money and lunch packs)
11:05 - 11:35	Lunch
11:35 - 12:00	Class meeting to share the morning accomplishments, story reading, rest with soft listening or sing-along music, then preparations for outdoor activities
12:00 - 12:25	Outdoor play
12:25 - 2:25	Work in learning centers. Completion of today's assignments. Assessment and feedback, work with small groups at the lesson table as needed. Integrated activities with 2nd grade students.
2:20 - 2:10	Completion of tasks and clean-up
2:10 - 3:00	Class meeting, review the day's goals and activities, share accomplishments, assign homework tasks (as appropriate), anticipate tomorrow's activities and inspect the centers for order and readiness for another day. Prepare for dismissal.
3:00	Dismissal

Working with Mandated Standards and Accountability Requirements

In as much as most states now require primary grade education in both public and nonpublic schools to meet predetermined learning goals (referred to as learning objectives, essential knowledge and skills, and other such terms), curriculum design must often come from a marriage of the teacher's insightful knowledge of the capabilities and interests of individual children in the class and the predetermined learning goals for the grade. During selected grades, student achievement of these learning goals is assessed through the use of standardized tests. Often these test scores are used to make student promotion and retention decisions, and to evaluate teacher effectiveness.

Quite understandably, teachers in these situations are anxious for their students to make appropriate scores on the state or school district tests. They worry that if they do not drill and utilize more direct whole group instruction, their children will not perform as well on the tests. Most scholars, however, believe that curriculums and tests need not be at odds with one another, that when young children are allowed to learn through their explorations and interactions with others, (adults and children), rather than in a format that is more appropriate for older children, their ability to process information, store it in memory, and utilize what they learn is fostered (Smith, 1998).

Fully enriched and creative curriculums that are taught in ways that tap the child-like ways of learning with which we are all familiar can be developed and carried out. Indeed, if primary education is to be successful, it must engage children's minds, be meaningful and relevant to them, and be challenging, yet achievable. Quality education depends on the teacher's ability to provide depth and breadth to the curriculum extending knowledge through a wide range of topics and experiences

and providing ample opportunity to learn and practice emerging skills.

So, how does one develop a challenging, meaningful, and child-friendly curriculum that meets standards for achievement? By creating a matrix or grid such as is partially illustrated here, the teacher can insert the learning centers in columns across the top of the page, and the learning objectives in the far left column. Grid lines are drawn and in each square created by this grid, an activity to promote the specific learning objective can be noted, along with the extensions and/or theme projects that augment the learning objectives through an enriched curriculum. Using such a grid assures that all knowledge and skill objectives are included in the curriculum through a range of options from concrete, hands-on materials to semi-concrete (e.g., picture cards, lotto games, magnetic letters, numerals, and symbols) to more abstract endeavors (connecting sounds/symbol puzzles, working simple mathematical problems).

The use of such a grid helps teachers to guard against narrow, test driven curriculums. Such curriculums deprive children of a broad knowledge base that is after all, the essence and purpose of a good education. Creating such a grid takes considerable thought, time, and planning. A quality education for young children demands such effort.

Curriculum Planning Grid

Learning Centers

Learning Objectives	Writing	Art	Science	Etc.
Understands that print conveys meaning	Write thank-you notes to ...	Dictate story with drawing	Label fish pictures	
Identifies phonemic sounds in spoken word				
Understands that written words are composed of patterns of letters				
Can retell a story in sequence				
Uses new vocabulary in many contexts				
Etc.				

Developmental Outcomes in Quality Primary Grade Education

Much of the preceding discussion addresses the cognitive and academic aspects of planning spaces and classroom experiences for 6- and 7-year-old children. But wait. What lies within the deep structure of these strategies? Do primary grade teachers no longer address the physical, social, emotional, and character needs of these young children?

Recall from you child development studies that 6- and 7-year-old children are developing what Erik Erikson referred to as *initiative* and *industry*. Some are still learning to *trust* and to be more *autonomous* (self-governing) (Erikson, 1963). The strategies described in the foregoing undergird and facilitate this psychosocial development through efforts at continuity, inclusion of children in decision-making processes, encouraging choice-making and problem-solving, and providing relevant, challenging, and meaningful learning tasks.

Further, as students are involved in a classroom that sets forth clear expectations and provides the supports for those expectations to be met, children have more opportunities to develop self-regulation and self-control (Bronson, (2001). As children work with others in a social context as well as an intellectual one, their thinking is expanded to include the perspective of others. Perspective-taking is an essential cognitive process along with attending, storing information in memory, finding solutions to problems, and setting goals and planning (Gauvain, 2000; National Research Council 2000). As children work through behavioral issues and expectations in class meetings that are free of affront, embarrassment, artificial rewards, or other manipulations, their sense of social justice and the common good are promoted and prosocial behaviors are fostered (Charney, 1997; Kohn, 1993, 1996; Developmental Studies Center, 1996).

Summary

Ms. Beck and Mrs. Ruiz have created classroom environments that meet the unique needs of 6- and 7-year-old-children. They have used their knowledge of child growth and development to guide their planning, arrangement of furnishings, and selection, storage, and display of materials.

They have spent a considerable amount of time creating a curriculum grid to guide and assure the inclusion of all mandated objectives. They capitalize on the primary grade child's unique ways of learning, interacting with one another, and pursuing information by providing relevant, meaningful, and mind-engaging materials and activities in each of the learning centers. They continually augment the learning centers with increasingly more challenging materials as the year progresses. They intertwine student assessment with curriculum planning, and they make every effort to create a child-friendly environment. Most important is the fact that they include children in an on-going process that leads to a community of learners whose ability to function appropriately within the classroom is fully supported.

References

Bronson, M.B. (2001). *Self-regulation in early childhood: Nature and nurture.* NY: Guilford Publications, Inc.

Bauvain, M. (2000). *The social context of cognitive development.* NY: Guilford Publications, Inc.

Charney, R.S. (1997). *Habits of goodness: Case studies in the social curriculum.* Greenfield, MA: Northeast Foundation for Children.

Developmental Studies Center (1996). *Ways we want our class to be: Class meetings that build commitment to kindness and learning.* Oakland, CA: Author.

Kohn, A. (1993). *Punished by rewards: The trouble with gold stars, incentive plans A's, praise, and other bribes.* Boston: Houghton Mifflin Co.

Kohn, A. (1996). *Beyond discipline: From compliance to community.* Alexandria, VA: Association for Supervision and Curriculum Development.

National Research Council, (2000). *How people learn: Brain, mind, experience, and school.* Washington, DC: Author.

National Research Council (2001). *Knowing what students know: The science and design of educational assessment.* Washington, DC: Author.

Puckett, M. B. & Black, J. K. (2000). *Authentic assessment of the young child: Celebrating development and learning* (2nd ed.). Columbus, OH: Merrill/Prentice Hall.

Checklist for Evaluating Spaces for 6- and 7-Year-Old Children

_____ 1. The classroom retains many of the features of the preceding grade.

_____ 2. The teacher has assessed the furnishings and room to establish an infrastructure that considers child health and safety.

_____ 3. The teacher assesses storage arrangements needed to support children's use.

_____ 4. The children are engaged in a planning process to provide needed materials in the learning centers.

_____ 5. Each learning center and its contents are explained or demonstrated to students with rules and procedures that are clear to them.

_____ 6. Arrangements and displays of materials are inviting to young learners.

_____ 7. Visual and auditory supports are meaningful and useful to learners.

_____ 8. Visual and auditory supports are culturally authentic and free of stereotypes.

_____ 9. The classroom, its contents, storage, displays, and other features facilitate use by each child regardless of ableness or specific challenges.

_____ 10. Mandated objectives are met through conscientious curriculum planning and strategic use of materials and instructional time.

About the Author

Margaret B. Puckett, Ed.D. is retired professor of education at Texas Wesleyan University, where she chaired the Elementary and Early Childhood Education programs, and Graduate Studies in Education. She is a founding member and past president of the Fort Worth Area Association for the Education of Young Children and has served as president of the Texas Association for the Education of Young Children and the Southern Early Childhood Association. She is the author of several textbooks on child development, assessment practices, and early childhood education. She currently serves as a consultant to school districts, universities, and Texas Education Region Service Centers.

Chapter 23

School-Age Extended Care

Frankie McMurrey

Defining Out-Of-School Time Programs

Programs before & after school and during weekends and summer hours are defined as out-of-school time programs. These programs may provide an opportunity to engage children and adolescents as partners in their own development by ensuring that they have access to the kinds of constructive learning and development opportunities that they both need and want during their out-of-school time.

The last bell of the school day has just rung and children rush to the other half of childhood – out-of-school time. Nine-year-old Collin serves himself his favorite snack of chips and cheese sauce and juice. As soon as he finishes his snack, he flops down on a sturdy but soft couch to read a book. Carleigh rushes to the craft table to finish a project she started yesterday and Preston sits down with Peyton to play a board game. Six children enjoy their snack but finish quickly and rush outdoors to the hill area to continue building the fort they started the day before. Ten-year-old Casey gives assignments to the other children. Over the next hour they work, stacking tires, laying planks, and lining up plastic milk cartons. The teacher, who has been watching from the sidelines, comes over to suggest they paint signs for their fort. With squeals of delight, Brendan and some of the children run indoors to start painting. The common comment they all have is "*It feels like I'm home. Sometimes I am having so much fun I don't want to go home.*"

If only all could be so positive about their out-of-school hours. A quality after-school program can provide the security and fun that adults and children want during out-of-school time. As caring adults, we seek to offer an environment in which children can grow to their best potential, one that taps their creativity and strengths and allows them to excel. The *Standards for Quality School-Age Care* developed by the National School-Age Care Alliance provides a baseline of quality, and the reassurance that programs are committed to providing each child with a unique growing and learning experience. These standards are designed to describe the best practice in out-of-school programs for children and youth between the ages of 5- and 14-years-old. They are intended for use in group settings where the children participate on a regular basis and where the goal of the program is to support and enhance the overall development of the child. There are a total of 36 *keys*, each divided into 6 basic areas: Human Relationships, Indoor Environment, Outdoor Environment, Activities, Safety, Health & Nutrition, and Administration. These components are known as the *keys of the standards*. This chapter will focus on the Indoor and Outdoor Environment keys.

Indoor Key

- *The program's indoor space meets the needs of children and youth.*

  ✓ There is enough room for all program activities.

  ✓ The space is arranged well for a range of activities: physical games and sports, creative arts, dramatic play, quiet games, enrichment offerings, eating and socializing.

  ✓ The space is arranged so that various activities can go on at the same time without much disruption.

  ✓ There is adequate and convenient storage space for equipment, materials, and personal possessions of children and staff.

- *The indoor space allows children and youth to take initiative and explore their interests.*

  ✓ Children can get materials out and put them away by themselves with ease.

  ✓ Children can arrange materials and equipment to suit their activities.

  ✓ The indoor space reflects the work and interest of the children.

  ✓ Some areas have soft, comfortable furniture on which children can relax.

- *The program's indoor space meets the needs of the staff.*

  ✓ There is enough room in the indoor space for staff to plan various program activities.

  ✓ Staff members have access to adequate and convenient storage.

  ✓ The indoor space meets or exceeds local health and safety codes.

  ✓ Written guidelines are in place regarding the use and maintenance of the facility.

Implementing the Keys

Once the space meets all of the requirements outlined in the Indoor Environment Key, the next task is to plan for enriching opportunities to occur in this environment. These opportunities can best occur in learning or interest centers. Sometimes these groupings are called *clubs* or *mini clubs* in order to attract the older child. The center approach is successful because:

✓ Centers meet individual needs while still meeting needs of the larger group.

✓ Centers give children opportunities to make decisions and evaluate the consequences of their choices.

✓ Centers use children's time effectively rather than have them waste time waiting turns.

✓ Centers are flexible enough to use whatever existing space is available.

✓ Centers allow children to work independently in small groups and one-on-one with the teacher or other special adults.

✓ Centers allow children to succeed in accomplishing tasks – primarily because they choose the tasks.

A center-based environment results in many benefits for children and teachers. Children exhibit many of the following characteristics, they

✓ are more cooperative,

✓ show less hostility and conflict,

✓ wander less,

✓ show more persistence in completing tasks or solving problems,

✓ make greater gains in acquiring skills,

✓ consider, contemplate, and discuss more, and

✓ do not have to engage in large-group transitions that are time-consuming and lead to disruption.

The benefits for teachers reveal that teachers:

✓ engage in more social interactions such as praising, questioning, and comforting children,

✓ spend less time managing children (commanding, correcting, monitoring),

✓ spend more time interacting with children and facilitating learning,

✓ are actively involved with children and become more sensitive to their cues, assist arriving and departing children with transitions,

✓ can set up the number and size of centers according to the number of children, (This is especially helpful when space is shared with another program.),

✓ guide children individually, rather than disciplining large groups,

✓ move freely to where they are needed, and

✓ are freed to deal with wider ranges of achievement, and developmental skills.

Space Requirements

According to Baden, Genser, Levine and Seligson (1982), designing an environment for a before-and after-school program is especially challenging because of the diversity in children's ages, abilities, needs and interest. When staff and children are both involved in making decisions about and organizing the program's environment, it can become a joint venture that provides an excellent, varied, and unique learning experience. Such collaborative planning allows children to feel a sense of ownership and profile in the environment they have helped create. Children's behavior in a space and their feelings about that environment are more positive and cooperative when activity choices are based on what they like to do. They discuss and set the rules and help build and paint the furniture. Children of different ages can participate as seems appropriate to their level of development, and with older children working beside younger ones, a "family" group atmosphere is encouraged.

How the space is organized is directly linked to what type of interactions and activities are intended to take place. Decisions about how to arrange the physical space should be based on the following guidelines:

- *Organize the space to match the program's priorities and goals.* For example, since it is important that children have a chance to spend quiet time alone (reading, resting, playing), the environment should have private places where such activity can occur without interruption. If a goal is to encourage children to be as independent as possible, materials such as scissors, glue, paper, and crayons should be accessible to them on low open shelves.

- *Organize the space into distinct activity or special project areas.* No matter how large or small the space is, dividing it into learning or interest centers for specific types of activities will encourage participation. It allows children to work productively in small groups without interruptions, and encourages continuity by permitting project and activities to be worked on over time. One should strive to create an environment that is predictable, yet not stagnant, flexible and changing, without the area being in constant upheaval.

- *Make the environment aesthetically pleasing.* Children and staff should feel comfortable in the out-of- school environment. Materials should have an order that makes sense to children. This helps children learn to care for things and allows them to function more independently. A space that is neat and orderly – blocks stacked according to size or shape on shelves, rather than dumped in a box – communicates a message to children about the purpose and proper care of materials.

- *Define clear boundaries within the space for specific activities.* Indoor space should be defined for energy-releasing activities (both noisy and quiet). For example, a block area should not be next to the quiet reading area.

- *Display materials so they are inviting to children.* For example, a woodworking area might be set up with hand tools displayed on pegboards, wood and nails in bins, and large woodworking tables for workspace. Others might have cooking areas in which cooking utensils and ingredients are arranged on shelves, with recipes written on large tagboard, easy for children to read.

Sharing Space

If the program must share space that cannot be modified, it is still possible – and necessary – to design an inviting environment. The space should always be adaptable to meet the diverse needs, ages, and capabilities of the children in care. Equipment such as locked storage closets, portable room dividers and shelves or cabinets on wheels provide flexibility and mobility and are essential for programs where the space and existing features cannot be changed.

For example, a program that operates in a school cafeteria can use ingenuity to provide a rich environment for children. A large metal closet with a lock and which contains supplies and materials can be opened after school and transform an empty cafeteria into an inviting space. Children can reach the lower shelves in the closet to help themselves to the supplies they need. A few rolled carpet remnants and pillows provide softness. Folded blankets can be draped over freestanding tables to create private spaces.

In situations such as this, where space has multiple uses, many programs successfully adapt the environment by including in the daily routine the time needed to set up and take down, e.g., hang pictures on the walls, place materials on tables, and roll out room dividers and storage cabinets. When space is shared, it is important that both users agree about how the program can claim its own area, where it will store equipment and supplies, who will clean the space and when, and in what condition the space is expected to be found by those sharing it.

When school is out for in-services, holidays or breaks, the full-day programs may be the only user of the shared area and daily transformation is not necessary. Additional materials and equipment may be brought out of storage to transform and enrich the area for the all-day school-age program.

Program Elements

To provide for the needs of school-age children, a program should contain these basics:

- variety in choices of activities, including snacks, manipulative materials, unit blocks, table games, arts and crafts, and cooking

- some freedom about length of time involved in activities as well as the freedom not to participate

- rules for behavior that are agreed upon by all

- quiet time and alone time in areas for homework, reading, doing nothing, or visiting with a friend

- activities that promote cooperation rather than competition

- activities that promote mixed-age interaction with peer teaching and role modeling

- real tasks that encourage productive behaviors and a sense of belonging such as preparing snacks, planning a project, hosting a parent meeting, writing thank-you notes to volunteers, building a clubhouse, sewing, setting tables, and conducting projects to earn money for field trips and other activities

- activities that promote appreciation of various cultures, such as celebrating holidays, preparing and tasting foods, and sharing stories and information about different types of clothing, traditions, and music

- a daily schedule that provides a balance between
  - ✓ indoor and outdoor activities, quiet and active time
  - ✓ individual, small-group, and large-group participation
  - ✓ large-muscle and small-muscle activity, and child-initiated and staff-initiated activities

Implementing Program Elements

The National Institute on Out-of-School Time, a leader in research and technical assistance, recommends the following:

1. Capitalize on the interest of the children.
2. Consider the range of experiences an activity can provide.
3. Use the community as much as possible.
4. Capitalize on the myriad of opportunities that present themselves for informal, social learning.
5. Build upon the special talents and interests of staff.
6. Allow for spontaneity and serendipity.
7. Agree upon and communicate to children clear, consistent, expectations and limits.
8. Take an integrated, total approach to planning and carrying out the program.
9. Balance the day's activities so there are structured and unstructured times, teacher-directed and child-initiated experiences and a range of activity options as well (Baden, et al., 1982).

Equipment and Materials

School-age programs should have a variety of materials available for the children.

Art and open-ended materials

Different types of paper, paints brushes, fabric scraps markers, crayons and clay should be available to school-age children. Supplies such as scissors glue, ruler, and pencils should be kept where children can reach them.

Other materials such as sand, water, and construction equipment (wood, tools) may or may not be available to the children without staff help. Materials are best organized on open shelves or in bins so that children can choose what they would like to do.

Manipulatives

Items such as Legos©, hardwood blocks, puzzles, tabletop blocks, and Cuisenaire rods© are excellent resources.

Library

A variety of books about a range of topics and written for different ages of children provide enjoyment and extend literacy development. Books need to be rotated regularly and displayed in inviting ways at children's eye level. Although it may be necessary to purchase books, libraries will usually lend the quantities needed. Other materials and equipment such as display racks, comfortable seating (rugs, pillows, beanbag chairs), pictures, table and chairs, paper, pencils, magazines, typewriters, computers and computers software, should also be a part of this center.

Dramatic play materials

Unit blocks, cardboard blocks, hollow blocks, block accessories, props and clothes, miniature furniture and people can be used with blocks and other items to create various theme settings.

Games

Games are fairly structured activities that provide opportunities for children to learn to follow rules, take turns, and settle disputes. These include teacher-made and children-made games as well as checkers, chess, Monopoly©, Sorry© and similar board games.

Science materials

Plants, scales, magnifying glasses, magnets, prisms, aquariums and cooking equipment provide opportunities for exploration.

Recycled Materials

School-age classrooms are especially enriched when they are well stocked with creative materials and resources for the project-oriented child. Gathering useable throw-way items is time consuming for most teachers. A systematic approach can assure a steady flow of supplies into the program. Such an approach consists of the following steps:

1. *Make a list of items the teachers and children want to use.* Distribute this list to parents and co-workers and ask them to help collect items. After-school programs should never want for items such as computer paper, boxes, packing materials, shredded paper, manila folders, and assorted envelopes, because these are the types of items most working parents can easily provide.

2. *Train the children to have a creative and imaginative eye, and they will see the creative potential in recycled items.*

3. *Establish contacts with local businesses to obtain free items.* Offer free advertisement for businesses in your program's newsletter in trade for the free materials and services and always send a thank-you note stating what was given to you and how much. The company might be able to use it as a tax deduction.

4. *Send a sample of pictures of what the children made with the donated materials.* This often helps the business understand what you are doing and encourages them to help again.

Sometimes teachers are reluctant to collect recycled materials because of the difficulty of storing them. Often these supplies are left in disarray on storage shelve, cluttering limited space. Other teachers are reluctant to dispose of excess materials after they have encouraged parents to bring these supplies. Both of these problems can be resolved.

Storage of materials will depend on how they are to be used. Materials gathered for children's self-directed activities will be displayed on shelves in each center. Materials for the teacher-directed projects with the children will need to become the responsibility of the teacher. In a shared space, the materials may have to be stored away from the center. A list of these stored items can be kept posted inside a cabinet door as a reminder of available resources. When supplies are well organized, they are used more often and inventoried more easily.

Safety

All adults involved with the after-school-program share the responsibility of setting up and maintaining a safe environment. Regularly, materials and equipment should be given safety checks. Unsafe equipment must be reported immediately to the appropriate person. Younger school-age children need specific instruction and supervision in the use of tools, scissors, and painting implements. Some activities such as woodworking and take-apart centers require adult supervision and safety measures such as having the children wear goggles. Children should never be left unsupervised. It is a good practice to show children how to carry their chairs safely from one area of the room to another; it's also wise to teach them to pick up objects from the floor to prevent stumbling and to wipe up spills immediately. Children should be taught to be aware of hazards to themselves and others.

Outdoor Key

The outdoor environment is an essential part of a school-age program. School-age children have an abundant amount of energy and need an opportunity for vigorous play. Activities on the playground allow children to enhance and develop physical skills, relieve tension, and provide an opportunity for social development.

Outdoor play is particularly valuable at the end of a structured school day. The time can provide a needed break before a homework session or other confining structured activity.

The NSACA standards identify the *outdoor environment keys as follows:*

- *The outdoor play area meets the needs of children and youth, and the equipment allows them to be independent and creative.*
  - ✓ Each child has a chance to play outdoors for at least 30 minutes out of every three-hour block of time at the program.
  - ✓ Children can use a variety of outdoor equipment and games for both active and quiet play.
  - ✓ Permanent playground equipment is suitable for the abilities and interests of both boys and girls.
- *The outdoor space is suitable for a wide variety of activities.*
- *The outdoor space is large enough to meet the needs of children, youth, and staff.*
  - ✓ There is enough room in the outdoor space for all program activities.
  - ✓ The outdoor space meets or exceeds local health and safety codes.
  - ✓ Staff use outdoor areas to provide new outdoor play experiences.
  - ✓ There is a procedure in place for regularly checking the safety and maintenance of the outdoor play space.

Program Elements

The outdoor area should serve as an extension of the indoor environment; therefore, children should have a variety of activities from which to choose:

- Interest areas for arts and crafts, cages and pens for pets, or a garden for planting,
- Privacy area such as a treehouse, sand pit, hammock, or pup tent (Regardless of type, the privacy area must be arranged so that staff can supervise it.),
- Large open area for games, sports, and large group activities,
- Apparatus area for climbing swinging and balancing, separate area for older children, (School-age children like having their own space. If this is possible, it can reduce conflicts and provide an added measure of safety for younger children.),
- Storage area such as a storage building or closet to store outdoor equipment, and
- A protected outdoor play area to allow active play when weather conditions prevent outdoor play, and which can serve as an extension for indoor activities that are excessively noisy, such as woodworking.

Outdoor Space Requirements

Plans for these areas should be considered part of the outdoor environment whether you are sharing the outdoor space with a school or designing a new playground. According to Baden, Benser, Levien, and Seligson (1982), the design of a new playground should take into consideration the following:

- Climbing structures should allow younger children to feel safe and older children to be challenged.
- Before obtaining or building any equipment, visit playgrounds and other day-care programs. Notice what kinds of equipment attract children.
- Equipment should be both single-purpose and multipurpose. The scale of the equipment should be appropriate for school-age children.
- Try to use large equipment that can be rearranged.
- Most playground equipment is expensive. Be sure to evaluate the cost against its versatility.

Since many after-school or recreation programs share the outdoor space with a school or park, there is little opportunity to change the existing equipment. However, one can find a number of ways to improve the existing outdoor play area.

- *Supplement the existing equipment from other sources.*

Volunteers can help make equipment from inexpensive or free materials.

- *Provide portable pieces from the indoor program that can be moved outdoors for activities.* Colorful cones can be used to add variety to spaces.

- *Allow children to bring bicycles or roller blades if the area can be used safely for those activities.* Be sure to provide protective safety equipment such as headgear, arm and leg protective pads.

- *Create different ways to use the playground.* For example, block part of a parking lot to have a skating rink. Bring music outdoors for an added touch.

Equipment and Materials

Providing a variety of equipment and materials for outdoor activities is important in meeting the developmental needs of school-age children. Suggested items to have as part of an outdoor program are the following:

- Climbing equipment such as ladders, ropes, and jungle gyms are not only challenging for children but also contribute to muscle development and hand-eye coordination.

- Equipment for active games including balls, bats, nets, chalk (sidewalk games), jump ropes, tumbling mats, horseshoes, hoops and a parachute.

- Building materials are essential and can be furnished inexpensively. Items might include boards, crates, large building blocks, bug cardboard boxes, sheets of paneling, large spools (from the electric company), and tires or tubes. Tires can be especially versatile. They can be filled with dirt for a garden or sand for a sandbox; they can be made into swings and climbing structures.

Keep in mind that a variety of materials contribute to creative and productive play — important ingredients in a child's development. Parents, local businesses, garage sales and other resources can provide these materials at little or no cost.

Materials should be available for hot and cold weather activities. Hoses, buckets, digging equipment, and sprinklers can give children added fun on a hot afternoon.

Quiet outdoor activities will require arts and crafts materials, books, science supplies for exploring (magnifying glasses and bug boxes, for example), and props for dramatic play.

Additional props that add to fun on the playground are an old bathtub with an open drain, a small boat (the children can restore it by sanding and painting), and an old car with windows and doors removed.

Outdoor Safety

Most playground-related injuries are caused by falls, particularly from equipment. Therefore, the type of playground surface, especially within the fall zone of the equipment, is important (Scofield, 1987). The fall zone can extend up to 7 feet, depending on the equipment. This area should be covered with material such as sand (6 to10 inches thick) wood chips, shredded bark, or rubber matting. It is also important to keep these areas maintained to prevent packing down or decomposing.

Close supervision is essential around high-risk equipment such as climber, slides, and swings. Children should be involved in writing clear safety rules for the playground. The rules should be posted outdoors and revised regularly to inform children new to the program as well as to remind all children and employees.

Special precautions must be taken for parking areas and entrances or exits. Barriers from traffic, deep water, or animals should be in place. Cones and barricades should be used to provide visual reminders to the children. If in a shared-space program you have no control over the repair of a piece of equipment, then consider the equipment off limits to the children.

Safety guidelines include:

1. Check playground daily for glass, trash, or other foreign materials.
2. Check equipment regularly for torn or broken parts.
3. Wrap exposed bolts, nuts, or sharp edges.
4. Replace heavy seats (swings) with light rubber canvas seats.
5. Anchor equipment properly and securely.
6. Locate equipment away from pathways and flow of traffic (Scofield, 1987).

Field Trips

School- age children are expanding their understanding of the world. Field trips and excursions in the neighborhood extend children's learning. However, taking children away from the program, crossing streets, or transporting them in vehicles to new and unfamiliar locations also involves risks. Risks can be minimized by having enough adult volunteers to supervise and assist the children, teaching children to walk and cross streets safely, and advance planning with children and volunteers assure a safe field trip or excursions.

School-age children often get excited about taking special trips away from the program site. Their excitement is in part due to the fact the situation is novel or unfamiliar. This may cause some children to be nervous and afraid. Adults also may be nervous about supervising the children in an unfamiliar location. Before taking a trip the teacher (and volunteers, if practical) can take a "dry run" trip to identify routes, potential hazards, points of interest, and so on. It is important to plan and go over procedures and what to expect with the children prior to the trip. The questions listed below can guide your planning.

- How will children be supervised?

- What should children do if they are accidentally separated from the group?

- What should children do if a stranger approaches them?

- What guidelines do children need for using public restrooms?

- How will children be kept safe while riding in program vehicles?

- What are the general guidelines for children's behavior?

Prior to each trip, take the following steps to ensure the children's safety:

- Discuss with staff the plans for the trip and be sure everyone agrees on the time and activity schedule.

- Inform parents well in advance of the trip, and require their signature on permission forms before the trip.

- If possible, travel to the site from the program using the same route you will follow on the trip. Check the amount of time it takes to get to the site. While at the site, locate the telephones, restrooms, food stands (or picnic tables), shelters for poor weather, and where to get emergency assistance. If you plan to separate into smaller groups, identify a convenient place to meet at the end of the visit. (On the trip adults may use walkie-talkies or cell phones to communicate with each other).

- Prepare a trip folder including the following information:

  ✓ Emergency telephone numbers (the program, police, etc.)

  ✓ Signed parent emergency forms

  ✓ List of all the children going on the field trip

  ✓ Some cash to cover unexpected expenses or an emergency

- Check the first-aid kit and replace missing or outdated items.

- Plan for the unexpected. Bring a list of five to ten familiar games and activities that require no equipment or supplies in case there are delays. Back-up activities such as guessing games, storytelling, and pantomimes will keep children calm and occupied during an unexpected wait.

- Plan how members of the group can be identified (for example, program T-shirts or name tags). To protect children, nametags should include their first names only. Write the program's telephone number on the back of the T-shirt. Preprinted plastic key chains can be put on a belt loop or on a ribbon around their neck.

On the day of the trip review the safety rules and emergency precautions with the children. Discuss the following calmly and clearly, and without alarming the children:

- Where children should go if they accidentally become separated from the group. An emergency or first aid area, the public telephone, or the main office of the building are good places to meet.

- Why it is important for security reasons to stay with a buddy at all times.

- Why it is important not to go into secluded areas for example, behind buildings, public restrooms (unattended) or into closed or deserted areas of a building.

- How to be safe while riding to and from the site:

  ✓ Use seat belts.

  ✓ Keep arms and heads inside the windows.

  ✓ Stay seated while the vehicle is moving.

  ✓ Refrain from shoving, throwing things, or behaving in ways, that disturb or distract the driver.

When you leave the site:

  ✓ Account for everyone. Count the children at least twice and call roll. (If you are gone over a 3- or 4-hour period, it is helpful to do the roll check once every hour).

  ✓ Give children the same vehicle safety reminder given before leaving the program site.

Planning for Children with Special Needs

The playground is one of the most natural areas for including children with special needs. By making minor adjustments for functional difficulties, all children can participate in planned activities. For example, a child in a wheelchair can participate in a ball game by getting a chance to bat and having a partner run the bases. Some communities have special playgrounds for children with disabilities. Locate these playgrounds and plan field trips to these sites as often as possible.

In designing an outdoor environment that will accommodate all children, include variations in the playground equipment. One example is a playscape composed of semi-abstract shapes in a compact arrangement of clam shell domes, ladders, and climbers. This is effective because it inspires cooperative play among all children, and it accommodates play at every level of physical ability. Apart from the environment, the activities conducted outdoors need to meet the developmental levels of all children (Fink, 1988).

The potential of out of school programs to contribute to children's lives is limited only by the prevailing concept of what these programs are supposed to do. If after-school programs are merely an extension of the school or just a safe place with adult supervision until either the parent picks up the child or the child is able to go home, then children are denied a host of developmentally supportive opportunities. Given the current economic and emotional stresses on families, in addition to the serious risks facing children each day, we must elaborate a more developmentally comprehensive concept of what before-and after-school programs should do and better utilize this daily opportunity to touch the lives of these children.

References:

Baden, R. K., A. Genser, J.A. Levine, & M. Seligson (1982). *School-age child care: An action manual.* Dover, MA: Auburn House Publishing Co.

Fink, D. B. (1988). *School- age children with special needs.* Boston: Exceptional Parent Press.

Newman, K. D. & L. Colker (1995). *Caring for children in school-age programs. Vol. 1.* Washington, DC: Teaching Strategies, Inc.

National School Age Care Alliance (1998). *The NSACA standards for quality school-age care.* Boston, MA: Author.

Scofield, R. T. (March/April 1989). Playgrounds and school-agers. *School-Age Notes.*

Indoor Activities

The School-Age News
(5-years-old and older)

Objective: To enhance children's language arts, problem solving, and planning skills

Materials needed: pencils, pens, markers, crayons, water colors, blank notepaper, newsprint, and other appropriate paper

What to do:

1. Have children interview playmates, staff, parents, teachers, and community persons to write feature stories.

2. Help children decide who will serve as reporters, editors, artists, publishers, and distributors. Younger children can orally dictate their stories to older children and can also serve as artists and distributors.

3. Teams can be assigned responsibility for different sections of the paper such as the front page, sports, and classifieds.

And still more:

Instead of newspaper, the children might prepare the program newsletter for parents or write and produce a play.

Hometown Board Game
(6-years-old and older)

Objective: To design and make various board games

Materials needed: cardboard, tag board, or other sturdy heavyweight paper approximately 2-foot squares, index cards; markers; small playing pieces; dice

What to do:

1. Encourage children to make a board game of their town or neighborhood.

2. Have them choose where players will start and stop (that is, start at home or school, and stop at Astroworld, Six Flags, or Sea World).

3. Suggest that they lay out a path of squares in snake fashion from start to finish across the cardboard. Along the path, draw and label landmarks in the neighborhood (Frank's Garage, City Zoo, Scott Elementary).

4. Create obstacles by coloring certain squares that designate what the occupant of that square should do – "Go back two spaces," "Go to the hospital."

5. Use index cards to tell the players what to do when they land on certain squares – "Win first place in the science fair," "Go to the art museum."

6. Let the children plan the game and set the rules.

And still more:

Children can develop other board games with different themes.

THEME ACTIVITIES
Theme: Space
Styrofoam Space Station
(5-years-old and older)

Objective: To create a space station.

Materials needed: Collection of Styrofoam© shapes and sizes including large flat pieces, pellets, balls, squiggles, and box liners; picture of space stations from magazines, variety of other materials such as toothpicks, straws, foil, and paper plates, adhesives such as glue and tape; stapler; scissors

What to do:

1. Place pictures of space stations in the art center.

2. Encourage children to use the materials to create what they think a space station looks like.

Space Craters
(5-years old and older)

Objective: To explore moon geography

Materials needed: plaster of paris, spoon, black tempera paint; mixing bowl, pitcher of water; 3-inch-deep box lids, collection of balls (e.g., golf, ping-pong, and waffle balls), pictures of the moon's surface.

What to do:

1. Mix a small amount of the tempera with the plaster of paris to tint the mixture light gray. Mix according to the package instructions, estimating the amount needed.

2. Fill the box lids at lest one-inch deep. Let the plaster begin to set.

3. Let the children push various balls into the plaster to resemble the pictures on display.

And still more:

Place the crater boxes on squares on the floor with a basket of Legos© nearby and encourage children create a space city.

Theme: Mardi Gras
Mask Making
(7-years-old and older)

Objective: To encourage creativity

Materials needed: balloons, white glue, water, newspaper, paints, glitter, scissors, construction paper, markers, cleaning materials, two buckets, string

What to do:

1. In advance, blow up the balloons for the children. (*Note:* Since balloons pose a choking hazard, it is best to have them already blown and ready to use.)

2. Have children cut strips of newspaper.

3. Mix a little water with glue.

4. Dip paper strips in mixture and cover half the balloon with paper strips. Put aside to dry.

5. The next day, have children pop the balloons and trim the edges, then cut out eyes, mouth, and nose.

6. Encourage children to paint and decorate the mask. Punch a hole in each side attach a string.

(*Note:* Younger children can make masks from paper plates or paper bags.)

And still more:

Children can wear their masks in a Mardi Gras parade.

Parade Floats
(5-years-old and older)

Objective: To encourage creativity

Materials needed: newspaper, glue, scissors, different size boxes, colorful crepe paper, paints, crayons, glitter, tissue paper, pictures of Mardi Gras parades and floats

What to do:

1. Display the pictures and talk about Mardi Gras parades.

2. Divide the children into groups and have each group decorate a box to look like a parade float.

And still more:

Some children might want to make or play musical instruments for the parade.

Mardi Gras Parade
(5-years-old and older)

Objective: To role-play a Mardi Gras parade.

Materials needed: dress-up clothes or children-made costumes, Mardi Gras masks, parade floats, and musical instruments made in the arts and crafts center

What to do:

1. Gather all materials and props. Schedule the order of events.

2. Have children dress up and parade around the building pulling their floats and playing musical instruments.

And still more:

After the parade, have children prepare and eat a Mardi Gras snack.

OUTDOOR ACTIVITIES

Soap Bubble Teams
(5-years-old and older)

Objective: To learn cooperative play

Materials needed: soap bubble pipe, soapy water, bucket or small container (*Note:* Homemade soap mixtures produce stronger bubbles than commercial ones.)

What to do:

1. Mark three parallel lines 3 feet apart. Have children divide into teams and line up on each side of the center line.

2. Each team takes turns blowing one bubble. Once a bubble is formed, members of the opposing team try to blow the bubble past the line behind the team blowing the bubble. Players may cross into each other's field. Each "goal" scored is one point.

And still more:

1. Stretch a rope across the field 3 feet above the ground.

2. Play the game according to the same rules as above, except that each team must remain on its own side of the rope and 2 feet away from it. The object is to blow the bubble into the opponent's side of the rope.

Human Pinball
(6-years-old and older)

Objective: To practice gross motor skills

Materials needed: red utility ball

What to do:

1. All players, except one, stand in a circle facing outward. Children spread their legs as wide as comfortable until their feet are touching the neighbor's on either side. All players bend down and swing their arms between their legs. They become the "flippers."

2. The single child stands in the center of the circle and is the target.

3. One of the "flippers" puts the ball into play, trying to tag the target with the ball. The "flipper" who tags the target becomes the next target and the game continues.

And still more:

Try having more than one target at a time.

Checklist for Evaluating Indoor & Outdoor School-Age Environments

Indoor:

_____ 1. There is enough room for all program activities.

_____ 2. The space is suitable for a range of activities: physical games and sports, creative arts, dramatic play, quiet games, enrichment offerings, eating and socializing.

_____ 3. The space is arranged so that various activities can go on at the same time without much disruption.

_____ 4. There is adequate and convenient storage space for equipment, materials, and personal possessions of children and staff.

_____ 5. Children can get materials out and put them away independently.

_____ 6. Children can arrange materials and equipment to suit their activities.

_____ 7. The indoor space reflects the work and interest of the children.

_____ 8. Some areas have soft, comfortable furniture on which children can relax.

_____ 9. There is enough room in the indoor space for staff to plan various program activities.

_____ 10. Staff have access to adequate and convenient storage.

_____ 11. The indoor space meets or exceeds local health and safety codes.

_____ 12. Written guidelines are in place regarding the use and maintenance of the facility.

Outdoor:

_____ 1. Each child has a chance to play outdoors for at least 30 minutes of every three-hour block of time at the program.

_____ 2. Children can use a variety of outdoor equipment and games for both active and quiet play.

_____ 3. Permanent playground equipment is suitable for the sexes and abilities of all children.

_____ 4. There is enough room in the outdoor space for all program activities.

_____ 5. The outdoor space meets or exceeds local health and safety codes.

_____ 6. Staff use outdoor areas to provide new outdoor play experiences.

_____ 7. There is a procedure in place for regularly checking the safety and maintenance of the outdoor play space.

About the Author

Frankie McMurrey is the executive director of Clayton Child Care Inc. – a not for profit agency collaborating with three public school districts to provide out-of-school care for over 1,200 children daily in Tarrant County. She is also a part time instructor at Tarrant County College. In the past, she has been owner-director of a child-care facility. She recently received her Masters Degree in School-Age Care from Concordia University. She is an advocate for school-age children and quality out-of-school care in the Tarrant County region and around the state.

Using
Room to Grow
for Professional
Development

Chapter 24

This chapter describes the manner in which Room to Grow is used for professional development in Texas. Perhaps, the policies and procedures herein described can serve as a prototype for other state personnel who are developing strategies to make professional development readily accessible.

Using *Room to Grow* for Professional Development

Linda Winkelman

Cindy Hansen

Note to Training Participant

Ongoing training for teachers and caregivers serves many purposes. It can improve your professional performance, enhance your understanding of young children, satisfy regulatory and program requirements, and offer opportunities for exchanging ideas and experiences with other professionals. However, many people who work with young children find it difficult to attend workshops, conferences, and other types of training opportunities. *Room to Grow* is designed to be used as a self-paced instructional tool enabling one to earn a certificate after 4 clock hours of training. The Texas Association for the Education of Young Children (TAEYC) is committed to the concept that a variety of training opportunities can best meet the needs of caregivers and teachers of young children. TAEYC encourages individuals to make use of the many training experiences offered through their local Associations for the Education of Young Children and other community agencies in order to further their professional development and earn additional training hours.

Guidelines for Using Self-Study and Self-Instructional Materials

- Accept responsibility for your own professional development.

- Select materials that relate to your teaching and that will help you meet your training goals.

- Allow yourself enough time for reflection and assimilation, testing ideas and methods, and building confidence in implementing new approaches.

- Document your learning with drawings, video recordings, journals, audiotapes, transcriptions of teacher-child interactions, interviews, field notes, checklists, portfolios, and photographs.

- Gather self-study groups for discussion and planning. Small study groups can maximize your training experiences. Take the time to build trust and rely on each other to solve problems and stimulate thinking.

- Meet with your supervisor to review your progress, get any questions answered, and discuss implementation of new ideas.

Types of Training Certificates

Three types of training certificates are available using *Room to Grow* as a self-instructional tool. Each is designed to meet the needs of particular individuals in specific environments. Each certificate requires that the participant read chapters one through five, as well as certain other chapters in the book, depending upon the type of certificate desired.

To earn a certificate, follow these steps:

1. Select the type of training certificate that best serves your needs. The choices are:
   - Environments for Children Younger Than 3
   - Environments for 3-, 4-, and 5-Year Olds
   - Environments for School-Age Children

2. Read chapters one through five. Also read the chapters related to the training certificate you select, as shown in the requirements below. For example, if you choose to earn the certificate for Environments for Children Younger Than 3, you would read chapters six, seven, and eight.

3. After reading the chapters, use the checklist at the end to identify specific ways that you can improve your environment (classroom, playground, family child care). If you need more information, visit the public library for additional books listed in Section V, Resources: Books, Journals, and Electronic Resources.

4. Make the changes suggested in the chapters to assure a developmentally appropriate environment for the children in your care. This might mean, for example, that you need to rearrange furniture or add materials to the art center, or make new equipment to use in the outdoor play area.

5. Ask an early childhood professional or a related professional to serve as a volunteer observer. Give the volunteer the chapter checklists and ask him or her to visit your program or family child care home and observe whether your environment reflects the suggestions in the checklists. At the end of the visit, the volunteer observer must sign the *Self-Paced Training Record* illustrated at the end of this chapter.

6. To be given credit for clock hours of training, send the training report to the TAEYC office and request a training certificate. The address is:

   Texas Association for the
   Education of Young Children
   P. O. Box 4997
   Austin, Texas 78765-4997

   For more information, phone TAEYC at (512) 451-2392 or 1-800-341-2392.

Learning Objectives

After completing this self-instructional course of study, you should be able to:

- design an environment that reflects the needs of children and adults;

- manage the use of space through scheduling and materials;

- arrange space according to 10 organizing guidelines;

- design and equip an indoor and outdoor environment that is developmentally appropriate for children younger than 3-years-old;

- design and equip an indoor and outdoor environment that is developmentally appropriate for children 3- to 5- years-old;

- design and equip an indoor and outdoor environment that is developmentally appropriate for school-age children (the primary grades: kindergarten, first, and second); and

- design and equip an indoor and outdoor environment that is developmentally appropriate for children of mixed ages in a family-child-care setting.

Requirements

Environments for Children Younger Than 3

Chapter One: Using Space

Chapter Two: Arranging Space

Chapter Three: Play and Neuroscience

Chapter Four: Literacy Development and Young Children

Chapter Five: Playground Essentials

Chapter Six: Infants

Chapter Seven: Toddlers

Family Child Care Providers can choose chapters 1-5 and chapter 8 (Family Child Care: Infants and Toddlers).

Environments for 3-, 4-, and 5-Year Olds

Chapter One: Using Space

Chapter Two: Arranging Space

Chapter Three: Play and Neuroscience

Chapter Four: Literacy Development and Young children

Chapter Five: Playground Essentials

Your choice of four chapters from Section III:

Environments for School-Age Children

Your choice of two chapters from Section III (chapters 9 to 21) listed above.

Volunteer Observer

Once you have made the suggested improvements in your environment, ask a volunteer observer to use the checklist at the end of each chapter that you have studied to evaluate your classroom environment. The volunteer observer could be a parent of a child in your program, a caregiver or director from another center or program, a registered family-child-care provider, a licensing representative, a CDA advisor, or an officer or chairperson from your local Association for the Education of Young Children. The volunteer observer could also be a professional from a related field, for example, a public school kindergarten teacher, nurse, or County Extension agent.

The volunteer observer should not be paid, should not be a relative, and should not be an employee at your program or home. The volunteer observer must make an on-site visit and must sign the *Self-Paced Training Report* at the end of this chapter.

Note to Supervisor

Investing in on-going training for those who care for young children is the single best indicator of a successful caregiver and quality program. The caregivers are a priority in any program, because they directly affect the children, family, and the facility. Other training benefits include lower turnover rates and greater levels of caregiver self-esteem. Challenges, however, are often overwhelming. Caregivers are reluctant to give up their time, and it is difficult to get everyone free to attend at a particular time. Here are some ideas to hurdle those obstacles and provide consistent and meaningful training for all caregivers.

Staff development is most meaningful when viewed on the basis of individual needs. Everyone has different needs, abilities, and learning styles. The best way to determine what topics are a training priority for each caregiver is to observe her/him in the classroom. Look for areas of need using the checklists at the end of the *Room to Grow* chapters to gain knowledge. When using the *Room to Grow* book for training caregivers, there are some critical points to consider:

- Take time to build trust with the caregiver. Let her/him know her/his success is important to you.

- Assess the skill level of the caregiver. An entry-level caregiver will need more concrete experiences while a more experienced caregiver may be ready for some theory.

- Balance topics that meet individual needs and interests *and* help meet center requirements and goals. This process facilitates team spirit. If a goal for the center is to foster children's creativity, training might be given on how to provide open-ended art experiences for children.

- Be specific about what the caregiver should take away from the training. A caregiver might be asked to look for ideas of how to provide non-mobile infants plenty of space for movement while keeping them safe from infants who are crawling and moving about.

- Identify the caregiver's strengths and build on them. For instance, if the caregiver does a wonderful job of enriching indoor learning centers, show her how she can use the same creativity to enrich outdoor environments.

The person providing the training should be knowledgeable about child development, an empathetic listener, and have the time to devote to the caregiver's development. This may not always be the supervisor. Many programs turn over training responsibilities to an educational coordinator or another competent caregiver who can become the trainee's mentor. Certainly, if there are classrooms with a particular strength, pair a caregiver from that classroom with another caregiver in need of guidance in that area. A visit might be arranged to a laboratory school or accredited center in your community where the caregiver can observe a model classroom. Check with your local Resource and Referral Agency, local licensing office, or call the National Association for the Education of Young Children to request a list of accredited centers near you or access accredited center information on the NAEYC website: www.naeyc.org. The trainer should use numerous examples, demonstrations, and illustrations of how the information fits the needs of the trainee and the children in her/his care. Through observation, feedback, and discussion, assist the caregiver in putting new knowledge into practice. Another way to facilitate learning and professional development is to design an adult learning center where the caregiver can have some quiet, uninterrupted time to study and read. Assist the trainee in providing proper documentation of the training using the form provided in this chapter. Encourage the trainee's further investigation into the topic using the Resources Section of this book or try highlighting a specific chapter or book. Assign material to be reviewed by a certain date and schedule a time to dialogue with the caregiver about the information. Caregivers could also discuss the material in assigned groups or write their interpretation of the information in a notebook or journal. Consider creating a worksheet over the material and using it to highlight information. One possible method to encourage creative ideas is to pose a question on a selected topic in a central area and ask staff to respond to it in writing. Explain to caregivers how the process will work, what will be done with the information, and how often the question will be changed. Caregivers read others' responses and expand their own perspectives. A question might be, "What are some ways the dramatic play area might be enriched?"

The needs of the caregiver and the goals of the center are constantly changing and growing. Be prepared to meet the challenges of having a well-trained staff and quality program by constantly evaluating those needs. Explore creative solutions to training obstacles by looking past ordinary methods.

Creative ways of providing training for staff are key in keeping them interested and motivated. On-going staff development will strengthen the center by improving the program and enriching the lives of the children with whom they interact.

Example for Using the Planned Learning Experience

Topic: Infant and toddler environment

Date: September 20-24

Place: Break room

Materials: *Room to Grow* book and infant/toddler environment video

Staff Participating: All infant and toddler staff

Trainer: Educational Coordinator

Objectives:

- To evaluate the center's infant and toddler classrooms using the checklists in *Room to Grow*, observing how space is used, and the experiences provided

- To identify what makes an infant and toddler environment high quality

- To develop a written plan to redesign the infant and toddler environment

Activities:

1. Use the checklists at the end of chapters 6 and 7 in *Room to Grow* to evaluate the environments.

2. Read and discuss chapters 1-7 in *Room to Grow*.

3. View video. (See Resources Section for suggestions.)

4. Visit a high-quality infant and toddler classroom preferably in a program accredited by the National Association for the Education of Young Children. Use the checklists at the end of chapters 6 and 7 to evaluate the environments. Note ways the host program has met the checklist criteria by asking staff to cite specific examples.

5. Brainstorm ideas to help enhance the quality of the infant and toddler environments using information gathered through checklists, observations, readings, and the video. Ask staff to evaluate what changes need to take place to make needed improvements.

6. Group staff by classroom and ask them to develop an action plan with ideas, estimated cost, who will be responsible, and dates targeted for completion.

7. Monitor the progress according to the schedule for completion.

Evaluation:

Ask each staff member to complete the following statements:

- If a parent asked me what was important in an infant or toddler environment, I would make these five suggestions:

- 1)... 2)... 3)... 4)... 5)...

- The best advice I could give a new caregiver about infant and toddler environments would be . . .

- The biggest challenge I faced in improving my environment was . . .

Follow-Up:

Follow-up by observing the classroom with the changes made. Is the classroom working for the staff and the children? Have necessary improvements been put into practice? Are there other changes that still need to be made? Establish a schedule to periodically use the checklists to document improvement. Provide resources for more information in upgrading environments.

Documentation:

After each planned learning experience, the trainer and participant need to complete the *Planned Learning Experience* form and place it in the participant's professional development file.

References

Alexander, N. P. (1999, November/December). Understanding adults as learners. *Child Care Information Exchange. (130)*, 82-84.

Bloom, P. M. Sheerer, & J. Britz (1991). *Blueprint for Action-Achieving Center-Based Change Through Staff Development.* Mt. Rainier, MD: New Horizons Educational Consultants and Learning Resources.

Center directors share staff training success stories: Management success stories from child care center directors (1995). Reprinted from *Child Care Information Exchange* pp. 9-14.

Getting the most bang for your buck: Make training count. (2001, Spring). *Texas Child Care Quarterly, 25* (3), 18-21.

Smith, C. J. (1999, May). Ongoing growing (1999). *Child Care Information Exchange, (127)*, 9-11.

Strickland, J, & S. Reynolds (1990). You gotta catch fire before you can burn out. In *The Best of Exchange: Child Care Information Exchange Developing Staff Skills Reprint Collection #7.* Redmond, WA: Exchange Press Inc.

About the Authors

Linda Winkelman is Vice-President of the Work/Family and Child Care Division at Camp Fire USA in Fort Worth, Texas. She holds a master's degree in Early Childhood Education from the University of Colorado (Denver). She is past president of the Fort Worth Area Association for the Education of Young Children and has served TAEYC as State Conference Co-Chair and Affiliate Representative. Past work experience includes classroom and college teaching, lab school director, and educational consultant.

Cindy Hansen is a child development specialist for Camp Fire USA in Fort Worth, Texas. She has over 25 years in the child-care field including directing a NAEYC accredited center. Cindy currently serves as a validator and commissioner for the National Association for the Education of Young Children. She is a contributing author for the Early Childhood Management Institute.

Self-Paced Training Report

My name is: _____

My mailing address is: _____City _____State _____Zip _____

My telephone number is: (_____) _____My e-mail address is: _____

I would like to be awarded a certificate for 6 hours of training in the area below *(check one)*:
❑ Environments for Children Younger Than 3   ❑ Environments for School-Age Children
❑ Environments for 3-, 4-, and 5-Year-Olds

I have studied and completed the checklist at the end of the chapters below. *(Check the ones related to your certificate.)*:

❑ 1.	❑ 5.	❑ 9.	❑ 13.	❑ 17.	❑ 21.
❑ 2.	❑ 6.	❑ 10.	❑ 14.	❑ 18.	❑ 22.
❑ 3.	❑ 7.	v 11.	❑ 15.	❑ 19.	❑ 23.
❑ 4.	❑ 8.	❑ 12.	❑ 16.	❑ 20.	❑ 24.

I have made the following changes in the environment where I work with children.
(Describe briefly, or, if needed, write on a separate sheet of paper and attach.):

Signature: _____ Date: _____

This section is to be completed by the Volunteer Observer

My name is: _____

My mailing address is: _____City _____State _____Zip _____

I am *(check one or more)*: ❑ an early childhood professional   ❑ a parent
❑ a related professional (nurse, social worker, etc.)

My qualifications to be a volunteer observer include.
(Briefly describe education, training, experience):

I observed the environment of *(name of person earning the certificate)*:_____
_____on_____ *(date of visit)*. I have evaluat-
ed the environment by using the checklist at the end of the following chapters *(list numbers of all chapters)*: _____

I observed the changes made to the environment described above. I am not a relative to the person earning the certificate, I am not employed at the same program or home, and I was not paid to make the observation.

Signature: _____Date: _____

Planned Learning Experience

Topic: _____ Date: _____ Time: _____

Staff Participating: _____

Trainer: _____

Objectives:

1._____

_____

2. _____

_____

3. _____

_____

Activities: _____

_____

_____

Evaluation: _____

_____

_____

Follow-up: _____

_____

_____

Documentation

Staff member's name:_____

Participated in the training session (topic): _____

Which was conducted on (date): _____(clock hours): _____

_____   _____
    Staff member's signature   Trainer's signature

Resources

Getting Started

American Public Health Association and American Academy of Pediatrics (2002). *Caring for our children: National health and safety performance standards: Guidelines for out-of-home child care programs.* Washington, DC: Author.

> Guidelines for the development and evaluation of health and safety provisions for children in family and group care homes and child care centers. Addresses issues such as infant sleep positions and SIDS, playground equipment specifications, standards relevant to children with special needs and many more.

Bergen, D. & J. Coscia (2002). *Brain research and childhood education: Implications for educators.* Olney, MD: Association for Childhood Education International.

> Provides educators with information relating to brain research that can guide decision-making and curriculum priorities in education.

Bredekamp, S. & C. Copple (1997). *Developmentally appropriate practice in early childhood programs* (Rev. ed.). Washington, DC: National Association for the Education of Young Children.

> Sets forth professional consensus about the developmental characteristics and needs of children in the context of early childhood education programs designed to be responsive to age and individuality.

Bronson, M. B. (1995). *The right stuff for children birth to 8: Selecting play materials to support development.* Washington, DC: National Association for the Education of Young Children.

> A handbook for planning and selecting age-appropriate materials for children of different ages from infancy through the primary grades.

Brown, W. H. & M. A. Conroy (Eds.). (1997). *Including and supporting preschool children with developmental delays in early childhood classrooms.* Little Rock, AR: Southern Early Childhood Association.

> A brief but thorough discussion of various issues important in planning for the needs of children with developmental delays, including such topics as family-centered practices, coordinating services, promoting language development, activity-based interventions, peer interactions, and the use of assistive technologies with preschool children.

Clayton, M. K. & M. B. Forton, (2001). *Classroom spaces that work.* Greenfield, MA: Northeast Foundation for Children.

> Describes creative physical environments that are welcoming, organized, and planned around the needs of children and adults to foster both social and academic learning.

Edwards, C., L. Gandini, & G. Forman (1993). *The hundred languages of children: The Reggio Emilia approach to early childhood education.* Norwood, NJ: Ablex.

> An introduction to the history, philosophy, curriculum, and methods of the city-run early childhood program of Reggio Emilia, Italy. This much acclaimed model for early childhood education, is described with attention to use of space and physical environments, the many ways children are encouraged to explore their environment and express themselves through music, movement, art, and creative curriculums.

Frost, J., S. C. Wortham, & S. Reifel (2001). *Play and child development.* Upper Saddle River, NJ: Prentice-Hall, Inc.

> An analysis and guide to play in relation to all aspects of child development; features a chapter on brain research and the implications of this emerging research for our understanding of, and provisions for play.

National Research Council, Institute of Medicine (2000). *From neurons to neighborhoods: The science of early childhood development.* Washington, DC: Author.

> An overview of research in the field of early brain growth and neurological development with implications for practitioners and policymakers. Emphasis is on using child development knowledge to provide nurturing interactions and appropriate education experiences during the early years.

Neuman, S. B., C. Copple, and S. Bredekamp (2000). *Learning to read and write: Developmentally appropriate practices for young children.* Washington, DC: National Association for the Education of Young Children.

> A joint position statement of the International Reading Association and NAEYC regarding best practices for early literacy development. Provides curriculum guidelines based on contemporary research on how language and literacy develop.

Puckett, M. B. & J. K. Black (2001). *The young child: Development from prebirth through age eight.* (3rd ed.). Columbus, OH: Merrill/Prentice Hall.

A text that provides a systematic way to study child growth, development, and learning from prenatal development through age eight. Each developmental domain - physical/motor, psychosocial, cognitive, language, literacy - is described with emphasis on the role of the adult in supporting growth, development, and learning.

Environments for Children Younger than 3

Bittenger, G., M. A. Hodege, & J. C. Rose (1998). *Terrific tips for toddler teachers.* Torrance, CA: Totline Publications.

Clear and easily implemented ideas for all areas of the toddler curriculum; includes classroom management, language development, discovery activities, dramatic play and large motor development.

Briggs, P., T. Pilot, & J. Bagby (2001). *Early childhood activities for creative educators.* Albany, NY: Delmar/Thomson.

Language arts, math, and science activities for children from ages two-years-old to eight.

Dodge, D.T. & Heroman, C. (2000). *Building your baby's brain: A parent's guide to the first five years.* Washington, DC: United States Department of Education.

Explains what scientists are learning about the infant's brain and the difference parents can make in the child's successful development. Emphasizes the importance of talking, sharing books, music, math, and playful interactions. A matrix describes child behaviors, what a parent can do in response to the behaviors, and why the responses are important.

Gellens, S. (2000). *Activities that build the young child's brain.* Sarasota, FL: Early Childhood Association of Florida, Inc.

Provides information about brain growth and neurological development and practical ways to translate research into daily activities with young children.

Herr, J. & Y. Larson (2000). *Creative resources for the early childhood classroom.* NY: Delmar/Thomson Learning.

Provides numerous activities to enhance curriculum themes with suggestions for field trips, group time, cooking, arts and crafts, large motor activities, sensory development, dramatic play, music, and science.

Hirsch, E. S. (Ed.). (1996). *The block book* (3rd ed.). Washington, DC: National Association for the Education of Young Children.

Practical tips for organizing and equipping the block center. Discusses the importance of block play to creativity, dramatic play, science, math, social studies and other learning domains.

Mayesky, M. (1998). *Creative activities for young children.* Albany NY: Delmar.

Presents information about how children learn language, and ideas for working with different preschool ages. Includes a section on how to read to an infant and how to share poetry with young children.

Miller, K. (1999). *Simple steps: Developmental activities for infants, toddlers and two-year-olds.* Beltsville, MD: Gryphon House.

An extensive collection of 300 activities organized by developmental domain and linked to child development principles; includes information on curriculum development and learning environments.

Pica, R. (2000). *Moving & learning series: Toddlers; Preschoolers & Kindergartners; and Early Elementary Children* (3 volumes). Albany, NY: Delmar.

The importance of movement activities for children is emphasized with numerous age-appropriate activities to enhance large motor development and learning.

Schickedanz, J. (1999). *Much more than the ABCs.* Washington, DC: National Association for the Education of Young Children.

Presents information about the early stages of reading and writing. Discusses developmentally appropriate approaches to literacy for young children.

Shore, R. (1997). *Rethinking the brain: New insights into early development.* NY: Families and Work Institute.

A description of brain research and its relationship to how adults respond to and care for infants and young children. Emphasizes the importance of early attachments and nurturing relationships.

United States Consumer Product Safety Commission. (1994). *Handbook for public playground safety.* Washington, DC: Author.

Provides comprehensive safety guidelines for public playgrounds. These guidelines can be used to plan safe playgrounds in nonpublic settings.

Wilson, L. C., L. Douville-Watson, & M.A. Watson (1999). *Infants and toddlers: Curriculum and teaching* (5th ed.). Albany, NY: Delmar.

A textbook providing an overview of infant and toddler care with information on the design of infant and toddler curriculum. Includes symbols throughout the text to indicate specific Child Development Associate (CDA) program functional areas.

Environments for 3-, 4-, and 5-Year-Old Children

American Association for the Advancement of Science. (1999). *Dialogue on early childhood science, mathematics, and technology education.* Washington, DC: Author.

Presents eleven papers representing current thinking about early childhood science, mathematics, and technology education. Includes an extensive bibliography and a list of resources for educators and parents.

Diffily, D., E. Donaldson, & C. Sassman (2001). *The Scholastic book of early childhood learning centers.* NY: Scholastic Professional Books.

A resource book with ideas and activities for creating environments that motivate young children to read, write, and learn.

Diffily, D. & Morrison, K. (Eds.) (1996). *Family-friendly communication for early childhood programs.* Washington, DC: National Association for the Education of Young Children.

Offers 93 messages for parents that demonstrate communication techniques on typical and timely topics; samples are ready to be adapted by individual programs for newsletters, bulletin boards, parent brochures and handouts, and to use in parent-teacher conferences. Includes many strategies for engaging parents in a partnership with the early childhood program.

Gargiulo, R., J. L. Kilgo, and S. Graves (1999). *Young children with special needs: An introduction to early childhood special education.*

Explains early childhood special education and intervention methods focusing on children from birth to age five.

Hall, N. S. (1999). *Creative resources for the anti-bias classroom.* Albany, NY: Delmar.

Developmentally appropriate interactions, curriculum topics, and materials are used to help children develop awareness of diversity and to acquire the skills necessary to interact in positive, affirming ways with others who may differ from themselves.

Haugland, S. W. & J. L. Wright (1997). *Young children and technology: A world of discovery.* Boston, MA: Allyn & Bacon.

Discusses the potential for discovery and enrichment in young children's use of technology.

Isbell, R. (1995). *The complete learning center book.* Beltsville, MD: Gryphon House.

An illustrated and comprehensive guide to planning, designing, and equipping learning centers in early childhood classrooms. Both traditional and non-traditional centers are included, and a total of 32 different learning centers are described.

Isbell, R. & B. Exelby (2002). *Early learning environments that work.* Beltsville, MD: Gryphon House.

Based on the Reggio Emilia model, the authors describe how to use furniture, color, materials, storage, and other elements to support learning and create spaces that are at once, child friendly and supportive, aesthetic, and functional.

Moomaw, S. & B. Hieronymus (1995). *More than counting: Whole math activities for preschool and kindergarten.* St. Paul MN: Redleaf Press.

Describes unique teaching ideas labeled as collections, grid games, path games, graphing, and grow-motor play. The Math Suitcase is a suggestion for involving the family in math learning.

National Research Council (1999). *Starting out right: A guide to promoting children's reading success.* Washington, DC: National Academy Press.

Provides specific recommendations on how to help children become successful readers; includes accomplishments checklists, activities, recommended children's books, and guide to computer software, CD-Roms and Internet resources.

Schiller, P. & L. Peterson (1997). *Count on math: Activities for small hands and lively minds.* Beltsville, MD: Gryphon House.

Describes a variety of math activities for young children, including sections on spatial relationships, classification, patterning, one-to-one correspondence, ordering, numeration, shapes, measurement, and time and money.

Scholastic, Inc. (1997). *50 math activities for your kindergarten classroom.* NY: Author.

Describes 50 math activities that are appropriate for five-year-olds; includes how to set up a classroom math center.

Silberg, J. (1998). *The I can't sing book.* Beltsville, MD: Gryphon House.

Easy activities to help adults (musicians or not) bring music and children together.

Trelease J. (1995). *The read-aloud handbook* (4th ed.). NY: Penguin Books.

Discusses many aspects of reading aloud with children and makes recommendations for wordless, picture, and other types of books, with guidelines for selecting read-aloud books.

Topal, C. W. & L. Gandini (1999). *Beautiful stuff! Learning with found materials.* Worcester, MA: Davis Publications.

Presents numerous ideas to enrich the creative experiences and activities of children.

Veitch, B. and T. Harms (1981). *Cook and learn: Pictorial single portion recipes: A child's cook book.* Menlo Park, CA: Addison-Wesley Publishing.

Provides single portion recipes that children can follow.

Environments for School-Age Children

Kirchner, G. (2000). *Children's games from around the world* (2nd ed.). Des Moines, IA: Allyn & Bacon.

An anthology of games from around the world with over 100 photographs and 150 illustrations showing teachers and students how to play the games. Describes traditional games and games invented by children. Authors seek to encourage multicultural perspectives, creativity and cooperative learning.

Gunning, T.B. (2000). *Best books for beginning readers.* Des Moines, IA: Allyn & Bacon.

Gunning, T.B. (2000). *Best books for building literacy for elementary school children.* Des Moines, IA: Allyn & Bacon.

These two books present extensive lists of books

of different genre and topics with annotations and suggestions on ways to foster reading development through appealing literature.

Puckett, M. B. & J. K. Black (2000). *Authentic assessment of the young child: Celebrating development and learning* (2nd ed.). Columbus, OH: Merrill/Prentice Hall.

An exploration of alternatives to large scale standardized testing of young children with emphasis on more child-centered, developmentally appropriate methods for assessing children's performance and achievements. Includes a master plan for assessment along with descriptions of various portfolio systems.

Seefeldt, C. A. (2000). *Active experiences for active children: Social studies.* Columbus, OH: Merrill/Prentice Hall.

Provides guides for planning meaningful learning experiences in the social studies emphasizing active experiential learning, includes experiences relating to history, geography, economics and living in a democracy.

Thonney, P. F. & T. J. Farrell, (1995). *Kitchen science for kids.* Ithaca, NY: Cornell University.

Projects and experiments for children ages five- to twelve-years-old, emphasizing explorations, science skills and concepts and scientific processes and techniques; includes checklists for organizing materials and conducting the experiments with extension ideas.

Professional Development

Alexander, N. P. (2000). *Early childhood workshops that work! The essential guide to successful training and workshops.* Beltsville, MD: Gryphon House.

The importance of planning for an effective workshop is stressed with numerous suggestions and illustrations for how to design, organize, conduct, and evaluate early childhood workshops and training seminars. Tips on how to deal with the unexpected are provided.

Beaty, J. J. (1999). *Prosocial guidance for the preschool child.* Columbus, OH: Merrill/Prentice Hall.

Practical and nurturing approach to guiding young children toward greater self-control and positive interactions with others. Addresses many typical behavior issues that arise in preschool groups.

Beaty, J. J. (2000). *Skills for preschool teachers.* Columbus, OH: Merrill/Prentice Hall.

    Discusses basic classroom skills built around the 13 CDA credential functional areas. Includes topics such as dealing with anger, promoting social skills, curriculum webs to plan emergent curriculum, the NAEYC Code of Ethics, and lists of children's books and computer programs.

Council for Early Childhood Recognition (1997). *The Child Development Associate assessment system and competency standards.* Washington, DC: Author.

    There are several titles in this series including: *Infant/Toddler Caregivers in Center-based programs; Preschool caregivers in center-based programs; Family child care providers; Home visitor; and Bilingual setting.*

    Describes the types of settings through which candidates for the Child Development Associate credential may pursue professional development. Competency goals and functional areas are described and the process for obtaining the CDA training and credential is delineated.

Developmental Studies Center (1996). *Ways we want our class to be: Class meetings that build commitment to kindness and learning.* Oakland, CA: Author.

    Intended for teachers of primary grades and above, the underlying principle in this small book of helping children to become more cognizant of the perspectives and needs of others while meeting their own goals and needs is an important concept and skill for educators at all levels. Illustrates how to use positive and affirming class meetings to teach children how to relate to one another in caring and prosocial ways.

Kohn, A. (1996). *Beyond discipline: From compliance to community.* Alexandria, VA: Association for Supervision and Curriculum Development

    Proposes a collaborative problem solving approach to helping children meet behavior expectations with the goal of helping children grow in self-control and a sense of belonging and community with others. Many anecdotes from real classrooms.

Leonard, A. M. (1997). *I spy something! A practical guide to classroom observations of young children.* Little Rock, AR: Southern Early Childhood Association.

    Becoming a keen observer of child development and behavior is a critical task for the early childhood professional. This author presents numerous strategies for developing observation skills and using observation information to benefit children.

MacDonald, S. (1996). *The portfolio and its use: Book II: A road map for assessment.* Little Rock, AR: Southern Early Childhood Association.

    A how-to book for developing the portfolio that assesses on-going growth, development, and learning of individual children. Many examples with instructions on how the portfolio is used to guide children, communicate with families, and inform curriculum.

Puckett, M. B. & D. Diffily (in press). *Teaching young children: An introduction to the early childhood profession.* (2nd ed.). Albany, NY: Delmar.

    Uses vignettes, stories, and examples to explore the principles of developmentally appropriate practices in early education. History, theory, contemporary trends, and every-day practices are discussed to introduce the reader to the knowledge base and the skills essential to becoming a professional early childhood educator.

Tertell, E.A., S.M. Klein, & J.L. Jewett, (Eds.). (1998). *When teachers reflect: Journeys toward effective, inclusive practice.* Washington, DC: National Association for the Education of Young Children.

    Eighteen teachers tell their stories of their efforts toward greater understanding of their roles and responsibilities as they strive for fully inclusive, developmentally appropriate practices.

Professional and Trade Journals

(with example titles)

ACEI Focus on Infants & Toddlers (Ages 0-3) (A quarterly newsletter of the Association for Childhood Education International)

    Connelly, E. B. (Spring 2000), Protecting the brain: Touring our environment. [12(3), 6-7].

ACEI Focus on Pre-K & K (Ages 4-6) (A quarterly newsletter of the ACEI)

    Morrone, M. H. (2000, Fall). More than cake and candles: Birthday celebrations with meaning. [13(1), 1-4)].

ACEI Focus on Elementary (Ages 7-10) (Quarterly newsletter of the Association for Childhood Education International)

    Kirkland, L. (1999, Fall). The role of autonomy in the elementary classroom. [12(1), 1-2, 4-5].

Byrne, K (1999, Spring). Benefits of foreign language in the elementary school [11(4), 1-6].

Child Care Information Exchange
Caesar, B. (2001, January/February) Give children a place to explore: Guides for preschool playground design. [#138].
Wardle, F. (2001, January/February). Giving your building a second chance: Guidelines for remodeling your center [#137].

Childhood Education: Infancy through Early Adolescence (Journal of Association for Childhood Education International [ACEI])
Adams, T. L. (2000/01, Winter). Helping children learn mathematics through multiple intelligences and standards for school mathematics. [77(2), 86-94].
Anderson, K. J. & D. Cavallaro (2002). Parents or pop culture? Children's heroes and role models. [78(3), 161-168].

Dimensions of Early Childhood (Journal of Southern Early Childhood Association)
McLean, D. (2002, Winter). Helping Aaron navigate: Including children with physical disabilities. [30(1) 9-15].
Fye, M. A. S., & J. P. Mumpower (2001, Spring). Lost in space? Design learning areas for today. [29(2), 16-22].

Early Childhood Education Journal (A trade journal of peer reviewed articles published by Human Sciences Press.)
Stroud, J. E. (1995). Block play: Building a foundation for literacy. [23(1), 913].
Berger, E. H. (1998, Fall). Don't shut fathers out. [26(1)57-61].

Early Childhood Research Quarterly (NAEYC)
Dickinson, D. K. & J. DeTemple (1998). Putting parents in the picture: Maternal reports of preschoolers' literacy as a predictor of early reading. [13(2), 241-261].
Odom, W. L., & K. E. Diamond. (1998, March). Inclusion of young children with special needs in early childhood education: The research base. [13(1), 3-25].

Journal of Research in Childhood Education (ACEI)
Readdick, C. A. & P. L. Chapman (2000). Young children's perceptions of time out. [15(1), 81-87].
Cassidy, D. J. & J. M. Lawrence (2000).

Teachers' beliefs: The "whys' behind the "how tos" in child care classrooms. [14(2)193-204].

Texas Child Care Quarterly (Published by the Texas Workforce Commission)
Brady, D. & Voss, B. (2002, Winter). The Americans with Disabilities Act: Overcoming barriers. [25(2), 10-16].
Kirk, E. W. & J. E. Stroud (1996). Water, sand, and so much more. [20(3), 14-20].
Warner, L. (2001, Fall). Classroom basics: How environments affect young children. [25(2), 2-9].

Young Children (Journal of National Association for the Education of Young Children)
Hewitt, K. (2001, January). Blocks as a tool for learning: Historical and contemporary perspectives [56(1), 6-10].
Nielsen, D. M. (2002, January). The journey from babysitter to child care professional: Military family child care providers [57(1), 9-14].

Zero to Three Bulletin (Bulletin of the Zero to Three National Center for Infants, Toddlers, and Families)
Theme Issue: Infant mental health and Early Head Start: Lessons for early childhood programs. [August/September, 2001, 22(1)].
Theme Issue: Babies, toddlers and the media. [October/November 2001, 22(2)].

Resources for Curriculum Materials

Audubon. National Audubon Society, P.O. Box 2666, Boulder, CO 80322.

National Geographic World. National Geographic Society, 1145 17th Street, N.W., Washington, DC 20036

Play safe! Be safe (Activities newsletter for teachers). Free from: BIC, 1 Grove Street, Suite 210, Pittsford, NY 14534.

Ranger Rick. National Wildlife Federation, 8925 Leesburg Pike, Vienne, VA 22184-0001.

Texas Parks and Wildlife. Austin TX: Texas Parks and Wildlife Department, P.O. Box 17668, Austin, TX 78760.

Electronic Resources

Editor's Note: There are numerous web sites relating to child development, early care, and education. The following list does not suggest endorsement, but includes a few of the recommendations of practitioners who have accessed them. Visitors to any of these sights are encouraged to evaluate the sites using the criteria suggested in Chapter 21.

Art, Music, and Dramatic Play

Crayola Company   www.crayola.com/ece/results.cfm

(Crafts)   www.freekidscrafts.com/preschool_crafts.htm

(Music)   www.music.com

(Puppetry)   www.puppet.com

Creative Drama and Theater Education Resource File
www.creativedrama.com

Child Growth and Development

The Child Development Web Site
http://www.idealist.com/children/

Early Childhood Intervention
http://www.eci.state.tx.us

I Am Your Child Foundation
http://www.iamyourchild.org

Mister Rogers   www.misterrogers.org

Ready for Life   http://www.kera.org

Zero to Three   http://www.zerotothree.org

Child Health, Safety, and Nutrition

American Academy of Pediatrics
http://www.apa.org

Child Health Alert   www.childhealthalert.com

Children's Environmental Health Network
http://www.cehn.org

Consumer Products Safety Commission
http://www.Cpsc.gov/

National Program for Playground Safety
www.uni.edu/playground

Sudden Infant Death Syndrome (SIDS)
http://www.nih.gov/nichd/

Texas Department of Health
http://www.tdh.state.tx.us

U.S. Center for Disease Control and Prevention
http://www.cdc.gov/ncidod/hip/abc/abc.htm

U.S. Department of Agriculture
http://www.nal.usda.gov/

Curriculum Resources

Association for Constructivist Teaching
http://www.users.interport.net/~roots/ACT.html

Disney Online   http://www.family.com/

Idea Box   http://www.worldvillage.com/ideabox

Teaching Strategies   www.teachingstrategies.com

Language and Literacy Development

American Library Association   http://www.ala.org

Children's Literature Web Guide
http://www.acs.ucalgary.ca/~dkbrown/index.html

National Clearinghouse for Bilingual Education
www.ncbe.gwu.edu/library/tolerance.htm

(Writing Process)
http://www.angelfire.com/wi/writingprocess/

Science and Math

Council on Competitiveness   www.getsmarter.org

Argonne National Laboratory/"The arithmAttack"
www.anl.gov/OPA/attack.htm

Conference on Standards for Preschool and
Kindergarten Mathematics Education
http://nctm.org

U.S. Department of Education, National Institute on
Early Childhood Development and Education
http://www.ed.gov/pubs/EarlyMath/

Space and Equipment Planning

Head Start
www.headstartinfo.org/publications/publicat.htm

Spaces for Children   www.spacesforchildren.com

Professional, Research, and Advocacy Organizations

Association for Childhood Education, International
www.acei.org

Children's Defense Fund
www.childrensdefensefund.org